NEW ZEALAND AT THE POLLS

The General Election of 1978

Edited by Howard R. Penniman

AEI's AT THE POLLS STUDIES

The American Enterprise Institute
has initiated this series in order to promote
an understanding of the electoral process as it functions in
democracies around the world. The series will include studies
of at least two national elections in each of nineteen countries
on five continents, by scholars from the United States and
abroad who are recognized as experts in their field.
More information on the titles in this series can
be found at the back of this book.

NEW ZEALAND AT THE POLLS

The General Election of 1978

Edited by Howard R. Penniman

American Enterprise Institute for Public Policy Research
Washington, D.C.

Library of Congress Cataloging in Publication Data

Main entry under title:

New Zealand at the polls.

   (AEI studies ; 273)
   Includes index.
    1. New Zealand.   General Assembly—Elections,
1978—Addresses, essays, lectures.   2. Elections—
New Zealand—Addresses, essays, lectures.   3. Political
parties—New Zealand—Addresses, essays, lectures.
4. New Zealand—Politics and government—1972-   —
Addresses, essays, lectures.   I. Penniman, Howard Rae,
1916-   II. Series: American Enterprise Institute
for Public Policy Research. AEI studies ; 273.
JQ5892.N5   324.9931037   80-16464
ISBN 0-8447-3376-8

AEI Studies 273

Printed in the United States of America

CONTENTS

PREFACE

New Zealand at the Polls: The General Election of 1978 is one of a continuing series of studies of elections in selected democratic countries published by the American Enterprise Institute. The series was launched in 1974 in the belief that examining particular elections in democracies with very different levels of electoral experience and economic and social development would offer scholars and policy makers a better understanding of electoral institutions and processes in all democracies.

Books on some nineteen countries have been published or are under way, and AEI expects to study at least two elections in each of them. Two books have already been published on elections in Japan, France, and Australia, and second studies are nearing publication on Great Britain and Canada. In addition, two related volumes are in progress: *Democracy at the Polls,* a comparative examination of democratic elections around the world, and *Europe at the Polls,* an analysis of the direct election of representatives from nine countries to the European Parliament in 1979. The titles in the series are listed at the back of this book.

In 1978 New Zealand, for the eighth consecutive time, held its general election on the final Saturday in November of the third and final year of the parliamentary term. New Zealand prime ministers, like their counterparts in other countries whose electoral systems are based on the Westminster model, have the authority to call elections at any time within a term that they consider advantageous for their party. British, Canadian, Australian, and Indian prime ministers have availed themselves of this advantage, but, according to Alan McRobie, in the hundred-year history of New Zealand's Parliament only in 1951 has a prime minister called an election before the last weeks of his term (though during the two world wars and the depression of the 1930s Parliament's term was extended because of the crisis).

Early in the 1978 campaign, public opinion polls suggested that the National party might escape the sharp decline in voter support that has plagued the party in power in virtually every election in the last three decades. Bill Rowling seemed an inept, bumbling leader and campaigner for Labour, while the National party prime minister, Robert Muldoon, came across as confident, capable, and strong. Shortly after the midpoint of the campaign, however, public attitudes changed. Rowling seemed to gain assurance on the platform, while Muldoon's aggressiveness offended more and more voters. Even rude attacks on the prime minister by students at National party rallies did little to restore his party's support. Still, the last polls published before the election all predicted a comfortable vote plurality for National.

Only the Heylen Research Centre's November poll forecast anything other than another big victory for Muldoon, and this poll was not made public. Instead, the director of the Heylen organization, who believed that opinion polls published near the end of an election campaign could improperly influence the outcome, distributed his poll results to the media with instructions that they not be published or announced before the balloting ended on Saturday, November 28. Nevertheless, rumors of Heylen's findings spread. Late Friday a Labour spokesman insisted that the poll showed Labour ahead and called on the media to report that development. The media refused but (what may have had much the same effect) reported Labour's claims and demands. When the Heylen poll results were announced at 8:00 P.M. Saturday, they showed Labour winning 38.5 percent of the vote to National's 38.2 percent and Social Credit's 17 percent, with other respondents either undecided or supporting the Values party or even more minuscule organizations. While both major parties received somewhat larger percentages of the actual vote, the difference between their shares almost exactly matched the Heylen findings: Labour won 40.4 percent of the votes, National 39.8 percent, Social Credit 16.1 percent, and Values 2.4 percent, with another 1.3 percent scattered.

In his sensitivity to the possibility that his findings might influence the election results, Heylen, so far as I know, is unique among private pollsters. In Germany, after some public controversy, market research organizations agreed "not to publish any findings on the current popular strength of the political parties during the last two months before the 1969 elections," and that agreement is still in effect in modified form; today no forecasts of election results are made public, although findings on the current popular strength of the parties may be published and German voters can draw their own conclusions.[1] French and Venezuelan laws prohibit publication of political polling data for two weeks just prior to elections, but they do not prevent the gathering of data, and the parties and polling organizations continue to study shifts in political opinion even though the public is left uninformed.

The distribution of the vote among New Zealand's parties in 1978 was a poor guide to the distribution of seats in the national legislature. Indeed, this election—like Britain's in February 1974 and Canada's in May 1979—was a textbook illustration of how the single-member-district system with plurality voting can distort the vote-seat ratio. In all three of these elections the party placing second in the popular vote won a plurality of the seats (belying the theory that the oddities of the single-member-district, plurality system work to the advantage of the party that wins the most votes). The distortion was relatively minor in Britain, where the Labour party won 37.2 percent of the vote and 301 seats in the House of Commons, the Conservatives 38.2 percent of the vote and 297 seats. But in Canada in 1979 the Progressive Conservative party took 136 seats with 35.9 percent of the votes, while the Liberal party won only 114 seats with 40.1 percent of the vote; and in New Zealand, National's 39.8 percent of the vote won it 51 seats, a clear majority, while Labour's 40.4 percent was worth only 40 seats.

New Zealand's results also illustrate the enormous disadvantage this electoral system imposes on third parties whose votes are relatively evenly spread across the country. Social Credit placed third in the popular vote with 16.1 percent, yet the party's leader, Bruce Beetham, was the only Social Credit candidate to win a seat. Its 16.1 percent of the votes netted Social Credit only 1.08 percent of the seats, whereas the two major parties, with 80.2 percent of the votes, won 98.9 percent of the seats. The seats in Canada in 1979 and Britain in 1974 were distributed slightly more proportionately, but the results in those two countries also demonstrate how the single-member-district system can defractionalize a legislature by heavily overrepresenting larger parties. This defractionalization of the legislature is lessened when the small parties' strength is geographically concentrated. Thus in Britain in 1974 the regional parties of Scotland, Wales, and Northern Ireland together won 5.8 percent of the vote

---

[1] Karl H. Cerny, ed., *Germany at the Polls: The Bundestag Elections of 1976* (Washington, D.C.: American Enterprise Institute, 1978), pp. 210-211.

and 3.6 percent of the seats, while the much larger Liberal party, with its 19.3 percent of the vote spread over the entire country, won a mere 2.2 percent of the seats.

Two-party domination of the New Zealand national legislature is so complete that Beetham's victories in a by-election in 1977 and in the general election of 1978 were the first by any third-party candidate in more than two decades. According to Douglas W. Rae, only the Republican and Democratic parties' domination of the U.S. House of Representatives has been more complete than the Labour and National parties' domination in New Zealand.[2] This situation has made for one-party governments; since both major parties are highly disciplined, as Stephen Levine points out, "no New Zealand Government has ever been forced to call an election by defeat on a parliamentary motion of no confidence."

A century ago four seats in the House of Representatives were set aside by law for New Zealand's Maori aborigines. In recent decades the Maori population has increased rapidly, and by 1971 it constituted roughly 8 percent of the total population. Under current law, according to McRobie, for electoral purposes a Maori is anyone of Maori ancestry who "wishes to be considered a member of the Maori race." Such a person may choose to register as an elector on either a Maori roll or a general roll. Regardless of their total number, those who register on the Maori rolls elect four Maori M.P.s from four districts superimposed on the eighty-eight "general electorates" and covering the entire country.

Labour candidates consistently win in all four Maori districts. In 1978 Labour won 77.6 percent of the 46,742 votes cast there—enough to turn the National party's tiny plurality in the general electorates into a small overall margin for Labour. Although abolishing the Maori districts and integrating the Maoris into the general electorates is often discussed, both major parties and some Maori politicians, for different reasons, decline to support such a move.

The authors contributing to this volume are all New Zealand scholars. Stephen Levine provides a brief history and description of New Zealand's political institutions. Keith Ovenden discusses the characteristics of the electorate. Alan McRobie analyzes the election rules, the registration of voters, and the drawing of district boundaries, and, in an appendix, the disputed elections that were decided

---

[2] Douglas W. Rae, *The Political Consequences of Electoral Laws* (New Haven: Yale University Press, 1971) p. 194. Rae refers to parliamentary majorities secured by parties or coalitions that have won less than 50 percent of the popular vote as "manufactured majorities," that is, created by the electoral rules.

five months after the general election. Keith Jackson describes the selection of candidates and some special problems of 1978. Gilbert Antony Wood, Roderic Alley, and Colin C. James, in separate chapters, discuss the National, Labour, and Social Credit and Values parties in the 1978 campaign. Brian Murphy describes public opinion polling in New Zealand and Les Cleveland the role of the mass media in the campaign. Judith Aitken discusses women in New Zealand politics. Finally, Nigel S. Roberts sums up and interprets the election and its results. The electoral data in Appendix C were compiled by Richard M. Scammon.

HOWARD R. PENNIMAN

NEW ZEALAND AT THE POLLS

1
New Zealand's Political System

Stephen Levine

The Development of a New Zealand Political Identity

New Zealand is a nation of slightly more than 3 million people situated on two islands in the southwestern Pacific. Like Australia 1,200 miles away, it was settled principally by immigrants from Great Britain. But even more than Australia, New Zealand has been marked by geographic isolation: its people are acutely aware of their distance from major centers of population and of their identity as a remote Pacific outpost of British culture and parliamentary democracy.

Constitutional Developments. Organized British settlement in New Zealand began in 1840, the year the Treaty of Waitangi between the British crown and certain Maori chiefs proclaimed British sovereignty over the country.[1] The native Maoris gradually found their control over the land diminished by the acquisitions of European settlers, and between 1860 and 1876 the Maori Wars were fought.[2] Although the Maoris were defeated, they were never forced to submit to unqualified domination, as the Australian Aborigines were, or to concede unquestioned military superiority to the whites, as the American Indians were. The Maori Wars were a more even match, and among their lasting consequences may be included a mutual (if grudging) respect between the adversaries. The Maoris have never been confined to

---

[1] The origins of British settlement in New Zealand are lucidly reviewed in Peter W. T. Adams, *Fatal Necessity: British Intervention in New Zealand 1830-1847* (Auckland: Auckland University Press, Oxford University Press, 1977).

[2] The histories of this intermittent conflict include James Cowan, *A History of the Maori Campaigns and the Pioneering Period* (Wellington: Government Printer, 1956) and Keith Sinclair, *The Origins of the Maori Wars* (Wellington: New Zealand University Press, 1961).

reservations, and while in the early days the settlers hoped the Maori race and culture might disappear through absorption into the dominant British ones, they were less arrogant and cruel in their dealings with the native people than settlers in many comparable situations.[3]

In 1846 the British Parliament passed an act providing for parliamentary government in New Zealand, but it was not until 1852, with the passage of "An Act to grant a Representative Constitution to the Colony of New Zealand," that the colony began to develop autonomous institutions. Known as the New Zealand Constitution Act, this law did not provide for a political constitution or even delineate broad purposes or commitments for government to implement on the people's behalf. Instead, in uninspiring language, it established a fundamental institutional framework of government, which has persisted, with formal amendment and alteration by custom, to the present.

The Constitution Act provided for six separate provincial assemblies (abolished in 1876) as well as a central Parliament for the whole of New Zealand.[4] The central government comprised a governor, appointed by the British crown, and two Houses of Parliament, a House of Representatives elected from single-member districts (known as electorates in New Zealand) and a Legislative Council with members appointed for life by the queen. This upper house was neither directly nor indirectly based upon the provincial councils and thus was in no sense analogous to a legislative body formed through a federal compromise to provide national representation for states or provinces. In addition, its members were not the "natural" proprietaries of political affairs, for there was in New Zealand no hereditary aristocracy: the country was too recently settled, and by people committed to egalitarian norms. Neither a Senate nor a House of Lords,

---

[3] The position of Maoris in contemporary New Zealand is one of incomplete absorption into the dominant *pakeha* (non-Maori) culture, complicated by simmering disputes relating principally to Maori lands and by a movement to revive the Maori language and culture. For recent analyses of Maori political and economic strategies and options, see Bernard J. Kernot, "Maori Strategies and Ethnic Politics in New Zealand," in Stephen Levine, ed., *New Zealand Politics: A Reader* (Melbourne: Cheshire Publishing Pty., 1975), pp. 228-234. Maori-*pakeha* relations are discussed in G. Antony Wood, "Race and Politics in New Zealand," in Stephen Levine, ed., *Politics in New Zealand: A Reader* (Sydney: George Allen & Unwin, 1978), pp. 333-342.

[4] The classic account of the Constitution Act by a political scientist is Kenneth J. Scott, *The New Zealand Constitution* (Oxford: Clarendon Press, 1962). See also Leicester C. Webb, *Government in New Zealand* (Wellington: Department of Internal Affairs, 1940); John L. Robson, ed., *New Zealand: the Development of its Laws and Constitution*, 2nd ed. (London: Stevens, 1967). For an account of the provincial system of government, see William P. Morrell, *The Provincial System in New Zealand 1852-76* (Christchurch: Whitcombe and Tombs, 1964).

the Legislative Council never managed to develop a coherent constitutional role,[5] yet it survived until 1950, a monument to political inertia.

The suffrage in New Zealand has expanded considerably since the passage of the Constitution Act, which reserved voting rights for adult men who owned or leased land or a dwelling above a stated value. The pattern of land ownership of the native population made these suffrage provisions totally inapplicable to Maoris, among whom land was owned not by individuals but by the tribe or some lesser collectivity. The only Maoris qualified to vote under its provisions were those few who owned or leased land under the European system of land titles. It was to deal with this anomaly and to guarantee Maoris some form of representation in the House that the Maori Representation Act of 1867 was approved. This legislation divided New Zealand into four Maori electoral districts, and the Maori population of each of these was entitled to elect one representative to the House. This experiment in separate ethnic representation has persisted although other features of the New Zealand electoral system have undergone major modifications.[6] While the four Maori districts guarantee minimal representation for the Maori population, Maoris may (and often do) choose to enroll to vote in non-Maori electorates instead. They may also run for election there. Two Maoris were elected in non-Maori seats in the 1975 general election, both representing the National party.[7] For several decades, the four Maori seats have been held by Maoris affiliated with the Labour party, which is associated with the Ratana church to which many Maori people belong.[8]

---

[5] An insightful history of New Zealand's experience with a second chamber is contained in W. Keith Jackson, *The New Zealand Legislative Council* (Dunedin: John McIndoe, 1972).

[6] For a review of the development of the Maori seats and some of the administrative difficulties affecting participation in them, see Alan D. McRobie, "Ethnic Representation: The New Zealand Experience," in Levine, ed., *Politics in New Zealand*, pp. 270-283. The future of the Maori seats may be emerging as a partisan and potentially bitter issue. A summary of New Zealanders' attitudes towards their abolition may be found in Stephen Levine and Alan Robinson, *The New Zealand Voter: A Survey of Public Opinion and Electoral Behavior* (Wellington: Price Milburn for New Zealand University, 1976), pp. 95-99, 152-153.

[7] See Stephen Levine and Juliet Lodge, *The New Zealand General Election of 1975* (Wellington: Price Milburn for New Zealand University Press, 1976), p. 10.

[8] An interesting account of the distinctive role played by Maori M.P.s in mediating between the social requirements of Maoris and the agencies and programs established by the government to serve Maoris is found in David Tabacoff, "The Role of the Maori M.P. in Contemporary New Zealand Politics," in Levine, ed., *New Zealand Politics*, pp. 374-383. See James M. Henderson, *Ratana: The User, the Church, the Political Movement* (Wellington: Reed, 1972), for discussion of this important political/religious movement among the Maori people.

Gradually, the electoral system has been modified to incorporate more democratic features: in 1879 universal male suffrage was introduced and the parliamentary term was reduced from five years (as in Great Britain) to three; in 1893 the term of legislative councillors was reduced from life to seven years, voting rights were extended to women, a full twenty-six years earlier than in U.S. presidential elections and well in advance of other Western democracies. A country quota system, which enlarged the voting strength of the rural population, was introduced in 1881, circumscribed in 1889, and abolished in 1946. The principle of equality of population of electoral districts—one person, one vote, as it is known in the United States—had otherwise been established, and since 1887 the regular reapportionment of electoral boundaries after the five-yearly census has been guaranteed by an independent, nonpartisan Representation Commission following criteria established by law.[9] The average size of electorates is approximately 35,000—roughly the size of American districts in the earliest days of the Republic and less than a tenth of their current size. The commitment to political action through the ballot remains firm in New Zealand, and participation in voting is exceptionally high.[10]

Parliamentary Democracy. There are few formal checks and balances in the New Zealand political system. Government is centralized, and only one legislative chamber remains. Nor is there any separation of powers between legislative and executive; the leader of the political party victorious at the triennial general election becomes prime minister and designates a cabinet from among his senior parliamentary colleagues. The remaining M.P.s of the governing party are backbenchers; true to their name, they occupy seats towards the rear of the legislative chamber.[11]

---

[9] The work of the Representation Commission is reviewed in Alan D. McRobie, "The Politics of Electoral Redistribution," in Levine, ed., *Politics in New Zealand*, pp. 255-269, while the political consequences of the 1977 redistribution implemented by the commission are skillfully explored in Alan D. McRobie and Nigel S. Roberts, *Election '78: The 1977 Electoral Redistribution and the 1978 General Election in New Zealand* (Dunedin: John McIndoe, 1978), pp. 33-39.

[10] The turnout at general elections was 88.9 percent of enrolled voters in 1969 (enrollment of eligible voters is required under New Zealand law), 89.1 percent in 1972, and 83.1 percent in 1975 (although in this election the extent of nonvoting may have been exaggerated by electoral roll inaccuracies). All of these figures are high by comparison with the turnout in U.S. presidential elections, which fail to attract even two-thirds of the registered voters to the polls.

[11] Interesting accounts of parliamentary rules, structure, and customs may be found in Thomas R. Smith, *Parliamentary Government in New Zealand* (Wellington: Government Printer, 1965); Alexander H. McLintock, *Crown Colony Government in New Zealand* (Wellington: Government Printer, 1958); and Anthony J. Dreaver, *Political People* (Auckland: Longman Paul, 1978).

These M.P.s together with the prime minister and cabinet (who, of course, remain members of Parliament) comprise the governing party caucus. If there is a check on executive power in New Zealand, it may be found in the power of the governing party caucus. The willingness of backbench M.P.s to challenge party leaders—on controversial questions and on trivial electoral matters, on partisan issues and on details of expenditure and taxation—determines how much autonomy the executive will have during its three-year term. In practice, however, party discipline and the pressures to conform imposed by the party struggle and by personal ambition make public dissent within a governing party especially rare in New Zealand.[12] Caucus meetings are secret and leaks rare, but even so the governing party caucus seems a feeble guarantor of restraint. The formal check provided by parliamentary approval of taxation, expenditure, and legislative proposals is if anything even more unsatisfactory:[13] support for executive initiatives is assured by the party system, so much so that no New Zealand Government has ever been forced to call an election by defeat on a parliamentary motion of no-confidence.

The judiciary plays a very limited role in New Zealand politics. Legislation is not reviewed by the courts to determine, through case-by-case adjudication, whether it may be sustained according to constitutional criteria. No constitutional document exists against which such a determination could be made, and in its absence the exercise of judicial authority and independence has been rare. Certainly it has not constituted a lasting impediment to parliamentary sovereignty.[14] The position of governor general remains, but the queen's representa-

---

[12] See Roderic M. Alley, "Parliamentary Parties in Office: Government-Backbench Relations," in Levine, ed., *Politics in New Zealand*, pp. 96-114, for a recent analysis of backbench participation reflecting the rise to dominance of the prime minister. A thorough treatment of the position of the backbench M.P. may be found in Robert N. Kelson, *The Private Member of Parliament and the Formation of Public Policy: A New Zealand Case Study* (Toronto: University of Toronto Press, 1964). Papers presented by two Government backbenchers suggest some of the frustrations and difficulties experienced by M.P.s seeking to enlarge parliamentary autonomy: Michael J. Minogue, "Information and Power: Parliamentary Reform and the Right to Know," and Marilyn Waring, "Power and the New Zealand M.P.: Selected Myths about Parliamentary Democracy," in Levine, ed., *Politics in New Zealand*, pp. 78-95.

[13] See Alan D. McRobie, "Parliamentary 'Control' of Public Expenditure," in Levine, ed., *Politics in New Zealand*, pp. 115-130.

[14] A review of the position of the judiciary as it has evolved over the past twenty-five years is contained in Ken J. Keith, "Constitutional Change," in Ian Wards, ed., *Thirteen Facets* (Wellington: Government Printer, 1978), pp. 3-37; Geoffrey A. Palmer, *Unbridled Power: An Interpretation of New Zealand's Constitution and Government* (Wellington: Oxford University Press, 1979) provides a critical treatment of government by regulation in New Zealand.

tive in New Zealand takes only a formal part in the affairs of state. Perhaps because the governor general has played a strictly passive and symbolic role, the maintenance of ties with the monarchy has not become the partisan issue in New Zealand that it has in Australia since the dismissal of Gough Whitlam's Labor Government by the Australian governor general in 1975. Admittedly, the crown seems most meaningful to older New Zealanders, yet for many it continues to provide a meaningful link with New Zealand's cultural origins.

In the end, the major check upon the Government is the requirement that it face the voters on a regular and relatively frequent basis. And beyond the sanctions of the ballot are the more subtle protections of political culture: the expectations of voters and politicians about what is permissible in politics. Behavior markedly at variance with those expectations will be resisted by the news media, by the opposition, and, ultimately, by the public. Although New Zealand does not have a strong civil liberties tradition, its British heritage of the rule of law and limited government is secure, and it is the people, by their vigilance and faith in their own fundamental decency, that serve as the essential barrier to tyrannical government. In any country, with or without a written constitution, these attitudes must be nurtured through positive acts of political participation.

Partly to encourage a sense of participation and of unmediated communication between the people and their representatives, broadcasting of parliamentary proceedings was introduced by the first Labour Government in 1938. Two premises underlay this initiative. One was the assumption that the people would be interested in what their representatives had to say; the other was a populist distrust of the media as a conveyer of impartial news and objective comment. The Labour Government was especially eager to circumvent what it saw as the conservative bias of the press.

While parliamentary proceedings are regularly broadcast, a formidable barrier of secrecy surrounds committee hearings, and media coverage of them is erratic. The haphazard character of parliamentary committee deliberations may be appreciated in the fact that most committees fail even to record their proceedings verbatim. In any case, since legislative initiative tends to be monopolized by the governing party through the cabinet, committees have little room for maneuver. Their work permits valuable pressure group participation and modification of legislative proposals, but House rules, unwritten political constraints, and inadequate institutional support (in the form of staff and investigative resources) limit their scope. Certainly for political bite, committee proceedings are far surpassed by the vivid confrontations that take place on the floor of the House. Most House debates are exceptionally well attended by M.P.s, who are forbidden by House rules to read prepared speeches, and the proceedings are punctuated by blunt exchanges and protracted speaker's rulings.

Of course lively debate is not the same thing as autonomy, and in a Parliament with disciplined parties the role of the individual M.P. is severely circumscribed. All Government measures are assured passage—indeed, Standing Orders of the House prevent proposals involving any expenditure from proceeding without Government support—and Parliament is principally a debating forum, where party antagonists can enunciate their views on issues and show off their verbal skills.

National-Local Government Relations. Since the abolition of New Zealand's provincial structure in 1876, local government functions have been performed by a range of elected authorities, of which there are two main types: territorial authorities (including city, borough, and county councils), which have general powers, and ad hoc authorities performing particular functions related to electric power, hospitals, catchment, pest destruction, rabbit control, rivers, and so on. But the authority of the central government to alter the powers and jurisdictions of these bodies is unquestioned; there are in fact no centers of countervailing power capable of challenging Wellington.

On the other hand, New Zealanders feel meaningful attachments to their local authorities, as reformist local government commissions and supporters of regional amalgamation have discovered when they have attempted to tamper with these "parochial" bonds in the name of administrative rationality. Referendums of ratepayers (property-owners, who provide the tax base for local government) regularly defeat amalgamation proposals, largely on the principle that government-sponsored reorganization for the sake of cost reduction is likely to be more expensive than apparently arbitrary practices with a basis in tradition.[15] Continuing efforts at local government reform, begun in 1974 under the Labour Government, are seeking to create regional authorities, a new layer of government amalgamating selected functions of the local authorities.

However, for the time being, the most distinctive feature of New Zealand local government remains the fact that (unlike those in

---

[15] A recent account of efforts at local government reform is contained in Robert J. Gregory, "Political Participation in New Zealand: The Democratic Idea in Local Government Reform" in Levine, ed., *Politics in New Zealand*, pp. 50-62. For a more general if dated view, see Raymond J. Polaschek, ed., *Local Government in New Zealand* (Wellington: NZIPA, 1956).

federal systems such as Australia and the United States) local authorities are not an obstacle to the exercise of power by the central government. In all areas of domestic politics, central government authority—ultimately, the authority of the political party that controls Parliament—is supreme and unopposed. No social policy, no economic practice of industry, agriculture, banking, or trade, is constitutionally beyond the jurisdiction of the central government, nor is the central government's regular involvement in these areas through management or regulation considered inappropriate.[16]

Egalitarianism and Modest Aspirations. During the early colonial years difficulties in transportation and communications and a relative absence of consistently divisive issues made provincial loyalties paramount, and support for the governor's program was far from predictable. Prior to 1890, life in Parliament revolved around shifting personal loyalties and commitments. This kind of maneuvering among a governing elite ended with the election of New Zealand's first political party—the Liberals—to Government in 1890.[17] Their opponents eventually formed an alternative political party, the Conservatives, but the Liberals dominated New Zealand politics from 1890 almost to the First World War. Since 1890 every Government has had its basis in majority party control in the House of Representatives.

The Liberal party's reign established much more than a tradition of party Government, for the Liberals sought to develop economic

[16] For an account of the growth of entrenched state power over the New Zealand economy, see William B. Sutch, *The Quest for Security in New Zealand* (Wellington and Harmondsworth: Penguin, 1942). A comprehensive review is provided as well by John Condliffe and Willis T. Airey, *A Short History of New Zealand*, 9th ed., (Christchurch: Whitcombe and Tombs, 1960), while an up-to-date paper with a narrower focus on public corporations is found in Irene A. Webley, "State Intervention in the Economy: The Use of Public Corporations in New Zealand," in Levine, ed., *Politics in New Zealand*, pp. 36-49. William P. Reeves, *The Long White Cloud* (London: Allen & Unwin, 1950) remains valuable despite its being superseded by experience in certain details.

[17] An authoritative account of the development of party government in New Zealand is found in Leslie Lipson, *The Politics of Equality* (Chicago: University of Chicago Press, 1948). Judith Bassett, *Sir Harry Atkinson 1831-1892* (Auckland: University of Auckland Press, 1975) underscores the small scale of New Zealand politics during the pre-Liberal party period. Works providing a more comprehensive survey of New Zealand politics include: W. Keith Jackson, *New Zealand: Politics of Change* (Wellington: Reed, 1973); Stephen Levine, *The New Zealand Political System* (Sydney: George Allen & Unwin, 1979); Austin V. Mitchell, *Government by Party* (Christchurch: Whitcombe and Tombs, 1966); Austin V. Mitchell, *Politics and People in New Zealand* (Christchurch: Whitcombe and Tombs, 1969). There are several excellent general histories, among them: John B. Condliffe, *New Zealand in the Making* (London: Allen & Unwin, 1959); William H. Oliver, *The Story of New Zealand* (London: Faber and Faber, 1963); Keith Sinclair, *A History of New Zealand* (London: Penguin, 1970).

democracy in New Zealand, alongside the political democracy that had evolved. In addition to granting women's suffrage, the Liberals laid the foundations for the welfare state, passing specific measures like old age pensions but also more generally embedding in the electorate the belief that Government was responsible for individual security. If political culture refers primarily to people's expectations about politics, then the Liberal Government made a central contribution to New Zealand's political culture, teaching its citizens that political decency requires Government to do what it can to provide the material basis for dignity and equality. The Liberals also passed legislation providing for industrial conciliation and arbitration which, like the Liberals' social security legislation, preceded comparable American legislation by four decades. The commitment to equality, not merely of economic opportunity but of material attainments, has persisted in New Zealand as the common inheritance of all political parties hopeful of attaining power. New Zealand politics has had as a central purpose protecting New Zealanders against adversity. New Zealand's welfare state is predicated upon the positive duty of government to ensure that health care, housing, education, employment, and a decent standard of living are not compromised by disability, old age, poverty, or illness. A genuine commitment to ensuring that ability to pay does not become a criterion for access to medical care or to basic community services has led to sustained government involvement in the provision of social services. Disparities of wealth have been limited (though not entirely removed) through taxation and social welfare measures—which have also taken a toll, discouraging independent initiative.

The commitment to government "of the people, by the people, and for the people," meanwhile, is unostentatious but genuine. The membership of Parliament, for example, has tended to reflect the occupational composition of the electorate. This was particularly true during the 1930s under the first Labour Government, although subsequently working-class representation in the Labour party declined. Today the membership of all the major parties is predominantly middle class in origin and attitudes. Even so, up until very recently the paucity of lawyers in Parliament has been striking: it has sometimes been difficult to find enough M.P.s with legal expertise to staff the ten-seat committee that reviews bills dealing with legal reform and the technical revision of legislation.

The American, Canadian, and Australian democracies, each in its own way, are based upon a fundamentally bold conception: that it is possible to govern a continent according to criteria conceived for the governance of a city-state. New Zealanders have only two islands to govern, and they abhor grand gestures and high-flown rhetoric. They ask government to ensure that life is no more uncomfortable than it need be. Perhaps they are oversensitive to the strategic insignificance of a country severed from its cultural and colonial roots; perhaps out of a sense of being irretrievably on the periphery of world affairs, New Zealanders have set their political sights low.

Americans may be puzzled by New Zealand patriotism, which strikes them as elusive at best. New Zealanders are unfamiliar with their flag and national anthem; their national holidays, largely imported from Britain and almost devoid of meaning for New Zealanders as such, include Guy Fawkes Day, commemorating a plot to blow up the British Parliament, and the Queen's Birthday. New Zealand is virtually bereft of indigenous political symbols above those of party, and, despite very substantial migration into and out of the country particularly between 1972 and 1979, the government has never initiated a formal program of political socialization in schools or communities.[18]

Few New Zealanders would be familiar with the names of the nation's founding fathers, although Governor George Grey has been more prominent than most since the dramatization of his life in a television serial. The one prime minister from earlier times whose name most people might know is Richard John Seddon, Liberal prime minister from 1893 to 1906 and the first New Zealand prime minister to serve more than six years in succession. Politically astute, crude, intuitively close to the public, practical, committed to the use and enjoyment of power for its own sake, domineering, occasionally eloquent, Seddon remains a dominant figure against whom contemporary political leaders are measured. Indeed, Seddon's hold on the public's affections is secure enough that television advertisers have tried to associate their products with his distinctive style.[19]

---

[18] Explicit support for such a program, which would no doubt inspire protests from civil libertarians and would reveal the considerable divisions in society (including those arising out of conflicts between Maori and non-Maori perspectives) about political and social values, is recommended by Marian Tower, "The Political Socialisation of New Zealand Schoolchildren," in Levine, ed., *Politics in New Zealand*, pp. 343-352. During 1979 a Government M.P., Ken Comber, sponsored a campaign for a more demonstrative style of patriotism, including more frequent flag demonstrations, while leading commercial interests have called upon New Zealanders to express faith and pride in their country and its future.

[19] For an account of Seddon by contemporaries, see David A. Hamer, ed., *The Webbs in New Zealand, 1898: Beatrice Webb's Diary with Entries by Sidney Webb* (Wellington: Price Milburn for Victoria University Press, 1974). As Lipson comments, with Seddon in mind: "The Prime Minister must build up a personal relationship with the citizens . . . He must also be an uncommon man where force of character and political shrewdness are concerned. But he should not possess

The Role of the State. The scantiness of resources and capital in New Zealand was the major fact in the economic development of the colony and in the enlargement of the role of the state beyond that normally encouraged by small farmers and small businessmen. Isolation was another feature of the colonial experience, along with the determined quest for economic security, motivated by the personal hardship the settlers experienced. One of the central paradoxes of New Zealand's development is that a fundamentally capitalist, free enterprise economic orientation has not merely coexisted with but actually served to foster an omnipresent state with the authority and the means to intervene in economic and social matters almost without restriction. As one political scientist has noted,

> the New Zealand dream has never been, for the majority of its inhabitants, the hope of making it big, going west or even rising up the class ladder. Essentially materialist, gentle, unambitious, it fixed upon a modest home on a separate plot of land, a protected job in both senses of limited competition and assured employment, free education for children, and a mild boom to make it possible for the restless to achieve spatial if not social mobility.[20]

These "bland, harmless and even boring aspirations" perhaps better than a recitation of constitutional or institutional differences distinguish New Zealand political life from the more restless competitive environment of the United States. In New Zealand it has never been assumed that anyone in principle might become president or a millionaire. Aspirations are more limited: social and political pressures, both informal and formal, discourage assertive behavior and encourage conformity.[21] Exceptional attainments tend to be deprecated by their

---

uncommon intellectual ability. If he does, he will find that his brains are, politically, a liability. In an equalitarian democracy the prime minister must carefully avoid or conceal anything that sets him too far apart from his fellows" (pp. 310-311). Imperfect but useful biographies of Seddon are: Randal M. Burdon, *King Dick: A Biography of Richard John Seddon* (Christchurch: Whitcombe and Tombs, 1955), and James Drummond, *The Life and Work of Richard John Seddon* (London: Siegler Hill, 1907).

[20] See John L. Roberts, "Society and Its Politics," in Wards, ed., *Thirteen Facets*, p. 71.

[21] Tendencies towards conformity have disturbed New Zealand intellectuals for decades. In his introduction to *The Pattern of New Zealand Culture*, Alexander McLeod, ed., (Melbourne: Oxford University Press, 1968), McLeod establishes the persistent estrangement of intellectuals from New Zealand society, and the New Zealand national character generally comes under bitter attack from David P. Ausubel in *The Fern and The Tiki: An American View of New Zealand National Character, Social Attitudes and Race Relations* (New York: Holt, Rinehart and

possessor as well as by others, and pressures against individuality extend from the schoolroom to Parliament.

Observers of American and British politics have contrasted the two nations' attitudes towards their political systems and leaders. The Americans, who are strongly critical of politicians as a professional group, take a deep, sincere pride in their political system. In Britain, on the other hand, an ingrained deference towards the political elite is accompanied by a lack of confidence in the responsiveness of the system.[22] New Zealand's political culture draws upon both of these orientations but is a little different from each. There has been confidence in the fairness of the political system and in the fundamental decency of the members of the Government and Parliament. In the absence of a constitution, a bill of rights, and a judiciary actively involved in the redress of political grievances, New Zealanders have tended to rely on these basic if untested assumptions about the character of their political leadership. Thus far they have not been outrageously affronted in their expectations; there has been no Watergate, no Teapot Dome, and suspicion of corruption in either the Government or the civil service (right down to the police force) is not an underlying feature of political life. Even that universally despised figure, the bureaucrat, tends to be viewed as one in whom integrity, if not industry and conscientiousness, may be taken for granted.[23]

Foreign Policy. New Zealand did not seize political independence through acts of rebellion; on the contrary, it had sovereignty virtually thrust upon it by an exhausted imperial power. New Zealand became a dominion in 1907 and in 1919 was given separate representation at the Versailles Peace Conference and subsequently in the League of Nations. While it was a keen supporter of the league, there were limits to the independence from Britain that its leaders and populace

---

Winston, 1965). New Zealanders are described as almost irretrievably damaged, psychologically, by their experience of themselves and their world in Gordon McLauchlan, *The Passionless People: New Zealanders in the 1970s* (Auckland: Cassell, 1976). A more light-hearted yet critical view of New Zealand identity and preoccupations is found in Austin V. Mitchell, *The Half-Gallon, Quarter-Acre Pavlova Paradise* (Wellington: Whitcombe and Tombs, 1971).

[22] A brilliant account of distinctive American and British orientations towards politics and government, centering on the theme of political distrust, has been produced by Vivien Hart, *Distrust and Democracy: Political Distrust in Britain and America* (Cambridge: Cambridge University Press, 1978).

[23] Thomas B. Smith, *The New Zealand Bureaucrat* (Wellington: Cheshire Publications Pty. Ltd., 1974), is a study of the New Zealand bureaucracy developed principally from interviews with civil servants. See also Robert S. Milne, ed., *Bureaucracy in New Zealand* (Wellington: NZIPA, 1957).

wished to achieve.[24] The Statute of Westminster was passed by the British Parliament in 1931, redefining dominions as equal, independent nations within the then British Commonwealth. It was not until 1947, however, after Britain's loss of power had been underscored by war and the imminent collapse of the Empire, that New Zealand chose to recognize the inevitable and ratify the statute confirming its political sovereignty.

While New Zealand has had overseas representation since 1876, through a consular office in Britain (principally responsible for raising overseas loans), the Ministry of Foreign Affairs was not established until 1937.[25] New Zealand's first foreign embassy was set up in 1942, in New York City, and the enormous expansion of its diplomatic representation during the 1960s and 1970s has placed considerable strain on the ministry's personnel and resources. Even so, in 1979 New Zealand was still without any direct diplomatic representation on the African continent (the ambassador in Rome is cross-accredited to Cairo) and had only a handful of representatives in the Arab world and Latin America.

If New Zealanders have long taken their country's relationships with other nations for granted, the casual self-confidence they express in the phrase "she'll be right" has provided a tenuous basis for security policy. In many respects, of course, "independent" diplomacy has simply meant dependence on the Americans rather than the British. However, the emotional consequences of dependence on the British have outlasted its geopolitical necessity, and relations between New Zealand and the United States have been less comfortable for New Zealand than may commonly be appreciated.[26] The transfer of al-

24 See, for example, Rex R. Cunninghame, "The Development of New Zealand's Foreign Policy and Political Alignments," and Alistair D. McIntosh, "Administration of an Independent New Zealand Foreign Policy," in Thomas C. Larkin, ed., *New Zealand's External Relations* (Wellington: NZIPA; London: Oxford University Press, 1962). The latter includes an interesting account of the origins of the Ministry of Foreign Affairs (pp. 34-44). Also useful is Neville Meany, *The Search for Security in the Pacific 1901-14* (Sydney: Sydney University Press, 1976).

25 An especially well-researched account of the origins of New Zealand diplomacy is Raewyn M. Dalziel, *The Origins of New Zealand Diplomacy: The Agent-General in London 1870-1905* (Wellington: Price Milburn for Victoria University Press, 1975).

26 U.S.-N.Z. relations have been the subject of several studies, varying in scope and historical content. These include: Mary P. Lissington, *New Zealand and the United States 1840-1944* (Wellington: Government Printer, 1972); Trevor R. Reese, *Australia, New Zealand and the United States: A Survey of International Relations 1941-1968* (Oxford: Oxford University Press, 1969); John H. Moore, *The American Alliance: Australia, New Zealand and the United States 1940-1970* (Melbourne: Cassell, 1970). For more recent commentaries on relationships under the ANZUS treaty, see Malcolm McKinnon, "Costs and Continuity: New Zealand's Security and the United States," *Political Science*, vol. 30, no. 1 (May/June 1977), pp. 15-18.

legiances was much simpler for Australians: one Australian prime minister was able to remark in 1941, "Without any inhibitions of any kind, I make it quite clear that Australia looks to America, free of any pangs as to our traditional links of kinship with the United Kingdom."[27]

New Zealand's self-image in world affairs has been curiously molded. New Zealanders proved their loyalty by fighting for the Empire (in the Boer War, for example), and their participation in Europe during the First World War was rightly taken for granted in London. At the same time their international orientations have reflected an awareness of their political and military insignificance. The major objectives of New Zealand's foreign policy have been to ensure national security through alliance with a great power and economic security through stable overseas markets for the country's exports (meat and dairy products, which continue to provide the bulk of New Zealand's foreign exchange despite efforts at diversification and the development of competitive manufactures). At home a deferential attitude to privilege may be uncommon, but in the international arena New Zealand's leaders have been only too willing to defer to the great powers in word and deed, choosing loyalty as a substitute for power.[28]

New Zealand has had few opportunities to develop autonomy in international relations. The constraints of dependency for security and trade, combined with the conviction of relative powerlessness, that is deeply rooted in the political culture, have tended to vitiate such opportunities as have arisen. Only in the South Pacific did New Zealand aspire to leadership and power—even at one point emulating Britain's imperial behavior so successfully that the British Foreign Office felt compelled to discourage New Zealand from acquiring further territory in the Pacific. More recently, New Zealand served as a colonial and United Nations Trust power for Western Samoa (which received independence in 1962); and other island territories have remained in close relationship with New Zealand.

Whether New Zealand retains a significant hold on the affections of Pacific Island peoples may be doubted, however. There is more self-flattery than realism in the belief that Samoans, Tongans, Fijians, and others see New Zealand as nonexploitative and the more pros-

---

[27] Lissington, *New Zealand and the United States*, pp. 97-98.

[28] Prime Minister Holyoake's remark "We can only have good allies by proving ourselves a good ally" seems typical of this orientation towards New Zealand's role in world affairs. See W. Theo Roy, "The Defence of New Zealand," in Levine, ed., *Politics in New Zealand*, pp. 383-395, for further elaboration of this theme. Holyoake's statement is quoted on p. 385.

14

perous Western nations as greedy and ruthless.[29] Moreover, recent New Zealand government policies designed to deter migration from the Pacific Island nations to New Zealand, including efforts to organize the compulsory deportation of Islanders overstaying their work permits, have been widely reported. The 1975 National party campaign, which identified Island immigrants as a source of problems in urban areas, was criticized, and subsequently the National party Government has been compelled to undertake diplomatic initiatives to restore cordial relations.

The Politics of Change in the 1970s

The 1970s have been a period of relative political upheaval in New Zealand—though in a country where participation in public life is muted and irregular and political protest rarely achieves a sharp focus, outsiders might be forgiven for thinking otherwise. Since 1890, competing partisan alignments have oriented New Zealand politics. The Liberals held power until 1912, to be succeeded by a coalition of anti-Liberal elements. In 1935, during the Great Depression, the Labour party came to power, and it held office until 1949. It was succeeded by the National party, formed in 1936 from the remnants of anti-Labour party organizations. But the predominance of one party is striking: by 1981, the National party will have held power in New Zealand since 1949 for all but two three-year terms (1957–1960 and 1972–1975), a total of twenty-six out of thirty-two years.[30]

The National party claims a membership in excess of 200,000 (about 10 percent of the voting age population), and roughly one in three of its votes in 1978 came from a party member. Despite its high membership, however, National cannot be considered a mass party. Like the other New Zealand parties, it is without a primary system permitting new candidates to challenge incumbent M.P.s or party nominees, which means that participation by the enrolled membership is limited. In the New Zealand Labour party, restrictions on public participation may be even more pronounced. In any conflict between

---

[29] New Zealand's imperialist aspirations in the Pacific are discussed in Angus Ross, *New Zealand Aspirations in the Pacific in the Nineteenth Century* (Oxford: Oxford University Press, 1964), and Angus Ross, ed., *New Zealand's Record in the Pacific Islands in the Twentieth Century* (Auckland: Longman for NZIPA, 1969). Also of value is Frank H. Corner, "New Zealand and the South Pacific," in Larkin, ed., *New Zealand's External Relations*, pp. 130-152.

[30] See Lipson, *Politics of Equality*, for a full account of these developments up to the end of the Second World War. In addition, Robert S. Milne, *Political Parties in New Zealand* (Oxford: Clarendon Press, 1966) discusses New Zealand political parties in depth, including their history, structure, membership, and functions.

an electorate organization and the party's central headquarters over the choice of a parliamentary candidate, the headquarters is authorized to make the selection.

The 1972 General Election. Labour's victory in the November 1972 general election seems to have triggered a process of change whose repercussions are still rippling through the political system. Labour had been expected to win, after twelve years in opposition. The National Government had virtually run out of ideas and energy, and the electorate seemed bored. At the same time, New Zealand's economy was buoyant, reserves of foreign exchange were at record levels, and business confidence in the stability and strength of the economy seemed well established. Even so, the magnitude of the victory in 1972 surprised independent observers and Labour strategists alike.[31]

The general elections of 1963, 1966, and 1969 had been characterized by stable electoral patterns; in each election the National party's support had slipped almost imperceptibly.[32] The 1969 election had nearly thrust Labour into power, but an industrial dispute in the final weeks of the campaign apparently deprived Labour of its brief advantage, and the party fell short by six seats.[33] In a by-election in 1970 a seat long held by a National cabinet minister fell to Labour, further reducing the Government's majority. An apprehensive National caucus found its anxieties about the party leadership fueled by media speculation; then in the casual manner so typical of New Zealand politics Sir Keith Holyoake, leader of the party for fifteen years and prime minister for twelve, gave up power to his long-time deputy, Jack R. Marshall.[34] But National's recognition that the voters felt it to be "Time for a Change" (the slogan used by Labour in 1972 in both Australia and New Zealand, with great success) was not enough. Marshall let the opportunity to reshape the cabinet and initiate new policies pass: the Holyoake cabinet was retained and the impression firmly established that the transition to Marshall was a matter of form, not substance. Marshall was not a dynamic leader. Like Holyoake, he had become adept at consensus politics New Zealand-style, drawing

---

[31] See, for example, the comments of John L. Roberts, "Labour after Nine Months," in Levine, ed., *New Zealand Politics*, pp. 418-427.

[32] See Nigel S. Roberts, "The New Zealand General Election of 1972" in Levine, ed., *New Zealand Politics*, pp. 99-114.

[33] See Tony Garnier, Bruce Kohn, and Pat Booth, *The Hunter and The Hill: New Zealand Politics and the Kirk Years* (Auckland: Cassell, 1978), pp. 70-71.

[34] Transitions of power in the National and Labour parties are analyzed in W. Keith Jackson, "Political Leadership and Succession in the National Party," in Levine, ed., *Politics in New Zealand*, pp. 161-181.

on an almost intuitive appreciation of the public and parliamentary mood. The leader allowed himself to be led by this mood, so that decisive measures that may have seemed long overdue to their earliest supporters were finally implemented only when they would be greeted with relief by all. Conducted in this manner, consensus politics involved few risks, and the commitment of political resources could be avoided until an almost irresistible momentum for action had developed. Emphasizing the virtues of caution and compromise, this "low profile" approach was unlikely to be suitable in an environment of unfocused public restlessness. Labour's slogan, "Time for a Change," could find support in virtually any kind of politically induced anger or anxiety. It specified neither programs nor policies and left even the direction of change to the voter's imagination.

Perhaps as significant as Marshall's gentlemanly approach to political debate was his demonstrable failure to acquire the full confidence of the National party in Parliament. As Holyoake's deputy, Marshall had been self-effacing: there had been no doubt of Holyoake's political supremacy within the cabinet. In selecting Marshall to succeed Holyoake, the National caucus also chose to elevate Holyoake's minister of finance, Robert D. ("Rob") Muldoon, to the position of deputy leader. By 1972 Muldoon was already famous for his enjoyment of vigorous debate on the floor of the House. Not a team player, he succeeded in politics as an individualist in a cultural environment that stresses cooperative endeavor bound by rules. Where Marshall's approach to parliamentary debate was often didactic, Muldoon's contributions, much appreciated by his colleagues, were blunt, forceful, often personal. The pairing of the two as a leadership team, particularly in an election year, proved to be inherently unstable. Marshall was frequently eclipsed by Muldoon, although the latter's curiously limited participation in the formal campaign allowed him to survive the defeat at the polls unscathed. It was Marshall, not Muldoon, whose political career was virtually ended by the 1972 Labour triumph. Muldoon's accession to the party leadership in 1973, following Marshall's lackluster performance as opposition leader against Labour's dynamic Norman Kirk, while not widely predicted by the media, seems to have been one of the very few options open to a reduced National party caucus unaccustomed to exile from the Government benches.

The 1972 election was a watershed. The period 1960–1972 had been politically quiescent, with relatively little legislative initiative coming from the central government. In part, this reflects the origins and political orientation of the National party, which regards the exercise of government power for positive social purposes less as an end in itself than as a means of taking the wind out of Labour's sails. But in its 1972 campaign, Labour, which had been an assertive and in some ways self-righteous opposition, encouraged voters to make a new personal commitment to politics and to work together to "get the country moving again" in reaction to years of comfort unequally enjoyed.

The Third Labour Government. The Labour party had been out of power for twelve years when it was elected in November 1972. So long a period in opposition had several consequences: brimming with ideas and proposals, the party envisaged a vigorous legislative program and new initiatives in international relations. Its leader, Norman Kirk, had several campaigns behind him, and his political style had evolved considerably. Initially awkward and inarticulate, Kirk had developed a direct, convincing approach to political argument, which became increasingly effective. By the 1972 campaign Kirk had emerged as the self-confident leader of a long-frustrated party assured of political success; only the margin of victory seemed in doubt. Another consequence of Labour's long exile from power, however, was that Kirk had few parliamentary colleagues with prior ministerial experience. An assertive leader, he was personally respected by the electorate but only indifferently supported by an inexperienced cabinet team. From 1972 to 1974 Kirk dominated the Labour party and the Government thoroughly in the Seddon manner; at the same time, his ministers found their portfolios unmanageable, and an elaborate system of overlapping responsibilities developed in an effort to minimize the likelihood of serious incompetence. In international relations, Kirk initiated a "new foreign policy" based upon moral principles; his bold departures in foreign relations represented an effort to distance the new Labour Government from its predecessor as rapidly and as totally as possible.[35]

All around, Kirk sought to show the public that his approach to politics was new. In his first 100 days, he severed relations with Taiwan with a minimum of fuss, ensuring that New Zealand would extend diplomatic recognition to the People's Republic of China, and opened a New Zealand Embassy in Moscow after a hiatus of twenty-two years. Conscription was abolished and the small New Zealand

---

[35] The immediate consequences of a change of Government in New Zealand are reviewed in W. Keith Jackson, "Government Succession in New Zealand," in Levine, ed., *Politics in New Zealand*, pp. 1-21.

contingent sent to Vietnam at the request of President Lyndon Johnson was withdrawn. Forthright opposition to France's nuclear testing program in the South Pacific became another major feature of Kirk's foreign policy. A New Zealand frigate with a cabinet minister aboard was sent to the testing area, and legal action was taken before the World Court in The Hague. At the United Nations, New Zealand added to its stand against nuclear weapons a proposal for a nuclear-free-zone in the South Pacific—despite an unsympathetic response from Australia and the United States, its partners in collective defense.

Domestically, the Kirk Government sought to implement a range of proposals, many of which had been features of Labour manifestoes for several elections. Controls on wages and prices were abolished, and a return to free collective bargaining by trade unions was inaugurated. Regional development programs were launched with some fanfare (although little was achieved to reverse the drift of population and industrial development away from the South Island), and a pet project of Kirk's, the establishment of rural communes known as *ohus*, was initiated to encourage a return to farming by people who could not afford to purchase property on their own. A new superannuation program improved the social security benefits available to the elderly, and spending on housing, education, and health was sharply increased.

For all the innovations of political style developed by Kirk under the influence of his campaign advisers, he remained very much a traditional Labour man bound to fixed political, social, and moral beliefs. These powerful loyalties, while a political asset for Kirk, deepening his rapport with New Zealanders, posed problems for his Government. For one thing, Kirk carried the usual view of the party manifesto to the extreme. Available in attractive, inexpensive editions, New Zealand party manifestoes summarize the promises and programs pledged by the party conference. Some of these promises are a package directed towards the interest groups that comprise the party's principal support, while others can be traced to the party's activists and membership, but even the manifestoes of the smallest parties address the whole range of the state's responsibilities. Moreover, New Zealand voters can be confident that the party elected to govern will have the will and the capacity to enact the commitments made in its manifesto since it will face little formal hindrance from opposition M.P.s, parliamentary committees, or "independent" members of the governing party caucus. Kirk viewed his party's manifesto almost literally as a contract between Labour and the voters, and when he at last achieved power, he was determined to keep faith with the electorate. Every promise, so far as was possible, was to be implemented, regardless of changing circumstances or altered requirements as viewed from the perspective of a party in office. This determination saddled the Labour party with difficult political choices as the country's economic distress deepened.

Norman Kirk had become leader of the Labour party in 1965, succeeding a former Labour minister of finance, Arnold Nordmeyer. Nordmeyer's misfortune had been that in the second Labour Government (1957–1960) he had introduced a relatively austere budget (known as the black budget) with which he had been identified ever after.[36] In addition, Nordmeyer had the handicap of not being conspicuously working class. Kirk, on the other hand, looked like a Labour party leader, and his working-class credentials were especially prized in an increasingly middle-class parliamentary team.[37] Kirk's third general election as leader of the Labour party, in 1972, was his most promising opportunity—and almost certainly his last if he were defeated.

On the campaign trail Kirk's style was personal. His connection with the public transcended party. In his way, Kirk contributed to the crumbling of traditional party loyalties in New Zealand by succeeding so well at communicating directly with the voters. When he suddenly died in office, Kirk was endowed with heroic stature by a public surprised at the magnitude of its own grief.

Kirk's successor was not in the Seddon mold, which Kirk had so comfortably filled in his last years. The new leader of the Labour party, Wallace E. ("Bill") Rowling, was a different sort of personality altogether: tentative where Kirk was firm, his voice high-pitched where Kirk's was deep and resonant, intellectual at least in demeanor where Kirk was attuned to the attitudes and instincts of the ordinary New Zealander. Rowling had been Kirk's finance minister, but he had lacked Kirk's full confidence and this had restricted his authority. When economic realities began to conflict with the long-frustrated commitments of the Labour party and with the dreams of a dying prime minister, economic realities were ignored, and Treasury Depart-

---

[36] See Keith Sinclair, *Walter Nash* (Auckland: Auckland and Oxford University Presses, 1976) for an account of the career of New Zealand's third Labour prime minister and second Labour Government.

[37] The development of the New Zealand Labour party has been the subject of several studies, including: Bruce Brown, *The Rise of New Zealand Labour: A History of the New Zealand Labour Party from 1916 to 1940* (Wellington: Price Milburn, 1962); Barry S. Gustafson, *Social Change and Party Reorganization: The New Zealand Labour Party since 1945* (London: Sage Publications, 1976); Douglas C. Webber, "Trade Unions and the Labour Party: The Death of Working-Class Politics in New Zealand," in Levine, ed., *Politics in New Zealand*, pp. 182-195.

ment recommendations were quietly filed away.[38] When the New Zealand economy felt the direct effects of the increase in oil prices (New Zealand imports all of its oil and gasoline) and of a severe downturn in its terms of trade (occasioned in part by Britain's entry into the European Community), the record surpluses in overseas funds that Labour inherited from the previous National Government were transformed into unprecedented deficits. Inevitably, when the National party chose to emphasize the Government's handling of the economy in the 1975 campaign, it was Rowling, Labour's finance minister during the period of greatest inflation, who became the central target.

The 1975 General Election. The economic adversity of the final eighteen months of the Labour Government provided the issues that brought National to power in 1975. It was ironic that Rowling was placed in the position of defending Labour's record, for Kirk had been most responsible for the failure to control inflation. Had a general election been held shortly after Kirk's death (as some Labour M.P.s had recommended) it is very likely that Labour would have been returned to power with a handsome majority, with Kirk's personal support transferred to Rowling. The moment passed, however, and the Kirk heritage became one in which all parties could share. Indeed, Muldoon used diffuse support for Kirk very shrewdly, contrasting Kirk's background and orientation to politics with Rowling's, to the latter's disadvantage. Perhaps more boldly, Muldoon suggested that despite partisan differences he and Kirk were more closely attuned to one another than either was to Rowling. In the eulogy he delivered in the House, Muldoon described Kirk in much the language he used to describe himself: "He will be remembered by the people of New Zealand as a great New Zealander, an ordinary man with no airs or graces who, in the New Zealand tradition, wanted none of the trappings of office but just the opportunity to serve his people."[39]

Rather like National party prime ministers prior to Muldoon, Rowling preferred to lead by consensus methods, influencing his parliamentary colleagues casually and indirectly. Rowling's own reluctance, or inability, either to override or to ignore his parliamentary colleagues as Kirk had, created the impression that an indifferent

[38] See Garnier, Kohn, and Booth, *The Hunter and The Hill*. Another useful account of the third Labour Government is by Labour backbencher (and historian) Michael Bassett, *The Third Labour Government* (Palmerston North: The Dunmore Press, 1976).
[39] Quoted in Garnier, Kohn, and Booth, *The Hunter and the Hill*, p. 303. An admiring view of Kirk is John Dunmore, *Norman Kirk: A Portrait* (Palmerston North: Dunmore Press, 1972).

cabinet "team" was floundering well out of its depth. By contrast, the National opposition was led in 1975 by a man with a reputation for decisiveness and assertiveness—another former minister of finance, Robert Muldoon. Muldoon's style of political attack left little to the imagination. His speeches, while repetitious, hit home and were remembered.[40] A loner by instinct, Muldoon made this potential liability into an asset: through his very domination of his parliamentary colleagues he appeared to elevate a team little changed from the one the electorate had rejected in 1972. Moreover, Muldoon's isolation from his colleagues appeared to some the fortunate inclination of a man well suited to present circumstances, one who would be more than capable of making "tough," unpopular decisions and defending them against the importunities of pressure group elites, cautious bureaucrats, electors, editorial writers, and National party M.P.s anxious about their prospects for reelection. Portrayed by cartoonists and photographers with his jaw thrust firmly out, Muldoon appeared to be strong and self-confident, capable of making solemn decisions that could only be entrusted to a man of character. To the voters in 1975 the choice was less between National and Labour than between Muldoon and Labour. The National party's conference concentrated wholly on Muldoon. What was described as a "presidentialization" of New Zealand politics transformed party gatherings into celebrations of the leader. In the process, the National party seized the initiative, never to surrender it, and morale at all levels of the party reached exuberant heights.

Rowling's identity in 1975 had been defined largely by Muldoon's onslaughts. In addition, however, the Labour party as a whole was associated with an array of concepts that had negative connotations for many voters. To begin with, it was associated with socialism—despite having moved so far from its working-class origins that Kirk avoided the term entirely, while Rowling, pressed by the younger elements within the party, reluctantly made it synonymous with compassion.[41] At the same time Labour was associated with economic disaster; its opponents repeatedly stressed the massive overseas bor-

---

[40] The Muldoon style may be appreciated by a glance through either of his autobiographies: *The Rise and Fall of a Young Turk* (Wellington: Reed, 1974) and *Muldoon* (Wellington: Reed, 1977).

[41] Norman Kirk's article "The Philosophy of the Labour Party," in Levine, ed., *New Zealand Politics*, pp. 142-146, is illuminating in establishing Kirk's very personal view of the purposes and principles of the Labour party in the context of New Zealand politics in the 1970s. Jim Eagles and Colin James, *The Making of a New Zealand Prime Minister* (Wellington: Cheshire Publishing Pty. Ltd., 1972) provides a complementary view of Kirk prior to his taking office.

rowing that had been instituted by the Labour Government to prevent economic collapse and severe unemployment. And the party was blamed by its opponents for the crime and other social problems that had arisen, particularly in Auckland, in the wake of the massive immigration permitted during Labour's term. In addition, the National party identified its own policies with freedom, which it claimed would be restored and vigorously defended under a National Government. By implication, Labour policies were likely to erode this value—in local government, where Labour favored forced amalgamation of local bodies; in sports, through interference with sports contacts with South Africa; in the economy, through rapidly increasing state ownership as capital accumulated under the superannuation program; and in other areas of social and personal life.[42]

In one television cartoon advertisement (prepared by the American firm of Hanna-Barbera, more often associated with children's programming), the Labour party was depicted running off with the ballot box—an image that underscored National's primary theme, that the 1975 election might be New Zealand's last opportunity to resist being shaped in a socialist mold.[43] Muldoon's slogan—"New Zealand—The Way *You* Want It"—carried the National party to victory. Its effectiveness lay principally in its ability to draw upon all kinds of frustrations, enthusiasms, and expectations without identifying specific policy commitments or objectives. Also unstated was the implication that there were elements in New Zealand politics and society who, given the chance, would impose their judgment on the average person. Cues of this kind gave the Muldoon campaign (and the National party campaign was principally that, despite the usual addresses by local candidates and the accumulation of political brochures in letterboxes) a populist flavor. What Muldoon described as "the ordinary bloke" was seeking to reclaim government for his own kind.

---

[42] The broad support for National's views, and the narrow base of support provided for Labour's perspective on these themes, is underscored by the opinion poll data on sports ties with South Africa, Labour's management of the economy and industrial relations, immigration, and political leadership, in Levine and Robinson, *New Zealand Voter*, pp. 23-28, 49-54, 69-88, and 142-162.

[43] See Chris Wilkes, "The Great New Zealand Melodrama: Television and the General Election of 1975," in Levine, ed., *Politics in New Zealand*, pp. 207-221 for a provocative account of the skillful use of television by the National party in 1975 and its apparent implications for the development of New Zealand politics. In the use of television by candidates and parties, New Zealand—which has had television since 1961—has been less sophisticated than the United States but, for good or ill, has recently begun to draw even. For an account complementary to Wilkes's looking at American experience, see Joe McGinnis, *The Selling of the President* (New York: Trident Press, 1969).

It was among the ironies of the 1975–1978 term that the Muldoon Government maintained a program of overseas borrowing that far exceeded the Labour record so overwhelmingly repudiated by the voters. During its term Labour had sought to finance its programs and promises at the risk of growing deficits and spiralling inflation, which in turn it had scarcely managed to control through a Speculators' Tax on property investors and an abortive scheme implemented in 1975 to fix Maximum Retail Prices on consumer goods. National, meanwhile, once elected, maintained internal and overseas borrowing at unprecedented levels (expanding deficits that even the Government had great difficulty in predicting, let alone controlling) while generating substantial unemployment in New Zealand for the first time since the 1930s. According to the Organization for Economic Cooperation and Development (OECD), New Zealand's rate of inflation from 1975 to 1978, while reduced under National through curbs on liquidity and a range of fiscal measures, was exceeded in the developed, non-Communist world only in Iceland, Greece, and Portugal, nations with unusual political conditions making for instability or associated with standards of living lower than those traditionally enjoyed in New Zealand.

The Third National Government. National's economic policies failed to restore New Zealand's "shattered economy" as the manifesto had promised they would, but in most other areas the party implemented its 1975 policy program with some success. In foreign affairs there was a retreat from the "independent" or "moral" foreign policy of Norman Kirk. A self-styled realist, Muldoon disdained the rhetoric of morality in foreign policy.[44] The purpose of his vigorous efforts to entrench New Zealand more securely in its alliance with the United States, he said, was to protect New Zealand from hostile powers: national security was the end of foreign policy. Certainly, Muldoon was as pragmatic as Richard Nixon and Henry Kissinger in his approach to détente with the Soviet Union and rapprochement with Peking. Though he had criticized Kirk at the time of his initiatives towards these two nations, Muldoon maintained and enlarged New Zealand's relations with China, while trade with the Soviet Union (despite Muldoon's alarm about the strength and deployment of the Soviet navy) continued to grow in a manner unusually favorable to New Zealand.

---

[44] See John Henderson, "The 'Operational Code' of Robert David Muldoon" in Levine, ed., *Politics in New Zealand*, pp. 367-382.

In domestic affairs, Muldoon moved rapidly to efface the record of the third Labour Government from the statute books. Labour's mandatory superannuation program was scrapped summarily and without legislative sanction, provoking a rare public expression of judicial displeasure. The New Zealand chief justice cited no less an authority than the English Bill of Rights as the basis for his judgment that Muldoon had acted improperly, though he refrained from taking action against Muldoon. When Parliament was eventually summoned, the National party enacted its own superannuation program (more generous than Labour's); by the end of the 1976 session it had repealed Labour legislation affecting local government, broadcasting, economic regulation, and criminal law. During three years in office, National fulfilled various electoral commitments: in industrial relations, for example, it modified the law in an effort to curb political strikes by trade unions and end compulsory union membership. It also enlarged the powers of the Security Intelligence Service and enacted legislation providing for a Human Rights Commission. Paradoxically, it named a privacy commissioner and at the same time established a data-processing facility consolidating government information about New Zealanders.

Despite a record of copious achievement, the National Government's 1975–1978 term was punctuated by a seemingly interminable succession of controversies. The Government was accused of improper intervention in the legal process, for example, when the prosecutions of workers for infringing new industrial relations laws (subsequently modified) and of protesters in a dispute over Maori land were not permitted to proceed. There were disputes relating to random checks of nonwhites in Auckland made by the police in an effort to deport illegal residents (known as overstayers), and a struggle over renewed sports contacts with South Africa led to an African boycott of the 1976 Olympics to protest New Zealand's participation. Retreating from its previous enthusiastic support for such ties, under Commonwealth pressure, the Government actually discouraged them while launching official attacks on "dissenters" accused of harming the country by providing information on sports contacts to black African nations. Finally, there were protests over visits to New Zealand by nuclear-powered and nuclear-armed American naval vessels, and the Government abandoned its efforts to promote a nuclear-free-zone in the South Pacific.

In addition, increasingly acrimonious conflicts occurred between the parties in Parliament. Relations between Rowling and Muldoon deteriorated, and bitter exchanges forced one senior Labour M.P. to resign from the House, while several other M.P.s were charged with breaches of parliamentary privilege. Ultimately, public confidence in the integrity of the parliamentary process declined. The breakdown of cooperation between the parties in Parliament—affecting the scheduling of legislation, the conduct of debate, and the issuance of official reports and proclamations by the Government—challenged venerable conventions and courtesies, toppling barriers to incivility which had long contained the expression of parliamentary conflict. By 1978 Muldoon, for all his innovations in policy and procedure, appeared to many to be a man sustained by turbulence and conflict rather than by their resolution.[45]

The Muldoon Phenomenon. Since the death of Norman Kirk, New Zealand politics has been dominated almost entirely by one figure: Muldoon has become the "sun" of New Zealand politics, around which a clustering of groups and orientations has revolved, drawn by his personality and approach to politics. Alternative parties and groups have been pale reflections of Muldoon, stressing issues and approaches less for their inherent worth than in reaction to his initiatives. Particularly in 1975, Labour and its leader acquired the shape and size ascribed to them by Muldoon. In 1978, some of the constellation of support gravitating around Muldoon began to fragment, with certain interests returning to Labour while others moved towards Social Credit.

The media's stress on Rowling's personality during the 1978 campaign may have been particularly important in making it possible for Labour to regain a majority-party potential at least temporarily. If National enjoys dominance through the coalition of support around Muldoon, it may well be that only a new and compelling personality in one of the other parties could serve as a rallying point for a new majority. In 1978, a defeat for National would almost certainly have meant a return to more accustomed patterns of party competition. It would have shattered the Muldoon phenomenon, which has reached beyond party labels and above the parliamentary processes with which Muldoon is so impatient, to emotionally involve many New Zealanders who otherwise stand outside political life.

Muldoon's campaign in 1978 was totally unlike his barnstorming of 1975; indeed the National and Labour leaders reversed their roles in 1978. In 1975 it was Rowling who was tentative, indecisive, and

---

[45] A recent biography of Muldoon aspiring to psychohistorical treatment is Spiro Zavos, *The Real Muldoon* (Wellington: Fourth Estate Books, 1978). See also the review by John Henderson of *Muldoon*, of Zavos's biography, and of Garnier, Kohn, and Booth's book about Kirk in *Political Science*, vol. 30, no. 2 (December 1978), pp. 111-114.

defensive, and Muldoon who drew the huge crowds and generated so much enthusiasm for his bold style. In 1978 Rowling became a positive political force for the first time, on a national scale, appearing eloquent, forceful, and decisive. As Muldoon admitted after the election, he had hoarded his energies and policy proposals until the final week of the campaign, by which time many voters had made up their minds or become bored even with a campaign as short as three weeks.

Muldoon and the Media. After the 1978 election, the prime minister attributed his party's reverses to the media's coverage of the campaign. In some respects this was a familiar verdict. Labour activists had interpreted their party's failure in 1975 not as a repudiation of its policies or priorities but as a consequence of its failure adequately to explain its intentions and initiatives. "We went too fast," was their complacent and self-serving rationale for defeat: the average voter (implicitly regarded as politically ignorant and unappreciative) was found wanting for a failure to comprehend. The party's advertising agency also came in for a share of the blame, for allegedly failing to package Labour's achievements of 1972–1975 with the necessary flair. In 1978 Muldoon similarly ascribed the five percentage point swing against National to the voters' failure to appreciate his Government's policies.

Muldoon's hostility towards the news media progressed through several stages during the 1970s. Initially it was expressed in attacks on the media as a whole for left-wing tendencies and remoteness from the concerns and beliefs of ordinary New Zealanders; journalists (along with economists, overseas experts, political scientists, and academics generally) were dismissed as effete and isolated. Gradually other charges were added: the media were excessively critical; they failed to emphasize the positive contributions of the National Government; they were obsessed with the prime minister and unwilling to rise above trivial matters to investigate the significant issues facing the country.[46] And there were personal antagonisms towards particular journalists; one television journalist became virtually persona non grata at prime ministerial press conferences after a series of confrontations with Muldoon.

Despite Labour's long-standing claim that the press was biased towards National, the current heir and beneficiary of anti-media sentiment in the political culture has been not Labour but National. Particularly during the 1975 campaign, Muldoon's political barnstorming included attacks on the media that were very well received

---

[46] These views are summarized and analyzed in Tony Garnier, "The Parliamentary Press Gallery," in Levine, ed., *Politics in New Zealand*, pp. 149-160.

by his audience. The 1975–1978 term was marked by frequent colli-
sions with the media as a whole and with individual journalists.
If attacks on the media during the 1978 campaign were less successful
than in 1975, this was more a reflection of changing attitudes towards
Muldoon than of any presumed rise in the public's esteem for the
media.

Muldoon's postelection analysis centered on the media (particularly television), which the prime minister accused of giving too much
favorable emphasis to Rowling's campaign and of covering his own
improperly. Bruce Beetham, leader of the Social Credit party, agreed
but went beyond this criticism to enunciate the predictable third-party
view that the media concentrated too much attention on the two
major-party leaders, slighting his own campaign. The Broadcasting
Corporation's postelection review found its coverage of the campaign
to have been proper and to have provided a service to listeners and
viewers, but Muldoon promised a further audit of programming
coverage along with proposed remedial measures. He also suspended
his press conferences for a while. These informal gatherings held
twice weekly following meetings of the cabinet and the party caucus
had not been televised live, but excerpts had sometimes been broadcast during the evening news. In an atmosphere of budget cutting, the
prime minister considered discontinuing one of the two television
channels, which are run as public corporations subject to review by
the minister and to discussion and financial control by Parliament.
He also had a crack at the press. In a letter printed on the front page
of Wellington's *Evening Post*, Muldoon attacked the "typically con-
temptuous language" of the paper's editorials, accusing the editor of
"unbounded arrogance." Whether these events have had the chilling
effect on freedom of expression that they might in the American
political climate is in dispute, but what can safely be said is that the
very real adversary position in which the tame New Zealand news
media have recently been placed is one of the central consequences of
the Muldoon Government.

The 1978 Election . . . And Beyond

Electoral Prospects. In a sense, all parties shared defeat in 1978. The
Values party alone of the four major contenders found its reversals
unsweetened in any way. Social Credit—its leader returned for a full
three-year term in Parliament, its vote more than doubled, and the
stigma of ridicule for its monetary policies at least momentarily thrust
aside—could take heart. With just a few more votes in the right

constituencies, Social Credit might have achieved enough seats to give it a working parliamentary team and the balance-of-power position in Parliament. In fact, it remained almost totally excluded from power, with only one seat in reward for the persistent and expensive organizational work that had netted it more than 16 percent of the popular vote. Moreover, the party's strength remained confined to rural areas, where votes from Labour supporters anxious to defeat an incumbent National M.P. (and perhaps the Government as well) swell its numbers beyond the converted. Whether Social Credit can build upon support for Beetham and widespread dissatisfaction with the parliamentary process and the two major-party alternatives remains the biggest imponderable in New Zealand electoral politics.

Labour could take comfort from the return of some of its more articulate M.P.s defeated in the 1975 disaster, including backbenchers Michael Bassett and Michael Moore and the former minister of overseas trade, Joe Walding. In addition, the party could be proud that it had not only disproved National's predictions of its demise but actually defeated National in the popular vote. Indeed, it is remarkable that this caused so little outcry. In the United States, consternation over the possibility of just such a discrepancy at a presidential election has preoccupied academics and politicians for years, inspiring a plethora of proposed constitutional amendments calling for the abolition of the electoral college even though only three presidents have ever been elected with fewer popular votes than their nearest rival (most recently, Benjamin Harrison in 1888). In New Zealand three such outcomes have occurred in this century. If they have not prompted widespread consternation, the 1978 controversies surrounding the preparation of valid electoral rolls and the discrepancy between Social Credit's share of the popular vote and its share of the seats in Parliament have nevertheless stimulated several official postelection inquiries into the principles and procedures of the electoral system.*

The Labour party could hardly have been heartened by its failure to improve on its 1975 popular vote total. Its slim advantage over

---

* EDITOR's NOTE: Under single-member-district, first-past-the-post electoral systems, a significant disparity between a party's share of the total popular vote and its share of the seats is not unusual. Two recent examples of Governments formed by parties that won fewer votes than the chief competing party are the Labour Government elected in Britain in February 1974 and the Progressive Conservative Government formed in Canada after the 1979 election. In Britain in February 1974, the Labour party won 301 seats with 37.2 percent of the votes while the Conservatives took 297 seats and 38.2 percent of the votes. In Canada in 1979 the Liberals won 114 seats with 40.1 percent of the votes, while the Progressive Conservatives took 136 seats with only 35.9 percent of the votes. See also Chapter 3, footnote 21.

National was a reflection of the steep rise in Social Credit's vote. Moreover, Labour may well feel that its failure to grasp power under the present economic circumstances condemns it to a long period in opposition; certainly it cannot be overly sanguine about the prospect of victory in 1981. Should a change in leadership occur in the National party, Labour might find itself deprived of one of its main electoral issues and, moreover, of one of the features that have given the party cohesion in recent years: opposition to Muldoon.

To National, the electoral results may seem most bewildering of all. Although the party was returned to power, most commentators reacted to the 1978 election as though a resounding verdict against the Government had been delivered. They had been too ready to accept Muldoon's prediction that, despite recent electoral experience, his Government might actually increase its strength. Swayed by his confidence, most were unprepared for the tight contest that developed on election night and the precarious character of the National victory. The outcome was a message to the Government, but, as so often occurs in politics, it was conveyed with more than one voice. Some voters objected to conservative policies and leadership, particularly towards abortion legislation and social welfare measures, while others were opposed to a softening of the conservative stands taken in 1975 on South Africa and industrial relations. How National interprets these contradictions will determine the character of its 1978–1981 Government and will have a central bearing on the party's electoral future. It seems unlikely that Muldoon can again lead National to the kind of dominance it unquestionably held over Labour and the electorate between 1975 and 1978. For National and for the country, the party's leadership problem may be critical. For the time being, a new leader of sufficient stature to unite both party and country has not appeared.

Crisis in the Welfare State. Muldoon has described the New Zealand voter as "prepared to forgive" the faults and weaknesses of politicians. This may normally be true, but it is not so with respect to Muldoon himself. Attitudes towards Muldoon are highly polarized, and his antagonists are unforgiving. Moreover, the impact of their opposition has been all the greater in that the Muldoon era has been a period of economic adversity severe enough to challenge people's faith in the welfare state. Generalizing from personal hardship to prognostications of national doom, they have called into question the state's ability to continue to provide the broad range of goods and services on which the community has come to depend.

But even before the recent economic difficulties set in, an awareness of inequalities based on sex and race had begun to erode confidence in the egalitarian society allegedly achieved during the 1930s and 1940s.[47] More recently, there has been growing doubt that New Zealand can sustain its present levels of social support for the disadvantaged, let alone extend them to new groups. Overseas and internal verdicts on the economy are uniformly gloomy; that New Zealand relied for too long on shrinking British markets for primary produce can no longer be doubted.[48] Overseas borrowing may be providing temporary, artificial support for an economy that is past salvaging, unable to compete in the manufacture of industrial products, unwilling to surrender its raw materials, unable to sell its traditional products at prices and in quantities necessary to maintain its standard of living. For decades New Zealand manufacturers have taken shelter behind

[47] See William B. Sutch, *Women with a Cause* (Wellington: Price Milburn for New Zealand University Press, 1973); Judith Aitken, *A Woman's Place* (Auckland: Heinemann, 1975); New Zealand Committee on Women, *Women in Social and Economic Development, International Women's Year Conference 1976* (Wellington: Committee on Women, 1976); David Pitt, ed., *Social Class in New Zealand* (Auckland: Longman Paul, 1977); Warwick A. McKean, ed., *Essays on Race Relations and the Law in New Zealand* (Wellington: Sweet and Maxwell, 1971); Graham Vaughan, *Racial Issues in New Zealand* (Auckland: Akarana Press, 1972). Along with books such as McLauchlan's and Ausubel's, studies like these establish a change in mood—a shift from the old self-congratulation towards a critical (in some instances, almost masochistic) awareness of the gap between intention and achievement in the welfare state.

[48] See, for example, S. Harvey Franklin, *Trade, Growth and Anxiety: New Zealand Beyond the Welfare State* (Wellington: Methuen, 1978); Report of the Task Force on Economic and Social Planning, *New Zealand at the Turning Point* (Wellington: Government Printer, 1976); New Zealand Planning Council, *Planning Perspectives* (Wellington: Government Printer, 1978); Reports of the OECD on the New Zealand economy for 1976 and 1978 entitled *New Zealand OECD Economic Survey* (Paris: OECD, 1976; 1978). While economic gloom is widespread, the principal alternatives—greater foreign investment on the one hand, and moves towards self-sufficiency on the other, with a range of alternatives running between and around these polarities—provoke considerable disagreement. While the studies cited above suggest a removal of barriers to foreign participation in the economy, and a reduction in the role of the state in the New Zealand economy generally, other perspectives reflect the very real misgivings New Zealanders have long felt about foreign involvement in New Zealand and the capacity of New Zealanders to compete with overseas interests. See several studies by William B. Sutch, including *Takeover New Zealand* (Wellington: Reed, 1972); *Colony or Nation? Economic Crises in New Zealand from the 1860s to the 1960s* (Sydney: University of Sydney Press, 1966); *The Responsible Society in New Zealand* (Christchurch: Whitcombe and Tombs, 1971). Other studies concentrating on the disparity between New Zealand's resources and the aspirations of the welfare state include Andrew D. Trlin, ed., *Social Welfare and New Zealand Society* (Wellington: Methuen, 1977); Geoffrey A. Palmer, ed., *The Welfare State Today: Social Welfare Policy in New Zealand in the 1970s* (Wellington: Fourth Estate Books, 1977); Geoffrey M. Fougere, "Undoing the Welfare State: The Case of Hospital Care," in Levine, ed., *Politics in New Zealand*, pp. 407-417.

barriers to competition, both international and domestic; whether any Government can now develop the will to expose the New Zealand economy to vigorous competition and impose a restructuring of the economy on groups wedded to old habits may be doubted. Meanwhile, the removal of government subsidies and pervasive inflationary pressures have made it inaccurate to regard New Zealand as a country guaranteeing its people essential commodities like housing, bread, dairy products, and meat at low cost.

Discontent and Development. The validity of this bleak perspective on New Zealand's future can be questioned: that it is widespread among New Zealanders cannot. As one television advertisement encouraging voluntary restraints on oil consumption argued: "We may not make it. It's tough but it's true." A recent collective analysis of New Zealand society and politics over the past twenty-five years coinciding with Queen Elizabeth's Silver Jubilee concluded for the most part on a pessimistic note. According to one author, "any honest review of events in the current reign must end in doubt if not despair."[49] A historian wrote, "Elizabeth reigns over a country more perplexed than it was when she came to the throne, a country that can only with great difficulty retain its image of itself as problem-free."[50] The conviction seems to be growing, too, that elections themselves may be declining in importance because of the allegedly decisive influence of external powers (such as the World Bank, trading partners, OECD, or the United States) over New Zealand's economic and political future.

Ultimately we return to political culture, the view people have of themselves as political creatures. How unrealistic New Zealand was to consider itself a uniquely privileged land, "problem-free" now and forever. It may be a sign of recovery that the impossible goals of the past are recognized for what they were: aspirations for security, equality, and economic justice, all of which may be achieved momentarily but never for all time. New Zealand has been beguiled by its view of its own past, involving a too ready acceptance of the virtues of protection by government and dependency on a powerful nation watchful from afar. What New Zealanders may now be achieving is

---

[49] Roberts, "Society and Its Politics," p. 97. Moreover, a nationwide poll conducted by the Heylen Research Centre found that only 18 percent felt "enthusiastic about the political future of New Zealand," and only one in three agreed that "New Zealand as a country has a very bright future ahead of it." See "The Mood of the People: A Pre-Election Survey," *New Zealand Listener*, November 11, 1978.
[50] William H. Oliver, "An Uneasy Retrospect," in Wards, *Thirteen Facets*, pp. 41-65.

a new form of independence,[51] with the realization that they themselves, through their own efforts and judgments, must determine the shape of their nation's future.

---

[51] This mildly optimistic view may simply reflect the well-known tendency for people to find what they seek. After all, Mitchell claimed to observe a similar national awakening several years earlier: "Hesitantly, reluctantly, the New Zealander is being forced to stand upon his own knees." (*Half-Gallon, Quarter-Acre Paradise*, p. 179).

2
The Electorate

Keith Ovenden

Often we see ourselves as the legatees of a mature, or at worst, a dying or decadent civilisation. But it may be that what troubles us most about the order of modern society is a consequence not of its maturity but of its relatively recent origin—that in many respects, as a human culture, it is still unfinished and quite primitive.
Charles W. Anderson, "Public Policy and the Complex Organization."

New Zealand is a modern society with, in comparative terms, a very brief history. Its natural history is remarkable, however. Lying apart from the great continental landmasses, it had little reptilian life and no mammals until these were introduced by man—which accounts for the survival of numerous rare bird species as well as of unusual indigenous trees, shrubs, and plants.[1] In the North Island there are extensive areas of thermal activity and many extinct and a few live volcanoes; in the South Island, a great range of mountains, numerous lakes and fiords, and vast areas of forest and park land. The two islands have a combined area of 268,519 square kilometers.[2]

The Maoris, a people of Polynesian descent, probably began their migration to New Zealand around 1300, and although they brought with them and subsequently developed a culture of great sophistication and depth of mythology, their lack of a written lan-

---

The author is grateful to Graeme Riley for research assistance in the preparation of this chapter. The complete title of the article from which the epigraph is taken is "Public Policy and the Complex Organization: the Problem of Governance and the Further Evolution of Advanced Industrial Society," in Leon N. Lindberg, ed., *Politics and the Future of Industrial Society* (New York: David McKay Co., 1976), p. 218.

[1] The kiwi, a flightless bird native to New Zealand, has become a national emblem, and it became common, especially during the Second World War, for foreigners to refer to New Zealanders as "Kiwis." New Zealanders seldom refer to themselves in this way any longer.

[2] The best guide to all of this background is Alexander H. McLintock, ed., *An Encyclopaedia of New Zealand* (Wellington: Government Printer, 1966), 3 volumes.

TABLE 2–1
AGE DISTRIBUTION OF THE MAORI POPULATION AND THE TOTAL
POPULATION OF NEW ZEALAND, 1976
(in percentages)

Age	Maoris[a]	Total Population
Under 15	45.3	29.7
15–19	12.3	9.6
20–44	30.9	33.2
45–59	7.9	14.6
60 and over	3.6	13.0
Total	100.0	100.0

NOTE: Columns may not add to totals because of rounding.

[a] Comprises persons who described themselves as half or more Maori as well as those who indicated that they were persons of the Maori race of New Zealand but who did not specify the degree of Maori descent.

SOURCE: Department of Statistics, *New Zealand Official Year Book*, 83rd annual edition, Wellington, 1978, p. 70.

guage precludes detailed historical knowledge of the period before the arrival of *pakeha* explorers, adventurers, and settlers.[3]

Systematic settlement, under British protection, began in 1840 and has continued to the present day. The population, which by November 1978 was just in excess of 3 million, is overwhelmingly European in origin, as Tables 2–1 and 2–2 show, and the great bulk of these Europeans are British. Ethnic minorities among the British are themselves still evident. Scots tended—and still do—to go to the south, where there are even more pipe bands and tartan-kilted marching and dancing teams than in the north, a strong Presbyterian church and annual celebrations of Burns's night and hogmanay in towns with names like Dunedin and Invercargill. Similar pockets of resistance to the melting pot are in evidence among the Irish, with their annual "colleen" beauty contests and St. Patrick's Day celebrations, but also among the Dutch settlers; the European Jews, refugees from Hilter's Germany, who have made a particularly great contribution in the arts and in the development of manufacturing; and the

[3] See Keith Sinclair, *A History of New Zealand* (Harmondsworth: Penguin, 1959), prologue, pp. 13-25; Sir Peter Buck, *The Coming of the Maori*, 2d ed. (Wellington: Maori Purposes Fund Board, 1949). *Pakeha* is the Maori term for white settlers; like many other words in the Maori language it has been assimilated into the local variant of English. New Zealanders of European descent, when in New Zealand, and when talking about social questions, habitually refer to themselves as *pakehas*.

TABLE 2–2

ETHNIC ORIGIN OF NEW ZEALANDERS, 1951, 1961, AND 1971

Ethnic Group	1951 No.	%	1961 No.	%	1971 No.	%
European	1,509,441	93.3	2,216,886	91.8	2,561,280	89.5
Maori	115,676	6.0	167,086	7.0	227,414	7.9
Other Polynesian	3,624	0.2	14,340	0.6	45,413	1.6
Chinese	5,723	0.3	8,524	0.3	12,818	0.4
Indian	2,425	0.1	4,179	0.2	7,807	0.3
Syrian and Lebanese	1,590	0.1	1,101	—	1,126	—
Fijian	—	—	746	—	2,021	0.1
Other	993	0.1	2,122	0.1	4,752	0.2
Total	1,939,472	100.0	2,414,984	100.0	2,862,631	100.0

NOTE: Columns may not add to totals because of rounding.

SOURCE: Department of Statistics, *New Zealand Census of Population and Dwellings, 1971, Volume 7, Birthplaces and Ethnic Origin* (Wellington: Department of Statistics, 1975), p. 39, and *Year Book*, 1978, p. 83.

Chinese, who have specialized in market gardening and the sale of vegetable produce.[4] It is only in the early 1970s that the proportion of British people among the immigrants arriving annually has fallen much below half. Even so, the dominant immigrant group has remained English, and what takes place in the melting pot is essentially a process of assimilation to English cultural, social, economic, and political values (see Table 2–3).

Social change has been occurring very rapidly in New Zealand in recent years, precipitating a widespread malaise in society and anxiety about the future. This anxiety about change, along with the ecology of New Zealand and the identity of "the real New Zealander," constitute the cluster of issues around which social values find their most intense expression in contemporary political life. They are the underlying determinants of what happens on the surface of politics in New Zealand. Differences in values touching on these matters constitute the major cleavages in the electorate. So what is this electorate like, and how are its circumstances changing?

[4] There was a gold rush in Otago beginning in 1861 and subsequently on the west coast of the South Island. On the whole settlement period, see Sinclair, *History*, pp. 29-145. The population at the first census (1858) was just under 115,500. It passed the million mark in 1908 and 2 million in 1952.

TABLE 2–3

IMMIGRATION TO NEW ZEALAND, BY COUNTRY OF ORIGIN, TOTAL EMIGRATION, AND NET MIGRATION, 1950–78

Country of Origin	1950	1960	1970	1971	1972	1973	1974	1975	1976	1977	1978
Immigration											
Australia	2,831	4,377	6,161	13,804	16,083	17,730	20,319	21,486	18,234	13,440	12,352
Canada	317	952	884	1,718	2,135	2,056	2,129	1,517	960	956	832
India	456	256	252	194	273	219	267	218	250	260	144
United Kingdom	9,640	9,261	13,626	13,276	15,209	21,676	31,811	27,486	14,554	9,156	9,792
Cook Islands and Niue	206	569	927	1,062	1,181	1,949	2,280	2,286	1,332	1,016	1,012
Fiji	381	811	385	795	784	970	1,189	1,324	1,236	1,168	860
Western Samoa	209	228	540	669	445	382	553	776	1,262	1,106	948
Netherlands	699	1,268	640	533	649	819	743	860	740	532	812
South Africa	120	370	—	331	516	641	847	731	620	576	792
United States	453	855	1,312	2,161	2,413	2,309	2,426	2,040	2,012	1,580	1,432
Other	2,922	2,477	3,785	4,834	5,411	5,900	7,251	7,176	7,260	7,230	7,996
Total	18,234	21,424	28,512	39,377	45,099	54,651	69,815	65,900	48,460	37,020	36,972
Emigration Total	7,786	14,838	38,164	38,165	37,546	35,483	42,338	43,461	43,160	56,092	63,680
Net Migration Gain (Loss)	10,448	6,586	(9,652)	1,212	7,553	19,168	27,477	22,439	5,300	(19,072)	(26,708)

NOTE: These are long-term (including permanent) arrivals and departures for years ending March 31.

SOURCE: Department of Statistics, *Monthly Abstract of Statistics: Population, Migration and Buildings*, appropriate years.

The Population

Controversy about the nature of New Zealand's social structure, of which there has been a certain amount among social scientists in recent years,[5] is a consequence of one major fact: that almost alone among high-income societies New Zealand is an industrial society where industrialization took place in the primary, or agricultural, sector. The result is that the benefits of industrialization—high income, welfare programs, consumption of consumer commodities, long life expectancy, and the politics of rising expectations—have been achieved without much evidence of its unattractive aspects— "dark satanic mills," slums, disease, pollution, and the visible despoliation of the countryside.[6]

Industrialization in agriculture occurred first as a consequence of technological innovation in the late nineteenth century, when refrigeration was introduced, opening up markets in the northern hemisphere to New Zealand producers; and second in response to the negotiation of bulk sale agreements with Britain at the outbreak of the Second World War. Agricultural products, particularly sheep meats, wool, beef, and dairy products, became the staples of New Zealand's overseas trade, and much of the manufacturing that followed in its wake was derived from agriculture—canned goods, woolens, and, more recently, forestry products of various kinds. The typical production unit, particularly in the North Island, was and still is the single-man or family farm, heavily reliant on both technology and capital investment, each unit locked into a national structure of producer boards, lending institutions, and farmers' representatives (called Federated Farmers), all producing for markets in which the government is heavily involved as bargainer, investor, court of appeal, mortgagor, and, ultimately, protector.

The long history of these arrangements, which in part go back to the Liberal administration of 1891, has produced a profound ambivalence in the minds of the industrialists (that is, the farmers),

---

[5] See for instance, David Pitt, ed., *Social Class in New Zealand* (Auckland: Longman Paul, 1977).

[6] In 1978, 44 percent of all factories employed 10 or fewer workers. Only 1.8 percent of factories had work forces in excess of 200. See Department of Statistics, *New Zealand Official Year Book*, 1978, 83rd annual edition (Wellington: Department of Statistics, 1978), p. 432. On trade unionism in New Zealand see Herbert Roth, *Trade Unions in New Zealand: Past and Present* (Wellington: Reed, 1973); Don Turkington, *Industrial Conflict: A Study of Three New Zealand Industries* (Wellington: Methuen, 1976), and Douglas Webber, "Trade Unions and the Labour Party and the Decline of Working Class Politics in New Zealand" (M.A. thesis, Canterbury University, Christchurch, 1976).

TABLE 2–4
Urban Population Growth in New Zealand, 1951–76

Year	Number of People in Urban Areas	Percentage of Population in Urban Areas
1951	1,406,516	72.7
1961	1,840,202	76.4
1971	2,328,876	81.5
1976	2,594,270	83.0

Note: The Department of Statistics defines urban population as "that of the 24 defined Main Urban Areas plus that of all boroughs, town districts, communities, district communities, and townships with populations of 1,000 or over." Department of Statistics, *Year Book*, 1978, p. 66. The Urban Areas are listed on pp. 60-61.
Source: Department of Statistics, *Year Book*, 1977.

who dominated, at least until recently, the cultural image that New Zealanders held of themselves. On the one hand there was a profound ethic of self-help, the idea that a man (the concept is unashamedly sexist) can stand up for himself, build, create, and find security. This fairly aggressive ethic lives on most visibly in New Zealanders' intensely competitive approach to their national sport, rugby, and to sports in general. Pushing in the opposite direction, meanwhile, is the widespread belief that if something needs doing, the government should do it. Thus, corporate structures have emerged in almost every area of New Zealand's economic and social life, and government intervention is the norm whatever political party is in office.

Continuing industrialization in the agricultural sector, coupled with the growth of ancillary manufacturing industries and import substitution industries, which were encouraged in the 1950s and 1960s, has produced a drift towards urban life. As Table 2–4 shows, even by 1950 less than 30 percent of the population lived in rural areas (communities with populations under 1,000), and by 1976 this percentage had almost halved again. At the same time urban areas have grown rapidly, with the number of towns over 25,000 more than doubling in the fifteen years after 1961 (see Table 2–5). This growth has been particularly rapid in the north of the North Island, where the cities of Auckland and Hamilton and the surrounding regions have become symbols of unrestrained urban development. The north of the North Island now contains almost half of the nation's population, and the North Island as a whole almost exactly three-

TABLE 2-5

POPULATION DISTRIBUTION, BY SIZE OF TOWN, 1926–76

Size of Town	Number of Towns						Percentage of Population in these Towns					
	1926	1961	1966	1971	1976		1926	1961	1966	1971	1976
1,000–2,499	63	45	44	43	48		7.5	3.0	2.5	2.4	2.4
2,500–4,999	23	47	41	40	39		6.2	7.2	5.5	5.0	4.7
5,000–9,999	11	34	34	35	32		5.9	9.6	8.9	8.8	7.4
10,000–24,999	12	21	23	23	25		13.3	15.0	13.5	12.8	12.5
25,000 and over	4	12	19	22	25		24.1	32.5	40.9	44.6	50.4

SOURCE: Department of Statistics, *Year Book, 1978*, p. 67.

TABLE 2–6
New Zealand Population, By Region, 1951–76

Region	1951	1961	1971	1976
Northern North Island				
Population	745,099	997,000	1,264,232	1,424,649
% of N. Z. population	38.4	41.3	44.2	45.2
Southern North Island				
Population	568,770	687,785	787,131	843,744
% of N. Z. population	29.3	28.5	27.5	27.3
Total, North Island				
Population	1,313,869	1,684,785	2,051,363	2,268,393
% of N. Z. population	67.7	69.8	71.7	72.5
Total, South Island				
Population	625,603	730,199	811,268	860,990
% of N. Z. population	32.3	30.2	28.3	27.5

SOURCE: Department of Statistics, *Census*, appropriate years.

quarters. Increasingly, the South Island's electorate sees itself as cut off from the areas of most rapid development—and sometimes as exploited by the North.

There is a great deal of misunderstanding among the electorate over urban growth. The popular notion that people are moving directly from the countryside to "the big smoke" of Auckland is probably false. Both Auckland and Wellington appear to have grown largely at the expense of smaller cities and towns or from immigration from overseas, and this pattern appears to be typical: migrants from the countryside go to small towns, and migrants from larger towns to the cities. There has also been a drift from the South Island to the North. The population of the South Island continues to grow, however, despite the popular myth that it is becoming depopulated (see Tables 2–6 and 2–7).

These points are important because it is sometimes argued that the ideology and value system of an electorate culled from rural society and set down in cities necessarily undergo rapid change. This does not appear to be happening in New Zealand, either among internal migrants or among immigrants coming from huge urban centers overseas—from London or Birmingham or Los Angeles. Newcomers tend to see New Zealand cities as small and manageable, not large, impersonal, and alienating.

TABLE 2-7

New Zealand Population, by Statistical Area, 1951–76

Statistical Area	1951	1961	1971	1976	1976, Percentage of N.Z. Total	Intercensal Percentage Increase 1971–76
North Island						
Northland	75,261	86,391	96,191	107,013	3.4	11.3
Central Auckland	382,014	514,507	698,400	797,406	25.5	14.2
South Auckland/						
Bay of Plenty	246,480	349,624	422,299	472,083	15.1	11.8
East Coast	41,344	46,478	47,342	48,147	1.5	1.7
Hawke's Bay	91,205	114,470	133,250	145,061	4.6	8.9
Taranaki	86,883	99,774	100,895	107,071	3.4	6.1
Wellington	390,682	473,541	552,986	591,612	18.9	7.0
Total	1,313,869	1,684,785	2,051,363	2,268,393	72.5	10.6
South Island						
Marlborough	22,891	27,748	31,642	35,030	1.1	10.7
Nelson	56,478	62,967	68,838	75,562	2.4	9.8
Westland	25,403	24,841	22,861	24,049	0.8	5.2
Canterbury	283,987	344,597	398,830	428,586	13.7	7.5
Otago	159,231	176,325	182,749	188,903	6.0	3.4
Southland	77,613	93,721	106,348	108,860	3.5	2.4
Total	625,603	730,199	811,268	860,990	27.5	6.1
Total, New Zealand	1,939,472	2,414,984	2,862,631	3,129,383	100.0	9.3

Source: Department of Statistics, *Census*, appropriate years.

TABLE 2–8

POPULATION DENSITY, BY STATISTICAL AREA, 1951–76

Statistical Area	Area (in square kilometers)	Persons per Square Kilometer			
		1951	1961	1971	1976
North Island					
Northland	12,629	6.0	6.8	7.6	8.5
Central Auckland	5,594	68.3	92.0	12.8	14.5
South Auckland/					
Bay of Plenty	36,760	6.7	19.5	11.5	12.8
East Coast	10,880	3.8	4.3	4.4	4.4
Hawke's Bay	11,303	8.1	10.1	11.8	12.8
Taranaki	9,721	8.9	10.3	10.4	11.0
Wellington	27,705	13.9	18.6	19.6	21.0
Total	114,592	14.1	17.1	20.0	21.4
South Island					
Marlborough	10,859	2.1	2.6	2.9	3.2
Nelson	18,046	3.1	3.5	3.8	4.2
Westland	15,415	1.6	1.6	1.5	1.6
Canterbury	43,371	6.5	7.9	9.2	9.9
Otago	37,100	4.3	4.8	4.9	5.1
Southland	29,136	2.7	3.2	3.7	3.7
Total	153,927	4.1	4.7	5.3	5.6
Total, New Zealand	268,519	7.2	9.0	10.7	11.7

SOURCE: Department of Statistics, Year Book, 1978, p. 68.

In terms of sheer numbers, however, the mobility in New Zealand in recent years has been remarkable. S. Harvey Franklin has shown that between 1966 and 1971 about a third of all New Zealanders were on the move, approximately 10 percent of these migrants coming from overseas.[7] But while the growth of urban areas has been great, it has not created big city life as that is understood in Europe or America. Table 2–8 shows that population densities remain low, with only central Auckland even beginning to compete with cities in other developed countries and all the other regions of the country far behind.[8] As Franklin points out, the South Auckland region, which

[7] S. Harvey Franklin, Trade, Growth and Anxiety: New Zealand beyond the Welfare State (Wellington: Methuen, 1978), p. 29.

[8] As long ago as 1961, over half of Britain's population—26,985,000 out of 51,284,000—lived in areas with population densities of more than twenty-five persons per hectare. See Government Statistical Service, Social Trends No. 6 1975, London, H.M.S.O., 1975, Table 10.15, p. 168.

contains 13 percent of New Zealand's population, covers an area the size of Holland, yet contains only about 2 percent as many people.[9] The question of urban growth and regional development, so earnestly debated in New Zealand politics, looks faintly ridiculous when seen in this light.

What is not ridiculous is the unquestioned and continuing impact of immigration. The National party's stated aim during the 1975 election campaign was to "pare immigration to the bone." Certainly there has been a spectacular reversal of previous immigration trends, and these in part reflect tightened regulations governing immigration (see Table 2–3). Once people are in New Zealand as legitimate immigrants, however, they cannot be forced to stay, so that the high figures for long-term departures recorded over the years from 1976 to 1978 reflect both the impact of the world recession and considerable anxiety about the future among New Zealanders.[10]

Public anxiety about the rate of immigration from Pacific Islands in particular was exploited by Muldoon, then leader of the opposition, during the 1975 campaign, and probably made a substantial contribution to his electoral success. A great deal of attention was directed at this issue, and yet, as the figures for long-term immigration show, in the years from 1972 to 1975 the combined immigration from the Cook Islands and Niue, Fiji, and Western Samoa was less than the immigration from the Netherlands, South Africa, and the United States: 14,199 as against 14,994. Both were, of course, insignificant alongside the inflow from the United Kingdom in those four years: 96,182. The implication, that Muldoon was tapping an anxiety founded upon racial hostility, was much commented upon at the time, and the public controversy was stoked by the National Government's handling of what is termed the "overstayer" issue during its first two years in office.[11]

Such potential as this issue held for provoking racial hatred and violence was probably checked by the effects of religious belief,

---

[9] Franklin, *Trade, Growth and Anxiety*, p. 241.

[10] The net migration losses for the calendar years 1977 and 1978 were 26,896 and 33,328 respectively. It is possible that in 1978 New Zealand recorded a net decline in its total population for the first time in its history outside of wartime. The net loss from migration for the nine months from April to December 1978 was 26,296, which suggests that for the year ending April 1, 1979, the total will be in the region of 35,000.

[11] An "overstayer" was a person resident in New Zealand without having gone through the proper immigration channels or without seeking an extension to an expired work permit. During the years of buoyant economic activity, from 1969 to 1974, many employers turned a blind eye to work permit irregularities because labor was in short supply. The vast majority of identified overstayers were Pacific Islanders.

TABLE 2–9

SELF-ASCRIBED RELIGIOUS AFFILIATIONS OF NEW ZEALANDERS, 1951–76
(in percentages)

Religion	1951	1961	1971	1976[a]
Anglican	37.5	34.6	31.3	29.2
Presbyterian	23.0	22.3	20.4	18.1
Roman Catholic	13.6	15.1	15.7	15.3
Methodist	8.0	7.2	6.4	5.5
Baptist	1.6	1.7	1.7	1.6
Ratana	0.9	1.0	1.1	1.1
Brethren	1.1	1.1	0.9	—
Salvation Army	0.7	0.6	0.7	—
Church of Christ	0.6	0.4	0.3	—
Latter Day Saints	0.5	0.8	1.0	1.2
Other Religions	3.3	2.8	3.3	9.5
Object/agnostic/ atheist/undefined	9.2	12.4	17.2	18.5
Total	100.0	100.0	100.0	100.0

NOTE: Columns may not add to totals because of rounding.
[a] Provisional.
SOURCE: Department of Statistics, *Year Book*, appropriate years.

which is generally strong among New Zealanders and particularly among the Maori and Pacific Island peoples. Self-ascribed religious affiliation is set out in Table 2–9, which shows that the decline in self-perceived religious belief since the middle of the century has been small.

As in other developed societies, the decline in religious worship has been much greater. In New Zealand the institutional authority of the church hierarchies remains strong, and the Anglican, Presbyterian, and Methodist clergy have been particularly active in trying to shape harmonious public attitudes on racial questions. The belief persists among the electorate, however, that racial tensions have reached a critical state in Auckland, and this belief, whether right or wrong, in turn helps to shape attitudes towards party politics. Maori electors and the Pacific Islanders who have come in recent years overwhelmingly support the Labour party.

The Quality of Life

New Zealanders argue among themselves about the cost of living and the standards to which they think they are entitled as much as people in Europe or North America. One thing is abundantly clear, however: in comparative terms, most New Zealanders live well. They have a kind climate, low population density, remarkable natural amenities (beaches, parks, mountains, forests, rivers, and sea), and a culturally ordained, compulsive interest in sports. In living accommodation, private property ownership is the norm (see Tables 2–10 and 2–11). At the 1976 census, 85 percent of all dwellings were single-unit private houses, more than a quarter of all dwellings were wholly privately owned, and a further 42 percent were in the process of being purchased on a mortgage. The idea of a property-owning democracy is further advanced by the widespread ownership of various consumer durables: by 1976, for example, the percentage of dwellings possessing freezers had risen to 70.2, clothes dryers to 38.0 (see Tables 2–12 and 2–13).

The television service, which began broadcasting in 1960, was expanded to two channels in 1975, by which time conversion to color transmission had also been completed. By December 1976 approximately a quarter of all households had color receivers. The audience is very large, and television programs attract a great deal of comment and discussion from both politicians and the electorate. As in other developed democracies, television plays a very important role in election campaigns, through paid advertising and through party political broadcasts of various kinds.[12] The high cost of providing this broadcasting service for a country with such a small population and such difficult terrain is in itself indicative of the electorate's capacity for a high level of consumption.

As Franklin points out, this ability to consume is not matched by an equal determination to produce. The average annual rate of growth in gross national product (GNP) measured at constant 1965-1966 prices for the eight years from 1970 to 1977, when much of the increase in consumption occurred, was only 1.85 percent. As a result New Zealand has a chronic balance of payments problem,[13]

---

[12] There is no systematic evidence on the audience effects of this political broadcasting, but it is widely believed that television advertising benefitted the National party in 1975, while Muldoon's lackluster performances on television in 1978 compared badly with Rowling's increasingly popular television image. Whether this widespread assumption is accurate, however, is anyone's guess.

[13] This demand for consumption is not, of course, the only cause of balance of payments deficits. Agricultural producers tend to be price takers, while manufacturers are price setters. As a result agricultural countries are vulnerable to movements in the terms of trade. In recent years these have been particularly adverse.

TABLE 2-10
Home Ownership in New Zealand, 1951–76

Nature of Dwelling	1951 No.	1951 %	1961 No.	1961 %	1971 No.	1971 %	1976 No.	1976 %
Private house	437,078	88.5	564,196	89.0	682,003	84.2	792,083	84.9
Private house, partly sublet	1,225	0.2	797	0.1	5,234	0.6		
Flat	35,021	7.1	52,936	8.4	105,459	13.0	117,970	12.6
Combined shop and dwelling, rooms attached to offices, etc.	8,040	1.6	6,830	1.1	4,736	0.6	8,278	0.9
Holiday residence ("bach"), hut	12,393	2.5	8,905	1.4	4,173	0.5		
Other	255	0.1	43	—	81	—	4,926	0.5
Total	494,012	100.0	633,707	100.0	801,686	100.0	923,297	100.0

NOTE: Columns may not add to totals because of rounding.
SOURCE: Department of Statistics, *Census, 1978*, and *Year Book, 1978*.

TABLE 2-11

Tenure of Dwellings in New Zealand, 1951–76

Tenure of Dwelling	1951		1961		1971		1976	
	No.	%	No.	%	No.	%	No.	%
Rented or leased	148,679	30.3	153,728	24.3	206,465	25.9	248,356	27.0
Provided free with job	31,502	6.4	34,087	5.4	34,683	4.4	22,678	2.5
Loaned without payment	9,122	1.9	8,586	1.4	13,171	1.7	8,649	0.9
Owned with flat-rate mortgage	56,296	11.4	86,359	13.7	82,151	10.3		
Owned with graduated mortgage	94,625	19.2	166,636	26.3	247,582	31.1	387,078	42.0
Owned with unspecified mortgage	279	0.1	433	0.1	—	—		
Owned without mortgage	150,985	30.7	181,793	28.8	212,374	26.7	253,567	27.6
Not specified	2,524	—	2,085	—	5,260	—	2,929	—
Total	494,012	100.0	633,727	100.0	801,686	100.0	923,257	100.0

Note: Columns may not add to totals because of rounding.
Source: Department of Statistics, Census, 1978, and Year Book, 1978.

TABLE 2–12

PERCENTAGE OF NEW ZEALAND HOUSEHOLDS POSSESSING MODERN AMENITIES, 1971

Amenity	Percentage of Households
Washing machine	90.5
Refrigerator	96.1
Television	84.6
Telephone	85.4
Motor-mower	64.6
Freezer	43.2
Clothes dryer	26.8
Private or business car	55.1
Two or more cars	24.0
Boat	9.7
Holiday residence ("bach")	4.4

SOURCE: Department of Statistics, *Census*, 1971.

which itself became the subject of acrimonious exchanges between party leaders at the general elections of both 1975 and 1978. It is not clear, however, that the electorate understands either the nature or the importance of this or the associated economic issues. In a regular survey of public opinion taken by the Heylen Research Centre voters were asked, at monthly intervals, "What would you say is the most urgent problem facing the country at the present time?" The answers to this question betray the absence of any clearly formed or stable view. In the two years from November 1976 to the election in November 1978 the proportion of people naming the economy (including inflation, the cost of living, overseas borrowing, exports, and the balance of payments) as the most important issue never rose above 48.6 percent (December 1976), and it had actually declined to less than a third (30.2 percent) by the election, despite the fact that these issues had been, more or less alone, at the center of the political arena continuously since at least 1975. Thus, consumer prices rose by an average of 16.9 percent in 1976, by a further 14.3 percent in 1977, and by almost exactly 10 percent in 1978. Over the same period the balance on the current account for overseas trade

TABLE 2–13

INCREASES IN PRODUCTION OF SELECTED ITEMS IN NEW ZEALAND, 1951–71
(in percentages)

Item	Increase in Production
Toasters	68
Irons	129
Electric radiators	788
Washing machines	116
Refrigerators	333
Radios	105
Blankets	86
Floor coverings	860
Soap	9
Daily newspapers	38
Other newspapers	144
Toothpaste	300
Stainless steel sinks	714
Stainless steel sink tops	258
Generation per capita of electricity	265

NOTE: Between 1951 and 1971 the population of New Zealand increased by 47.6 percent. For these items and years, the production figures are also a fair measure of consumption.

SOURCE: Calculated, with his assistance, from S. Harvey Franklin, *Trade, Growth and Anxiety: New Zealand beyond the Welfare State* (Wellington: Methuen, 1978), p. 125.

showed annual deficits of $1,362.7 million, $1,011.0 million, and $842.7 million,* figures that range from 6.4 percent to 14.2 percent of gross domestic product.[14]

By the time of the election unemployment had caught up with the economy as "the most urgent problem"; it was named by 30.3 percent of a sample in November 1978. The number of registered unemployed rose from a monthly average of 4,166 in 1975 to 26,307 by July 1978, when there were also 20,587 people employed on special work schemes. In a total labor force of 1.23 million (1977) this represented an unemployment rate of 3.81 percent during the run-up to the general election. This is low by international standards, but the figure needs to be seen in the light of three important factors.

---

* EDITOR's NOTE: Throughout this volume, dollars means New Zealand dollars. In November 1978 one New Zealand dollar was worth approximately US$0.96.
[14] *Year Book*, 1978, pp. 606, 642, and 951-952.

First, unemployment at this level is far higher than anything New Zealanders have experienced since before the Second World War. Even during the brief recession in 1968 the number of registered unemployed did not rise above 1.0 percent, and for almost every year through the fifties and sixties the economy was characterized by total employment and a shortage of labor. Second, the figures for recent years certainly underestimate the degree of real unemployment since married women cannot register for unemployment benefits. And third, a true measure of the recent decline in job opportunities must also take into account the rates of emigration, whereby New Zealand has been, in large measure, exporting its unemployment problem. Of the 56,092 people who left the country permanently in the year ending March 31, 1977, 35,666 were aged between twenty and forty-four (see Table 2–3). Indeed, only 19 percent of these emigrants were under fifteen or over sixty-five and therefore almost certainly outside the work force. The "true" rate of unemployment is thus far higher than the 3.8 percent recorded just before the election.

It is impossible to overemphasize the importance of historical experience here: New Zealand simply had not had *any* unemployment during the lifetime of the majority of its citizens. Still, despite the sudden rise in unemployment and despite the relatively poor performance of the economy as a whole during the mid-seventies, only three-fifths of all respondents named either the economy or unemployment as the most important problem facing the country at the time of the last election, and even among this small majority the data suggest that stability of opinion was weak.

Part of the explanation for this curious state of affairs must have to do with the quality and style of Muldoon's political leadership, which is taken up elsewhere in this book; but much must also be a result of the kind of information the electorate receives on political and economic matters. In New Zealand, as in Britain and other European states, the press is a crucial element in the equation of public opinion formation, and New Zealand's newspapers do not see it as one of their principal functions to provide the public with the kind of serious and sustained treatment of difficult problems that citizens in other advanced societies have come to expect.[15]

---

[15] There are thirty-five daily newspapers in New Zealand, each published on a regional basis, and none fulfilling the role of a national press. Papers seek to achieve saturation coverage of households in their region and perceive, probably correctly, that the way to do this is to concentrate on local issues at a fairly low level of comprehension. There are five weekly publications that cover current affairs, but three of these are popular tabloids that would be familiar to Rupert Murdoch readers anywhere in the world; one of the others, the *New Zealand Listener*, is owned and published by the Broadcasting Corporation

TABLE 2–14

HIGHEST LEVEL ATTAINED BY PUPILS LEAVING SCHOOL, 1963–71

(in percentages)

Highest Level Attained	1963	1965	1967	1969	1971
University entrance	14.6	17.2	21.4	22.0	25.0
School Certificate or better	18.6	20.5	22.5	21.5	22.0
Other, none	66.8	62.3	56.1	56.5	53.0
Total	100.0	100.0	100.0	100.0	100.0

NOTE: Both university entrance and School Certificate are granted on the basis of examinations conducted by the Department of Education. The marking is controlled so as to pass set proportions of the students competing, though the figures are complicated by "single-subject passes." School Certificate is a certification of proficiency in up to six subjects taken by most pupils at age fifteen.

SOURCE: Allan Levett and Eric Braithwaite, "The Growth of Knowledge and Inequality in New Zealand Society," *New Zealand Libraries*, vol. 38 (April 1975), p. 55.

This situation is accentuated by the fact that the electorate is, at least according to the statistics, highly educated. By 1971 fully a quarter of all pupils leaving secondary school had qualified to go on to university at age seventeen and almost a quarter more had reached the level of School Certificate at age fifteen (see Table 2–14). The number of people attending technical institutes had increased by half between 1961 and 1975, and after a quarter of a century of rapid growth, the number of students attending universities had quadrupled (see Table 2–15).

These figures disguise a growth record that is considerable. It is as if a European city with the population, say, of greater Birmingham were to have six separate universities, including two large faculties of engineering, two medical schools (with two additional clinical units), and two schools of architecture; nine teacher training colleges; fourteen technical institutes and a community college; an agricultural college, and three agricultural research institutes. In the year ended March 31, 1976, students in universities or in full-time training at technical institutes or teachers colleges constituted 1.85 percent of the whole population and almost 5 percent of people aged between fifteen and forty-four.

and has a publication lead time of more than a month, which means that public issues may come and go before it can offer comment; the fifth, the *National Business Review*, is aimed at business and commerce and has a very small circulation indeed.

TABLE 2–15

ENROLLMENT IN HIGHER EDUCATION IN NEW ZEALAND, 1961–76

Type of Institution	1961	1971	1974	1975	1976
University	17,411	37,257	39,612	42,122	46,207
Technical institute					
Full-time		1,882	3,561	3,840	4,513
	82,618				
Part-time		101,695[a]	106,194	119,450	123,298
Teachers college	3,814	7,791	8,004	7,779	7,521

[a] 1970.

SOURCE: Department of Statistics, *Year Book*, 1975, 1978.

Government expenditure on the entire education system that year ran at $627 million, or 5.7 percent of GNP. And these figures exclude most of the private sector, which is itself flourishing. Between 15 and 20 percent of primary and secondary school pupils in New Zealand attend private schools. Despite the enormous investment in higher education there is an almost continuous demand for more. The last Labour Government (1972-1975) actually had plans (which have since been dropped), to found a seventh university, in Auckland, and as of September 1978 six new technical institutes were planned for the coming decade.

Such social indicators as these are evidence not just of the electorate's ability to consume public as well as private goods, but also of the changing demands imposed by the evolution of the economy. As Table 2–16 shows, the proportion of the work force

TABLE 2–16

LABOR FORCE, BY MAJOR INDUSTRIAL SECTOR, SELECTED YEARS, 1901–76
(in percentages)

Industrial Sector	1901	1921	1951	1971	1976
Primary production	27.7	24.8	18.6	12.0	10.5
Secondary industry	35.0	29.4	34.3	34.7	34.1
Services	35.2	42.2	46.4	53.3	55.4
Unclassifiable	2.1	3.6	0.7	—	—
Total	100.0	100.0	100.0	100.0	100.0

SOURCE: Department of Statistics, *Census*, 1971, 1976.

employed in the service sector of the economy exceeded 50 percent by the census of 1971 and five years later had reached 55.4 percent. The numbers actively involved in primary production meanwhile fell to 10.5 percent of the work force, fully seven percentage points less than the share employed in the professions or as administrators and managers.

Nor are these changes in the structure of employment the only indicators of the society's transition to what has become known, perhaps unfortunately, as the "postindustrial" era.[16] Given the electorate's enthusiasm for interventionist government, it is worth noting that fully a third of the work force is employed directly by the government, that in excess of 40 percent of GNP is accounted for by government activities, and that the government wholly owns the railway system, the national airline (Air New Zealand), the mail and telephone services, the Broadcasting Corporation (all television and all the national radio services), and the generation and supply of electricity. The government is also a major shareholder in shipping, the forestry industry, the exploitation of natural gas, the provision of insurance and banking facilities, and, through its newest creation, Petrocorp, the supply of liquid fuels.

In the private sector a small number of large corporations have emerged and New Zealand subsidiaries of multinational corporations have proliferated. In most branches of industry, trade union membership is compulsory and the government intervenes frequently—sometimes exercising legal powers, sometimes merely exhorting—in the process of wage bargaining and wage fixing. At least up until the 1978 election the government also sought to fix prices.

So strong has this instinct for corporatism been with the electorate that much state control goes unnoticed. To give an example from the numerous cases that exist: New Zealand, like other advanced

---

[16] The principal texts that are of interest in the New Zealand context, drawn from what is now a very large literature, are Daniel Bell, *The Coming of Post-Industrial Society* (New York: Basic Books, 1973); Ralph Dahrendorf, ed., *Scientific-Technological Revolution: Social Aspects* (London: Sage Publications, 1977); John Kenneth Galbraith, *The New Industrial State*, 2d ed., rev. (Harmondsworth: Pelican, 1974); Jonathan Gershuny, *After Industrial Society? The Emerging Self-Service Economy* (London: Macmillan, 1978); Jean Maynaud, *Technocracy* (London: Faber and Faber, 1968); Theodore Roszak, *Where the Wasteland Ends: Politics and Transcendence in Post Industrial Society* (London: Faber and Faber, 1973); Alain Touraine, *The Post Industrial Society* (New York: Random House, 1971). The degree to which it is possible to misunderstand this literature— or ignore it altogether if it fails to bend reality to the "scientific laws of history"—is superbly illustrated in David Bedggood, "State Capitalism in New Zealand," in A.D. Trlin, ed., *Social Welfare and New Zealand Society* (Wellington: Methuen, 1977).

societies, makes a fairly substantial effort in the area of scientific research and development. According to statistics collected by the Organization for Economic Cooperation and Development (OECD), New Zealand's stock of scientific research workers (6.2 per thousand of the total labor force) places it exactly in the middle of the range (which goes from 1.6 for Spain to 10.8 for West Germany).[17] Canada (at 4.0) and the United States (at 5.6) actually come below New Zealand on this measure. In New Zealand, however, 71.6 percent of the funds for research and development in the natural sciences and engineering come directly from the government, and 62.9 percent of all research scientists in these areas are employed directly by the state. The equivalent figures for Britain are 47 percent and 30.3 percent, and for the United States 52.6 percent and 12.1 percent. Further, whereas in New Zealand only 10.1 percent of scientific researchers work in higher education, in the countries of Scandinavia, which are in some degree comparable in size and wealth, the equivalent figure is almost exactly 27 percent. OECD's figures indicate that in this matter New Zealand is a special case: indeed it is tempting to think that the proper comparison here lies not with the countries of the Western world but with the centrally planned systems of Eastern Europe.[18]

The electorate, however, is happily unaware of these facts of New Zealand's position in the international league of emergent corporatism, except perhaps in one regard: the provision of social welfare. Broadly speaking, the social security system in New Zealand conforms to Harold Wilensky's description of those in the United States and the United Kingdom:

> . . . a welfare mess characterised by inadequate benefits for most of the poor and gross inequities in the flow of cash and services to various groups. Unfairness is compounded by a misplaced accent on work disincentives for some, which inspires an expensive, punitive apparatus of investigation and surveillance for all—a bewildering array of programs and agencies which recipients must negotiate when they need help, and an enormous waste of everyone's time and money. Added to inadequacy, inequity, punitive-

---

17 See OECD, "International Survey of the Resources Devoted to R&D by OECD Member Countries," *Denmark*, DSTI/SPR/77.37/05 (Paris: OECD, October 1978), Tables 1, 2, and 3.

18 See Keith Ovendon, "The Politics of Funding Scientific Research," in Wren Green, ed., *Focus on Social Responsibility in Science* (Wellington: New Zealand Association of Scientists, 1979).

ness, and inefficiency is an unfortunate lack of fiscal and policy control.[19]

Expenditure on welfare and medical benefits accounted for 10 percent of New Zealand's national income by April 1977, after almost 2 percent growth in real terms over the previous decade (see Table 2–17). This was in excess of $350 per capita and was sure to continue to rise through 1978 and 1979 as the full effects of the National Government's new pension scheme were felt. Despite this commitment to welfare programs, Wilensky has estimated that New Zealand moved from fourteenth to nineteenth of the twenty-two richest countries of the world ranked for social security spending as a proportion of GNP between 1966 and 1971.[20] The myth of the right to universal welfare persisted, but in comparison with that of other advanced countries New Zealand's performance has not been outstanding. There is, for instance, no provision of dental care for people over the age of sixteen outside of the private sector; charges for visits to the doctor except for pregnancy rose sixfold between 1949 and 1975; and the family benefit payment to mothers ($3 per child per week in 1978) as a proportion of average weekly earnings fell from 7.7 percent in 1947 to 3.2 percent in 1975.[21]

In the absence of systematic interview data on the beliefs of the electorate about the provision of social welfare the best that can be said is that the public appears to be ambivalent. On the one hand there is pride in the system and a belief, now largely misplaced, that it is modern and innovative. On the other hand the increasing comment in newspapers and from politicians about "welfare bludgers" suggests antagonism to the redistributive aspects of social welfare benefits. The minister of social welfare in the National Government of 1975-1978, Bert Walker, launched a campaign to persuade citizens

[19] Harold L. Wilensky, "The 'New Corporatism,' Centralization, and the Welfare State," Sage Contemporary Political Sociology Series (London: Sage Publications, 1976), p. 10. In this chapter the use of the terms "corporatism" and "corporate sector" follows the definition set out on pp. 1 and 2 of Wilensky's paper. He is following Philippe C. Schmitter, "Still the Century of Corporatism?" in Frederick B. Pike and Thomas Stritch, eds., The New Corporatism: Social-Political Structures in the Iberian World (Notre Dame, Ind.: University of Notre Dame Press, 1974), pp. 93-94 and 103-105.

[20] Wilensky, "New Corporatism," Table 1, p. 11. For a range of views and judgments on New Zealand's social security arrangements, see Trlin, Social Welfare, passim. The best short account of the evolution of the system and its original intellectual justification is in William B. Sutch, The Responsible Society in New Zealand (Christchurch: Whitcombe and Tombs, 1971).

[21] P. Avery Jack and J. H. Robb, "Social Welfare Policies: Development and Patterns since 1945," in Trlin, Social Welfare, pp. 29, 30. The family benefit payment was doubled, to $6, effective October 17, 1979.

TABLE 2–17

New Zealand's Net National Income and Social Security Expenditures, 1968–77

Year ending March 31	Net National Income at Factor Cost	Social Security Expenditures				
		Medical benefits	Family benefits	Other benefits	Total	$ per capita[a]
1968						
Amount[b]	3,468	44.4	71.4	163.5	279.3	102.04
Percentage[c]	—	1.3	2.1	4.7	8.1	
1969						
Amount	3,649	47.4	68.3	174.5	290.2	105.03
Percentage	—	1.3	1.8	4.7	8.0	
1970						
Amount	4,051	53.1	72.3	190.2	315.6	112.10
Percentage	—	1.3	1.8	4.7	7.8	
1971						
Amount	4,656	61.7	70.4	217.6	349.7	123.52
Percentage	—	1.3	1.5	4.7	7.5	
1972						
Amount	5,392	66.3	73.8	253.2	393.4	136.77
Percentage	—	1.2	1.4	4.7	7.3	
1973						
Amount	6,481	77.2	128.7	315.1	521.0	177.98
Percentage	—	1.2	2.0	4.9	8.0	
1974						
Amount	7,514	90.4	160.1	383.7	634.3	212.40
Percentage	—	1.2	2.1	5.1	8.5	
1975						
Amount	8,184	111.0	153.2	464.7	728.9	239.22
Percentage	—	1.4	1.9	5.7	8.9	
1976						
Amount	9,541	139.8	164.7	611.4	915.9	295.70
Percentage	—	1.5	1.7	6.4	9.6	
1977						
Amount	11,149	161.3	156.6	787.1	1,105.0	354.10
Percentage	—	1.4	1.4	7.1	9.9	

[a] Based on mean population.

[b] In millions of dollars.

[c] Percentage of national income.

Source: Department of Statistics, *Year Book*, 1973, 1978.

to report any woman living on the single mother's benefit who was known by neighbors or relatives to be cohabiting with a man. Under such circumstances a woman would lose her entitlement to the benefit. Walker's approach, although it aroused controversy, attracted a great deal of support.[22]

Social Structure

One element of the English legacy that has not taken root in New Zealand is the class system. Politicians of all the main political parties insist that New Zealand does not have a class system, and it is certainly true that in everyday life questions of class rarely arise. The public may be acutely conscious of differences in income, but class distinctions in all the major areas of social intercourse are difficult if not impossible to detect.

Again, there is only very sketchy survey evidence on the issue of class related beliefs, but that evidence, perhaps surprisingly, suggests that beliefs about class are more pervasive than is generally admitted. In a survey of members of the Values party one researcher found that only 17.3 percent were not prepared to place themselves in a social class and that fully 30 percent of those who had attended a university placed themselves in the upper-middle class.[23] Another survey, this time of white-collar workers in a large private corporation, found that although 96 percent of the 422 respondents believed there was a class system in New Zealand, fully 80 percent of them exhibited only "a weak and ambiguous class consciousness."[24] None placed themselves in the working class, although one-third of the sample were working class by reasonably objective criteria.

Historically, subjective views of class have probably been important in helping to shape party allegiances at times of crisis. It is certainly, and not unreasonably, a part of Labour mythology that, when it came to power in 1935, during the depression, the party drew the overwhelming bulk of its support from people who saw themselves as working class. The National party, whose whole purpose in coming into being in 1936 was to shape a coalition to keep

---

[22] Walker lost his seat in the 1978 election. He was, however, opposed by an attractive young candidate, and the issue of benefits for single mothers did not figure at all in the campaign.

[23] Suzanne Mackwell, "Radical Politics and Ideology in the Coming of Post-Industrial Society: The Values Party in Perspective" (M.A. thesis, University of Canterbury, 1977).

[24] Willi Sutherland, "Political Consciousness in Capitalist Post-Industrial Society" (M.A. thesis, University of Canterbury, 1978), pp. 50-51.

the socialists out of office, unashamedly looked for its support among the middle classes in urban areas and among the rural population.[25]

As in other advanced countries of the Western world, however, traditional party allegiances have been weakening in both scope and intensity over the past twenty years. The decline in strong party identification has probably gone hand in hand with a decline in class sentiment generally. Today most New Zealanders are reluctant to see themselves as anything other than middle class. This makes sense in a social context where a strong streak of social egalitarianism has been coupled with changed economic and social conditions in the past two decades. In a society formerly isolated from the rest of the world, the impact of technology is felt particularly hard. The acceleration in communication symbolized by television, the sudden accessibility of the northern hemisphere through jet transportation, the rapid expansion in tourism (both visitors to New Zealand and opportunities for New Zealanders to travel abroad)—all of these have served to accentuate changes that were simultaneously occurring elsewhere in the economy.

We have drawn attention to as many of these changes as space permits: the movement from producing to servicing industries, the growth of city life and environments, increases in higher education, the emergence of value-laden issues having to do with the preservation of the environment, and changes in sexual and social mores. This cluster of concerns, of course, has attracted increased attention in recent years in all the "postindustrial" democracies.

This term is particularly liable to misinterpretation in New Zealand, where industrialization occurred in the agricultural sector and thus produced unfamiliar results. To suggest that the society is moving into a postindustrial phase appears to offend against both appearances and reason. But of course what all the postindustrial theorists have had in common is a concern to account objectively for the new structure of society that is bound to emerge under the impact of technology. This process is visible enough in societies where class feeling was deeply rooted, and it is much more so in a society where this sentiment was weakening rapidly.

It is possible to formulate a tentative, hypothetical scheme that takes account of the new circumstances of the society and links changes in the demographic base, the industrial infrastructure, and the social perceptions of the electorate with changes in party support. Such a

25 Austin Mitchell, *Politics and People in New Zealand* (Christchurch: Whitcombe and Tombs, 1969), pp. 104-105.

scheme is set forth in Figure 2–1.[26] The hypotheses advanced in this figure are: (1) the traditional aristocracy, composed of great land-owners, has remained a stable and numerically negligible element in the social structure; (2) the traditional middle class, composed of lawyers, doctors, teachers, managers and executives of traditional industries, and the great bulk of farmers, has expanded steadily from small beginnings in the colonial period and at a slightly more rapid pace since 1935; (3) over the same period a wholly new middle class, the theory and knowledge elite, the managers of the new technology-based industries (in New Zealand they include horticulturalists, agricultural engineers, botanists, agrarian chemists, and so on) as well as the systems analysts, university scientists, and computer engineers, has grown to be a significant element in the work force; (4) the traditional working class, which had New Zealand almost to itself 100 years ago, was in a very stable if small majority up until about the end of the depression, then shrank and is still shrinking; (5) this working class has been joined by a new working class of office employees and shop assistants, who see themselves as middle class and have adopted middle-class lifestyles, although their place in the productive process and the amount and value of property that they own distinguish them from the middle class; and (6) a class of marginals, comprising temporary and seasonal workers and drifters, drawn as often as not from ethnic minorities, after having been almost eliminated by the end of the fifties, is returning in ever larger numbers and performing the dirty and unwanted jobs, a pool of reserve labor in the big cities that is increasingly composed of women and of temporary migrants from Pacific Islands.

Together, A and C in Figure 2–1 constitute the old industrial sector—mainly farming and the derivative and supporting industries; B is the new corporate sector, substantially in state hands, but even where it is not, as in building, banking, insurance, and the retail trade, conforming to the pattern of the modern corporation anywhere in the world.

---

[26] This proposed scheme for New Zealand's social structure owes much to David Apter, *Choice and the Politics of Allocation* (New Haven: Yale University Press, 1971), passim, but see especially Figure 3-1, p. 82, and the associated discussion. Franklin's interesting attempt at a model that makes sense for New Zealand conditions (Franklin, *Trade, Growth and Anxiety,* p. 72) seems to this author to be extremely simplistic and not to take account of historical and generational factors. The categories outlined in Figure 2-1 are not, of course, so clearly delineated in the real world. Categories shade off into one another, particularly at the cutting edge of the economy where traditional industries in the old industrial sector are retooling, transforming their production techniques, and altering their marketing strategies as well as their products.

FIGURE 2-1

A MODEL OF NEW ZEALAND'S SOCIAL STRUCTURE, 1858–1978

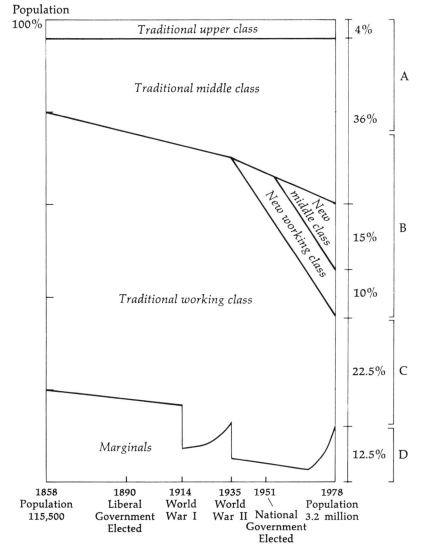

NOTE: A and C together constitute the old industrial sector, B is the new corporate sector, and D is the marginal work force. The figures given here are rough estimates and include both members of the work force and their dependents. For the sake of simplicity, the effects of the Great Depression of 1886–1891 have been smoothed out. For further explanation of this model, see text and footnote 26.

SOURCE: Author. See Keith Ovenden. "Politics and New Zealand Social Structure: A Preliminary Analysis," forthcoming.

The political parties, three of which (National, Labour, and Social Credit) have their roots firmly planted in the depression of the 1930s, still compete for the support of the various groupings in the old industrial sector. The realignment that has been taking place in the social structure, however, particularly in the past twenty years, challenges all of the assumptions on which the old coalitions were founded. Thus, for instance, the Labour party, locked into a traditional association with the Catholic (Irish) element of the old working class, finds itself hamstrung in appealing to members of the new corporate sector when it comes to the issue of abortion law reform. In turn, the National party, with its traditional allegiance to the farmers, finds businessmen and entrepreneurs in the new and technologically sophisticated manufacturing and servicing sector unwilling to give it their undivided support. When it seeks to woo that support by, for instance, intervening in industrial disputes that might harm the new manufacturing sector by damaging the level of trade generally, it risks losing the allegiance of the farmers.[27] Meanwhile, underneath them all, there is a steadily growing class of marginals. These are the dispossessed in a property-owning democracy, the uneducated and inarticulate in a highly educated and literate society; many of them brown-skinned, female, unorganized, they move in and out of the work force as opportunities expand and contract in an economy where most workers' employment is secure, ultimately supported by the state. Who, if anyone, is going to represent them?

The impact of postindustrial developments is a major cause of the political anxiety among New Zealanders that has given rise to dramatic shifts in electoral support. It can also account for the ambivalent and contradictory positions that voters assume on a broad range of issues. They appear to support individualism in some areas, collectivist policies and state centralism in others, welfare policies one day and laissez-faire the next; to couple egalitarianism with incipient racism and a status-conscious consumer mentality, repressive moralism with casual tolerance. In this complicated setting, electoral com-

---

[27] One technique for coping with the extensive and politically damaging ramifications of this problem, and one practiced by both parties when in office, is to try to define contentious new issues out of the political arena altogether by passing them on to "experts." The Labour Government did this, unsuccessfully, with its Royal Commission on Contraception, Sterilization and Abortion, and the National Government is doing it with its Planning Council and its Commission for the Future which deal with medium-term and long-term economic and social policy respectively. Not surprisingly, the "solutions" advanced by these supposedly nonpolitical bodies keep bouncing back into the political arena, where they create profound misgivings among the paralyzed political elite.

petition between politicians, the vast majority of whom still talk the old language and appeal to the old allegiances of traditional politics, is nothing if not confused—and the electorate's profound confusion is hardly surprising.

3

The Electoral System and the 1978 Election

Alan McRobie

Elections are an important and conspicuous element of New Zealand's political life; indeed, for the great majority of its citizens, the country's triennial general elections represent the quintessence of democracy. Public interest in politics and the political process quickens perceptibly in an election year, reaching its peak on election night as the results of the day's voting begin to flow into the Electoral Office from polling places throughout the country. The outcome is usually known within a few hours (or, at the very least, the overall trend is sufficiently clear for the eventual result to be predicted with a high degree of certainty), the leaders of the vanquished political parties concede defeat, and the electorate slides back into a state of political somnolence that will characterize it for the next two to two-and-a-half years. Another general election has been fought and won or lost, the electorate's voice has been heard, and democracy has been preserved for three years more.

But if the electorate evinces little interest in political affairs between elections, the same cannot be said of the political parties. Party politics is a constant battle to wrest the initiative from the other side and, having won it, to retain it. Interparty tensions form an integral element of New Zealand's political life, and although they may wax and wane with the passage of time, they are always present. The 1970s have been characterized by steadily rising discord between the two major parties, a central element of which has been fundamental disagreement over a number of provisions contained in the country's electoral law. Dissension in this area is by no means new, but, after a period of quiescence lasting nearly two decades, it has again boiled over into open conflict. During the past five years the Electoral Act has been amended three times, as first the Labour Government and then the National Government have sought to reshape the electoral system to their own perceived advantage. The underlying currents of suspicion and distrust thus created were aggravated in the eighteen months prior to the 1978 election by a redistribution of electorates (redistricting) and by instances of maladministration in the preparation of the electoral rolls. Together, these seriously exacerbated the tensions that already existed.

The 1978 general election campaign was a long drawn-out and often bitter affair. Disagreements over the content and interpretation of the electoral law had played a key role in creating a unique climate of opinion within the electorate between 1975 and 1978. The purpose of this chapter is to examine in detail three elements of the electoral system—the statutory provisions, the procedures for redistributing electorates, and the regulation of the elections themselves—which together provide the essential backdrop to the 1978 general election.

The Electoral Framework

States differ in the status they accord to the laws regulating their electoral systems. In some countries, of which Sweden is an example, the electoral law is part of the constitution. In others, like Australia, the general principles of the electoral system are prescribed in the constitution but the details have been left to subsidiary legislation. For most countries, however, the overall structure of the electoral system is regulated through statute law alone. Where this is the case, the electoral rules are in no way superior to any other laws and, unless special arrangements are included to give crucial clauses some protection, they can be amended by Parliament at will.

New Zealand clearly falls into the last category. Its electoral system is prescribed in considerable detail in the 1956 Electoral Act, itself a major consolidation and amendment of earlier legislation. Like most laws governing the electoral process this act comprises a number of interlocking sections which together specify the procedures to be followed at every stage, from the definition of electorate boundaries to the resolution of disputed elections.[1] One clause fixes the life of Parliament at three years "and no longer"; other clauses govern the compulsory registration of electors, the preparation of electoral rolls, the qualifications for candidacy, the administration of the election itself, and the maximum amount a candidate may spend on his campaign in the three months immediately prior to polling day. Eventualities such as by-elections and the death of a candidate are also

[1] In New Zealand *constituencies* or *districts* are commonly referred to as *electorates*, although the official name is *electoral district*.

provided for, as are definitions of corrupt and illegal practices and other election offenses. Even the process of actually casting a ballot is spelled out with meticulous attention to detail.

The Electoral Act also governs the size and composition of the House of Representatives. The populations of the two main islands have been growing at different rates for years, and this fact has important political repercussions. Between 1900 and 1966, when the number of general electorates[2] was fixed at seventy-six, one or more of the South Island's seats were transferred to the North Island after each quinquennial census.[3] This steady erosion of the South Island's representation finally persuaded Parliament to stabilize it at twenty-five seats and allow the number of electorates allocated to the North Island to increase gradually in proportion to its population. By 1978 the number of general electorates had risen to eighty-eight. In addition, four seats are reserved for the representatives of the native Maori people.

A number of provisions in the Electoral Act cannot be amended by a simple parliamentary majority. These—the life of Parliament, the composition and terms of reference of the Representation Commission, the method of voting, and the minimum age for registration—have all been the subject of bitter personal and interparty disagreements in the past. They are now given limited protection from wanton amendment by a party with a narrow majority in the House of Representatives by being "entrenched" in the 1956 Electoral Act. None of these provisions may be altered or repealed unless the proposed amendment is either supported by 75 percent of the *total* membership of the House of Representatives or carried by a majority of valid votes cast in a referendum to determine the question. Since the entrenching clause, however, is not itself entrenched, its sanction is moral rather than legal. Its strength rests on the fact that, in the twenty-two years since the clause was inserted into the act, the political parties have respected its intent. So far six amendments to entrenched provisions have been proposed: three were passed unanimously by Parliament, the others failed to satisfy the requirements of the entrenching section and were abandoned.[4]

---

[2] Until 1976 general electorates (that is, all but the four special electorates reserved for Maoris) were known as European electorates.

[3] This form of reapportionment, in which seats were transferred from one part of the country to another, is identical to that employed by the United States to reallocate seats in the House of Representatives between states.

[4] It should be noted here that, in 1975, the National opposition effectively vetoed a proposal to increase the size of the House of Representatives by nearly one-third. This was one of the points of conflict between the two parties which helped make the electoral system an important source of friction in 1978.

FIGURE 3-1
New Zealand Electoral Districts, 1978

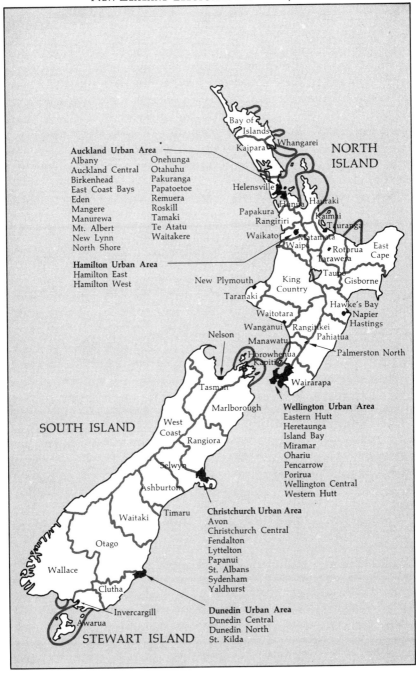

Auckland Urban Area
Albany	Onehunga
Auckland Central	Otahuhu
Birkenhead	Pakuranga
East Coast Bays	Papatoetoe
Eden	Remuera
Mangere	Roskill
Manurewa	Tamaki
Mt. Albert	Te Atatu
New Lynn	Waitakere
North Shore	

Hamilton Urban Area
Hamilton East
Hamilton West

Bay of
Islands
Kaipara   Whangarei   **NORTH
ISLAND**
Helensville
Hunua Hauraki
Papakura   Kaimai
Rangiriri   Tauranga
Waikato   Matamata
Waipa   • Rotorua   East
Tarawera   Cape
New Plymouth   King   Taupo
Country   Gisborne
Taranaki
Hawke's Bay
Waitotara   • Napier
Wanganui   Rangitikei   Hastings
Nelson   Manawatu   Pahiatua
Horowhenua   Palmerston North
Kapiti
Wairarapa

Tasman

SOUTH ISLAND

Marlborough   **Wellington Urban Area**
West   Eastern Hutt
Coast   Heretaunga
Rangiora   Island Bay
Miramar
Selwyn   Ohariu
Pencarrow
Ashburton   Porirua
Wellington Central
Timaru   Western Hutt
Waitaki
Christchurch Urban Area
Otago   Avon
Christchurch Central
Fendalton
Wallace   Lyttelton
Papanui
Clutha   St. Albans
Sydenham
Invercargill   Yaldhurst
Awarua
STEWART ISLAND   **Dunedin Urban Area**
Dunedin Central
Dunedin North
St. Kilda

The primary purpose of New Zealand's electoral law is to ensure that, as far as is humanly possible, electoral arrangements are fair to all and the election result is a just one. To this end electoral boundaries are drawn by an independent commission which works within very strict limits and whose decisions are final in law. The central element of the redistribution procedure is the requirement that all votes should have the same value. General electorates are therefore obliged to contain the same total population, subject only to a variation of plus or minus 5 percent from the prescribed quota. Nevertheless, a single-member, simple-plurality electoral system like New Zealand's is notorious for inflating the parliamentary majority of the leading party at the expense of all others. In 1972, for example, the Labour party won only 48.4 percent of the total vote but took 63.2 percent of the parliamentary seats; in 1975 the relative position of the two main parties was almost exactly reversed. On the other hand, minor parties and candidates without party backing secured 10.1 percent of the votes cast in 1972 and 12.8 percent three years later, but in neither election did they win any seats. "First-past-the-post" electoral systems can even give one party a clear majority of parliamentary seats with a smaller share of the total vote than its nearest rival, as New Zealand's did in 1978 (see Table 3-1). Thus, while New Zealand's

TABLE 3-1

RESULTS OF NEW ZEALAND GENERAL ELECTIONS, 1966–78
(in percentages)

Year	Labour	National	Social Credit	Independent and Other
1966				
Votes	41.5	43.6	14.5	0.4
Seats	43.8	55.0	1.2	—
1969				
Votes	44.2	45.2	9.1	1.5
Seats	46.4	53.6	—	—
1972				
Votes	48.4	41.5	6.6	3.5
Seats	63.2	36.8	—	—
1975				
Votes	39.6	47.6	7.4	5.4
Seats	36.8	63.2	—	—
1978				
Votes	40.4	39.8	16.1	3.7
Seats	43.5	55.4	1.1	—

SOURCE: Appendices to the Journals of the House of Representatives, 1967-1979.

electoral system invariably produces a decisive outcome, it often fails to measure up to its acknowledged objectives. A great deal of time and effort is expended in maintaining equality between the general electorates, but remarkably little concern is evinced at the obvious distortions resulting from this fetish.

This concern for detail—and lack of concern for the larger issues of representation—is characteristic of an electoral system that has evolved in a piecemeal and pragmatic way. In recent decades in particular, attention has focused on minutiae. Issues such as whether teachers should be defined as public servants (and therefore obliged to take leave without pay for the duration of the formal campaign if they wish to stand for election), whether candidates should be permitted to use loudspeakers during campaigning without first having sought permission to do so from the requisite local authority, whether the qualifying period for registration as an elector should be one or three months' residence in an electorate, or whether prisoners should be given the right to vote have all been debated at length. On the other hand, calls for electoral reform designed to make the composition of Parliament reflect public opinion more accurately have received only scant attention.[5]

Separate Maori Representation. A decidedly anachronistic feature of New Zealand's electoral system, one that does not even pretend to uphold the ideals of equality, justice, or fairness, is the continuing presence of the four Maori electorates. It is curious, to say the least, that in a country which has always prided itself on its racial harmony and integration two totally separate and distinct patterns of parliamentary representation—one based on universal and equal suffrage regardless of race, the other established solely on the basis of ethnicity —should still exist.

The Maori electorates were created in 1867, towards the end of the Maori-*pakeha*[6] land wars, "to give [the Maoris] a voice in the

---

[5] See *Appendices to the Journals of the House of Representatives*, 1975, I.15, "Electoral Act Committee, 1975: Final Report." In February 1979 Prime Minister Robert Muldoon announced that the Prime Minister's Department had set up a Committee of Inquiry to make "a practical examination of the mechanics of the electoral law in order to ascertain whether it has been and can be effectively and efficiently administered." The committee, comprising the privacy commissioner, a retired public servant, and a computer expert, was also empowered to recommend changes in the Electoral Act or in the regulations and procedures normally followed in the administration of elections if these were considered necessary. See the *Press* (Christchurch), February 14, 1979, and the *Christchurch Star*, February 15, 1979.

[6] On the term *pakeha*, see Chapter 2, footnote 3.

administration of the Colony and make them feel they have a voice in the management of public affairs."[7] From the beginnings of representative government in 1854 Maoris were permitted to enroll as electors and stand for Parliament under the same conditions as Europeans. In practice, however, very few were able to do so because until 1879 there were property qualifications for voting and, since virtually all Maori land was held in common by the tribes, only a few Maoris were eligible. The seats were therefore intended as a temporary expedient to guarantee Maoris some parliamentary representation until their landholdings could be converted to individual titles. Once this had happened they would be eligible to enroll as electors under the same conditions as the European settlers.

Although the Maori Representation Act had a finite life of five years, the individualization of Maori land tenure was an exceedingly slow and complicated business which was nowhere near completion when the expiry date loomed up. In 1872 the House approved a continuation of the measure for a further five years, and in 1876 it was again reenacted, this time without limit. When universal adult male suffrage was introduced in 1879 (a step which brought the European franchise qualification into line with that already enjoyed by Maoris for twelve years), Parliament could easily have merged the two representation systems. It failed to do so, and in 1893, when legislation was passed to prohibit Maoris from enrolling in general electorates, the separation of the two distinct systems of representation was completed. For the next seventy years the many questions raised by the continuing presence of special representation for the Maori people were almost totally ignored.

Recent changes in Maori society. The early European settlers believed that the Maoris were a dying race, and the steady decline in the number of Maoris recorded in each census during the nineteenth century seemed to confirm this view. By the beginning of the twentieth century, however, the trend had been arrested and the Maori population was beginning to increase. Since 1945 spectacular advances in Maori medical and health care and a continuing high birth rate (nearly half as high again as that of the population as a whole) have resulted in a significant increase in the proportion of Maoris in

---

[7] *New Zealand Parliamentary Debates*, 1867, vol. 2, pt. 1, p. 459. This is a charitable view of the creation of the Maori seats. The cynical view holds that they were established as a quid pro quo for the North Island to balance the creation of four goldfields electorates in the South Island (established to give gold miners parliamentary representation even though they did not meet the formal property qualification for voting).

the total population. By the 1971 census the number of Maoris had risen to over 227,000—7.9 percent of the total population compared with only 5.8 percent twenty-five years earlier.[8]

Maori urbanization, stemming largely from the influx into the cities of younger Maoris seeking better employment opportunities, is another recent trend with important sociological and political implications. Between 1936 and 1971 the number of Maoris living in urban centers rose from 10 percent to slightly under 60 percent. This change has meant that the group dynamics of traditional Maori society have been largely transferred into the urban setting, principally through urban *maraes*,[9] Maori culture clubs, and gangs. At the same time a new style of Maori leadership has emerged, more assertive than in the past. Educational standards among Maoris have also risen markedly over the last two decades, and while there is still a long way to go before Maoris as a group reach parity with their *pakeha* counterparts, several highly educated and articulate younger Maoris have emerged to spearhead Maori demands for equality of opportunity in all walks of life. A growing pride in "being Maori" and the continuing existence of the four Maori seats have combined to cause some embarrassment to successive Governments in recent years.

Maori electoral districts. While the boundaries of the general electorates are meticulously redefined every five years, the four Maori electorates have been virtually ignored (see Figure 3–2). Their boundaries are defined by Government proclamation, and since 1867 there has been only one boundary revision of any real significance: in 1954 the "rotten borough" of Southern Maori (which then comprised the whole of the South Island and Stewart Island, and which had a mere 1,420 registered electors in 1951, compared with an average enrollment of 15,347 in the general electorates) was enlarged to incorporate much of the southern half of the North Island. At the same time, and as a direct consequence of this change, the boundary between the Eastern and Western Maori electorates was also adjusted. The Northern Maori electorate, on the other hand, has remained unaltered since it was established in 1867. The Maori electorates thus fail completely

[8] Until 1974 a Maori was defined as "a person belonging to the aboriginal race of New Zealand; and includes a half-caste and a person intermediate in blood between half-castes and persons of pure descent from that race." Today, however, a Maori is defined as "a person of the Maori race of New Zealand; and includes any descendent of such a person. . . ." The 1971 census figures are used here because this was the last census to employ the ethnic definition. In terms of the ethnic definition of a Maori used before 1974 there were 270,035 Maoris living in New Zealand at the time of the 1976 census.

[9] A meeting place, a focal point for Maori activities (literally, a courtyard in front of a Maori meeting house).

to meet the requirements demanded of general electorates. They do not contain approximately the same total population as the general electorates, their boundaries are not revised regularly to maintain equality between them, and the rare boundary changes that have been made have been decided upon by the Government of the day, not by an independent commission.

In recent years opinions on the future of separate Maori representation have become more sharply divided. Some sectors of the population (principally small groups of highly politicized younger Maoris) contend that the number of Maori seats should be increased because, in terms of population, Maoris are currently underrepresented in Parliament. On the basis of the formula used to calculate the number of general electorates, they argue, Maoris should have seven parliamentary seats. Those opposed to any increase plead their case from a different perspective: on average, Maori electoral rolls are 20 percent smaller than those of general electorates, and voter turnout is over 40 percent lower. In this context it is argued that Maoris are actually overrepresented[10] and that, rather than the number of Maori seats being increased, Maoris should be encouraged to transfer to and stand for election in general seats. Once this happens the need for separate Maori representation will wither away. The presence in Parliament, since 1975, of two Maoris representing general electorates is regarded by the proponents of this argument as clear evidence that Maoris can win representation through the general electoral system and that the abolition of separate representation is only a matter of time.

Labour and National are both vaguely committed to the ultimate abolition of separate Maori representation. Neither party, however, has been willing to make any positive moves in this direction, and their reluctance can be traced largely to their perceptions of their own interests. Electorally, the four Maori seats are the safest in the country. Labour, which has held all four by wide margins since 1943, effectively enters every general election with a headstart that it is reluctant to forgo. For National, the advantage in retaining the Maori seats lies in the fact that they lock up in just four electorates a sizable number of solid Labour votes which would otherwise be spread through a large number of general electorates (including a number of marginal ones where they could conceivably alter the delicate balance). Legislation governing the Maori electorates has been tinkered with twice during the past five years—by Labour in 1975 and National in

---

[10] This argument, of course, totally ignores the fact that the size of general electorates is determined by *total* population, not the number of registered voters.

FIGURE 3–2
The Maori Electoral Districts

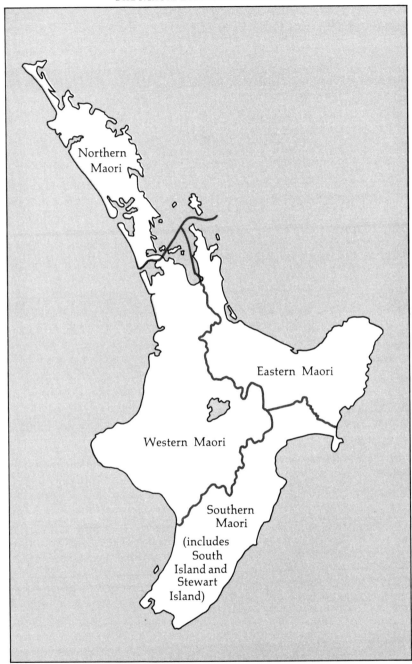

Northern Maori

Eastern Maori

Western Maori

Southern Maori (includes South Island and Stewart Island)

1976—and on both occasions the change made was dictated almost totally by partisan self-interest.

In its 1972 election manifesto the Labour party promised to amend the Electoral Act to permit Maori electorates to be determined on the basis of "eligible population." Legislation passed by the House of Representatives in 1975 implemented this pledge in four important ways. First, the definition of "Maori" was altered to include all persons of Maori ancestry *who wished to be considered members of the Maori race.* Henceforth, the key element in deciding who was, and who was not, a Maori would be cultural affinity, not ethnicity. Second, Maoris who wished to retain separate parliamentary representation could choose to register as electors on a Maori roll, while those who believed that this was no longer necessary could choose the general electoral roll. In this way the number of Maori seats could rise, fall, or remain static depending on the number of Maoris favoring their retention. Third, starting with the 1977 redistribution, the number of Maori electorates and their boundaries were to be determined by the Representation Commission in exactly the same way as those of general electorates. Finally, where the Maori partner of a mixed marriage chose to be enrolled on the Maori roll, all the children of the marriage were to be counted as Maoris for redistribution purposes.

Without doubt Labour expected to be the chief beneficiary of these changes. The National party, on the other hand, was visibly alarmed by the possible electoral consequences. In particular, it believed that the Labour Government's decision to allow children of mixed marriages to be included in Maori population totals for the purposes of calculating the number of Maori electorates was little more than a thinly disguised device to secure an increase in the number of Maori electorates. Consequently, one of its early legislative moves following its return to office was to repeal this provision and reinstate the clause fixing the number of Maori electorates at four. Ironically, the population statistics released a few weeks after the amendment had been passed indicated that, on the basis of completed electoral enrollment cards, Maoris would have been entitled to only four seats had the provisions of Labour's 1975 legislation still applied. This difference of opinion only increased the atmosphere of suspicion and distrust that was developing between the two major parties and which was intensified by each attempt to secure an electoral advantage. More important, it tended to undermine any confidence Maoris may have had that their legitimate interests could be represented adequately through general electorates, and it has almost certainly delayed the inevitable demise of separate Maori representation.

The Redistribution of Electorates

Wherever political representation is based on single-member constituencies the procedures adopted for drawing and revising constituency boundaries have a significant influence on the composition of the resultant assembly. Over a long period of time, and largely through trial and error, New Zealand has evolved a strategy for revising its electoral boundaries in a way that is generally accepted as being fair and equitable to all concerned. These procedures are based on four key principles: that redistributions will take place regularly and frequently (in practice, immediately after each quinquennial census), that the overriding consideration in any redistribution will be the arithmetical equality of electorates, that redistributions will be carried out by an independent and impartial statutory commission, and that its decisions will be final and have the force of law. It is this last principle that effectively removes electoral redistribution from the arena of party politics and makes New Zealand's procedures unique.

Nevertheless, M.P.s and political parties have sometimes been less than wholly satisfied with the results. Individual and party dissatisfactions have surfaced from time to time, and during the early 1950s the entire redistribution process came perilously close to collapse. Although this particular conflict was ultimately resolved through the establishment of a special interparty parliamentary Select Committee, which drafted amendments to the rules acceptable to both sides, party tensions continued to rest rather uneasily just below the surface. This fragile concord was shattered in 1977 following the most extensive and disruptive redrawing of the electoral boundaries in more than thirty years.

The Rules of Redistribution. Redistributions are carried out by an eight-member Representation Commission, a quasi-judicial body whose composition is intended to underpin the impartiality of its decisions. The five "official" members owe their appointment to the fact that they are senior public servants (civil servants) whose departments are directly concerned either with population movements and their consequences or with the conduct of elections.[11] Because they are not beholden to the Government of the day for their positions, they are

---

[11] The official members are the government statistician, the surveyor general, the director general of the Post Office, the chief electoral officer, and the chairman of the Local Government Commission. Strictly speaking, since the chairman of the Local Government Commission is appointed by the Government of the day he is not a public servant. To ensure that the Representative Commission is seen to be impartial, the chairman of the Local Government Commission does not have a vote.

considered politically neutral and constitute one guarantee that the commission's decisions will be nonpartisan.

Since 1956 two "unofficial" members have been appointed on the nomination of Parliament, one to represent the Government and the other the opposition. In practice they represent the two major political parties—Labour and National—for neither Social Credit nor Values has any say in their appointment. Ostensibly, their role is to satisfy themselves (and their respective parties) that the redistribution has been carried out fairly, impartially, and in accordance with the rules laid down by Parliament; in practice both participate actively through-out all stages of the redistribution process in an attempt to establish an advantage, however slight, for their "political masters."[12]

As a final and perhaps ultimate guarantee of its political neu-trality, the Representation Commission is chaired by a stipendiary magistrate.[13] His task is to satisfy himself (and, indirectly, the country) that the criteria for redistribution as set out in the Electoral Act have been adhered to faithfully and have not been colored by partisan political considerations.

The rules governing redistribution are simple and straightforward. The overriding consideration is that all electorates must be as nearly equal as possible in population. Since the number of electorates allocated to the South Island is fixed at twenty-five, the quota for each electorate is obtained by dividing the South Island's electoral popu-lation[14] by that number. The number of electorates to be established in the North Island is then calculated by dividing its electoral popula-tion by the South Island's electorate quota.[15] No electorate may vary from the prescribed quota by more than 5 percent, by world standards an extremely narrow tolerance.

In addition, the commission *may* take account of existing electoral boundaries, community of interest, communication links, and topog-raphy. The primacy of the arithmetical requirement, however, means that these factors can play only a relatively minor role in shaping the

---

[12] It should be noted that the quorum of four must include both unofficial members.

[13] The equivalent of a district court judge in the United States.

[14] Sometimes known as European population, the electoral population in this sense excludes Maoris, prisoners, hospital patients, and a number of transient groups such as guests in hotels but includes children under eighteen. In 1977 the number of non-Maoris excluded from the electoral population totalled over 42,500, the equivalent of nearly one-and-a-third electorates.

[15] Because the South Island's electorate quota seldom if ever divides evenly into the North Island's electoral population, the number of seats allocated to the North Island is rounded off to the nearest whole number. The North Island's quota therefore differs slightly from that of the South Island.

country's electoral geography. Of the four, the preservation of community of interest is usually given the greatest weight, but this can only be applied to the extent that the quota limits are not breached. Certainly, the commission tries wherever possible to locate any identifiable community within a single electorate, but its terms of reference are so tight and its room for maneuver so limited that this is frequently impossible.

A number of informal constraints further limit the commission's scope for change. Some electorates, for example, those formed from peninsulas, are largely predetermined, as are the electorates of secondary cities whose populations closely approximate the electoral quota. Another important constraint arises from the fact that the boundaries of one electorate invariably dictate part of the boundary of at least one, and frequently more than one, other electorate. These limitations add to the Representation Commission's difficulties, particularly since there is no latitude whatsoever between the two main islands. The population of the last electorate in each island, like all others before it, must fall within the limits set by the tolerance.

In every electoral redistribution there are a number of clearly defined stages. The earliest ones, like the surveyor general's preparation of draft proposals and the commission's formal scrutiny and amendment of these, take place behind locked doors. After tentative agreement has been reached, however, the proposed boundaries are published throughout New Zealand, and comments and objections are invited. In this way the electorate may participate directly in the redistribution process, but, somewhat surprisingly in view of the widespread dislocation of boundaries that accompanies nearly every redistribution, comparatively few objections are ever lodged. While all those received are considered carefully, the number acceded to wholly or in part is only about one in three. Many suggested alternatives are impractical because of the adjustments that would flow from them, while others are rejected because they would be likely to upset an even greater number of people than would be affected by the original plan. Because there is no right of redress against any variation of the draft boundaries, this is an important consideration. Thus when the commission reconvenes to review the objections it has received, its principal concern is to tidy up any anomalies that have become apparent. Only where a significant body of local opinion suggests an alternative division of an area, and only where a new proposal can be implemented without causing extensive disruption to the remainder of the new electoral map, are major departures from the original plan countenanced. Nevertheless, this act of public participation is important as a means of establishing the legitimacy of the new boundaries in the eyes of the electorate.

Although electors, M.P.s, political parties, and those who administer the electoral law are all affected to some degree by boundary changes, New Zealand's arrangements for the regular and automatic adjustment of its electoral districts compare extremely favorably with those of other countries. Within the narrow limits of its discretion the Representation Commission does a creditable job in maintaining a generally acceptable balance between considerations that are frequently in conflict with one another. Certainly the constraints under which it operates would rule out any possibility of deliberately drawing up a set of boundaries that would favor one political party at the expense of all others.

Nevertheless, after most redistributions it is alleged that gerrymandering has occurred. Of course it is virtually impossible to maintain precisely the preexisting political balance, and it is *not* the commission's responsibility to attempt to do so. Alterations to the political balance occur, but they are of nonpartisan origin stemming primarily from the changes in population distribution that have taken place during the previous five years. Such changes have their greatest impact at the level of individual electorates, where in some circumstances the future of an incumbent M.P. may be severely compromised. Over the entire country, however, a party's losses in some electorates are almost invariably offset by gains in others. The electoral boundaries determined by New Zealand's Representation Commission are almost certainly imperfect, but they are not drawn to consciously favor any political grouping.

The 1977 Redistribution. The redistribution announced in April 1977 was the most sweeping for thirty years. Apart from the four Maori electorates, only five seats completely escaped alteration. This large-scale disruption had two main causes: intercensal demographic change and the new provisions governing Maori electoral enrollments. Changes in population distribution between 1971 and 1976—principally the more rapid growth of the North Island (especially the northern half), the continuing population drift from rural to urban areas, and the rapid growth of the suburbs at the expense of the inner cities—left as many as fifty electorates outside the population range permitted by the Electoral Act. This situation was compounded by the fact that a large number of Maoris had failed to reenroll at the time of the census and consequently were counted as part of the general electoral population for redistribution purposes. Since over 90 percent of all Maoris live in the North Island, the disparity in electoral population between the North and South Islands was accentuated significantly.

Altogether, five additional electorates were established in the North Island, two in the Auckland urban area and the remaining three slightly to the south, in the Waikato-Central Plateau-Bay of Plenty areas. These were the regions of greatest population growth. Inevitably, the addition of these five electorates affected most of the island, seriously disrupting the preexisting pattern of electoral boundaries. Many electorates had to be regrouped, and some had to be abolished and new ones drawn so that the statutory requirements could be met.

Because the South Island's parliamentary representation is fixed, the Representation Commission's task there was not as difficult as it had been in the North Island. Even so, above average population growth in and around Christchurch (and, to a lesser extent, around Nelson and Blenheim), coupled with static and even declining populations in parts of Otago and Southland, resulted in a general northward movement of electorates towards Christchurch. The overall effect was to further enlarge many of the already geographically huge rural electorates and to regroup established communities of interest into new electorates. Only one electorate remained totally intact, and, as in the North Island, many others were so altered by the redistribution that they had to be renamed.

The Political Consequences of the Redistribution. Although the Representation Commission discharges its responsibilities meticulously and without favor, its decisions inevitably create political difficulties and tensions. Electorates are often so radically altered that they bear little resemblance to their predecessors; some even disappear completely, leaving the incumbent M.P. without a seat to which he or she can claim to be the rightful heir. In a number of instances the political complexion of an electorate still bearing an old name changes from "safe" for one party to "marginal" or even to "safe" for the opposing party. Thus, while the regular quinquennial adjustment of electoral boundaries maintains reasonable equality between electorates, the accompanying dislocation of established political patterns has a highly significant effect on New Zealand's political life.

An unusual aspect of the 1977 redistribution was the extent to which the political elites of both major parties were prepared to comment publicly on its possible outcome long before the commissioners had even met for the first time. The National party's president, George Chapman, was particularly free with his widely publicized "helpful hints," so much so that the president of the Labour party,

Arthur Faulkner, accused him of seeking to influence the commission to draw boundaries that would entrench the National party in power.[16]

This altercation was symptomatic of the increasing tension between the two parties. From the time the provisional census figures were published it was apparent that a major electoral upheaval was imminent. Naturally, sitting members were keenly interested in the outcome of the commission's deliberations. Pressure was applied somewhere, and the unofficial commissioners (apparently with the blessing of the full commission) informed M.P.s, in confidence, of the proposed changes nearly two months before the provisional boundaries were released for public scrutiny. This confidence was soon breached as M.P.s from both sides publicly clashed over the political effects of the new electoral map. Many Labour spokesmen alleged that gerrymandering had occurred: one party official went so far as to claim publicly that every marginal National seat in the Auckland area had been made safe for the sitting National M.P.[17] National party spokesmen, on the other hand, predictably and emphatically denied all suggestions that the boundaries had been gerrymandered in the Government's favor.[18] After the new boundaries were finalized, however, Chapman acknowledged that the redistribution had been "very favorable" to his party. Faulkner agreed. Labour's chances, he said, had not been improved by the changes, but, he added, "the new boundaries will ensure that the party which gets most votes will become the next government."[19]

These partisan assessments of the political effects of the 1977 redistribution were subsequently confirmed in an independent study of 1975 voting patterns and their bearing on the new boundaries.[20] After the 1975 general election Labour required a swing of 4.7 percentage points to win a majority of the two-party vote—more than

[16] Alan D. McRobie, "The Politics of Electoral Redistribution," in Stephen Levine, ed., *Politics in New Zealand* (Sydney: George Allen & Unwin, 1978), pp. 264-265.

[17] *Press* (Christchurch), January 10, 1977.

[18] Ibid.

[19] Ibid., April 20, 1977. Insofar as the National party won both a majority of votes in the general electorates and a majority of parliamentary seats, Faulkner's assertion was correct. But when the four Maori electorates are included, Labour's share of the total vote was greater than National's. Shortly after the general election one Labour M.P. challenged the Representation Commission to explain how the National party could win a six-seat parliamentary majority with 10,000 fewer popular votes than Labour. *Christchurch Star*, November 30, 1978.

[20] Alan McRobie and Nigel S. Roberts, *Election '78: The 1977 Electoral Redistribution and the 1978 General Election in New Zealand* (Dunedin: John McIndoe, 1978).

TABLE 3–2

SWING TO LABOUR REQUIRED FOR A LABOUR VICTORY
BEFORE AND AFTER THE 1977 REDISTRIBUTION
(in percentage points)

	Swing Required by Labour:	
	To win a majority of the two-party vote	To win a majority of parliamentary seats
All electorates		
Before 1977 redistribution	4.7	4.4
After 1977 redistribution	4.7	5.2
General electorates		
Before 1977 redistribution	5.8	5.3
After 1977 redistribution	5.8	5.8

SOURCE: Alan McRobie and Nigel S. Roberts, *Election '78: The 1977 Electoral Redistribution and the 1978 General Election in New Zealand*, pp. 37-39.

enough to capture a majority of parliamentary seats under the old boundaries (see Table 3–2). The 1977 redistribution significantly altered this balance: Labour now needed to generate a two-party swing of 5.2 percentage points in its favor if it was to recapture office, significantly more than it needed to secure a majority of the two-party vote. Labour's electoral task, therefore, was made more difficult by the redistribution. Nevertheless—and this is an important point—if the eighty-eight general electorates directly involved in the redistribution are examined, it is clear that no overall bias towards either major party existed *after* the redistribution. In 1978 Labour needed a two-party swing of 5.8 percentage points to win *both* a majority of the two-party vote *and* a majority of the general electorates. Unwittingly, the 1977 redistribution had eliminated a preexisting bias in the general electorates favoring Labour by one-half of one percent: it was as fair to both major parties as it could possibly be.[21]

[21] In the 1978 general election the two-party swing to Labour over all electorates was 5.0 percentage points. Although Labour won more votes in total than any other party, it still failed by seven to win an absolute majority of the parliamentary seats. In the general electorates, where Labour took 49.1 percent of the two-party vote, the two-party swing was 4.8 percentage points, and here Labour was eleven seats short of a majority. This marked discrepancy between the percentage of the two-party vote and the number of parliamentary seats results from a number of factors. Voter support for the two main parties is far from

The effects were by no means uniform across the country. In the South Island the redistribution slightly favored Labour, but in the North Island, where boundary changes were generally more substantial, the National party was the chief beneficiary. National's gains were greatest in the northern half of the island, and especially in urban Auckland. It was here, a region where National has been increasing its support steadily over a number of years, that the five additional electorates were established.

Redistribution can affect individual M.P.s in a number of ways. Some are delighted to discover that their hold on their seats has been made considerably more secure by the changes, while others find that their position has been weakened. The difficulties arising from a redistribution appear to be most acute when an M.P.'s parliamentary career is placed in jeopardy. Electoral defeat stemming from a loss of voter support is accepted as an occupational hazard, but no M.P. relishes the prospect that his political demise will be occasioned by boundary changes which undermine his organizational power base. Yet, after nearly every redistribution, a number of M.P.s find themselves in this predicament. Their options are clear: find new, safer electorates where the local party organizations are prepared to accept them as their candidates, or retire from politics as gracefully as possible.

The upheaval emanating from the 1977 redistribution brought more than its fair share of difficulties to a number of sitting members on both sides of the House. Three of the twenty cabinet ministers had their electorates abolished both in name and as geographic units, one of them for the second time in successive redistributions. The National party's hierarchy moved swiftly to decide in which electorate each minister would run.[22] Some Labour M.P.s faced the same problem.

---

evenly spread over the country. Traditionally, Labour piles up huge majorities in a number of its safe electorates while losing narrowly in many others; National's electoral support is much more uniform. It may be argued that Labour's dominance of the four Maori seats goes some way towards redressing this imbalance. Another factor contributing to the discrepancy is the degree of support (and its geographic distribution) accorded to the minor parties, especially Social Credit.

[22] Immediately following the 1972 redistribution two National cabinet ministers (Allan McCready and Leslie Gandar) were involved in an unseemly public squabble over who should be nominated in the restructured Manawatu electorate, which included part of the electorate each minister was currently representing. This dispute was ultimately resolved by the intervention of the prime minister and leader of the National party, Jack (later Sir John) Marshall, who decided in favor of McCready. Gandar subsequently won the newly created Ruahine electorate and retained it in 1975. The 1977 redistribution, however, abolished Ruahine, and Gandar was selected to represent National in neighboring Rangi-

In urban Auckland, the inner-city electorate of Grey Lynn was abolished and its voters were divided between three adjacent (and substantially altered) electorates, all of which had sitting Labour M.P.s. Grey Lynn's sitting member, Eddie Isbey, sought his party's nomination in three central and west Auckland seats before being chosen by the party hierarchy to contest the southern Auckland seat of Papatoetoe, which on paper was marginally National. Similarly, Roger Douglas's southern Auckland electorate of Manukau was split between three new ones, and he had to accept nomination in the restructured Manurewa electorate. It included only one-quarter of his old electorate, and the boundary changes had made it, like Papatoetoe, marginally National. The effects of the redistribution are highlighted by the fact that, until 1975, Labour could win all three seats in the southern Auckland urban area quite comfortably. After the 1977 redistribution had created an additional seat in this region and the boundaries had been radically redrawn, Labour could count on winning only one of the four new seats. Thus, two sitting Labour M.P.s in previously "safe" electorates found themselves fighting for their political lives.

This was the pattern in many parts of the country. Many M.P.s who had expended a great deal of time and effort in building up their party's organization in the electorate they represented, were faced with having to rebuild their local power base (sometimes from practically nothing) before they could begin their 1978 campaigns. Where an electorate underwent a major alteration, and particularly where its name was changed, the incumbent M.P. generally moved with remarkable rapidity to establish his, and his party's, credentials in the

---

tikei where the incumbent National M.P., Sir Roy Jack, was retiring. This satisfactory arrangement was upset by Jack's untimely death in December 1977. In the subsequent by-election the Social Credit leader, Bruce Beetham, won Rangitikei against a "stand-in" National candidate. Having already publicly indicated that Gandar would be nominated in Rangitikei in the general election, the National party found itself in the somewhat embarrassing position of having one of its senior ministers pitted against Social Credit's sole parliamentary representative. To have changed direction and nominated Gandar for another electorate (probably Manawatu, where National had still to choose its candidate) would have been tantamount to admitting that Social Credit posed a threat; to do nothing meant that two sitting M.P.s would be competing directly against each other in the general election—a most unusual situation in New Zealand politics. It meant, too, that Beetham had eight months as member for the old Rangitikei electorate to work towards establishing himself as the legitimate heir to the new Rangitikei electorate. Gandar, on the other hand, could be labeled a carpetbagger and interloper because, until the end of the 1978 parliamentary session, he was still M.P. for Ruahine.

new electorate. In one new electorate, Yaldhurst, on the outskirts of Christchurch, the first meeting of the Labour party's Yaldhurst branch was held within three weeks of the *provisional* boundaries' being made public, ten weeks before these were confirmed, and twenty-one months before the electorate actually came into existence. Throughout this period, Michael Connelly, M.P. for Wigram (which was to be abolished), described himself as "M.P. for the new Yaldhurst electorate" as a means of establishing his legitimate claim to the seat. And well he might, for on paper the new Yaldhurst electorate had a National majority by some 750 votes!

The consequences of the 1977 redistribution were felt throughout the political system. They manifested themselves most clearly in the interparty tension that built up as the election approached. National's goal was to cement its claim to be the natural party of government in New Zealand, and its leading spokesmen seldom missed an opportunity to remind the electorate that the redistribution had provided the party with a unique opportunity for destroying Labour once and for all. For its part, Labour alleged repeatedly that the redistribution had been unfair. Allusions to gerrymandering, foul play, and "political perversion" were heard frequently as Labour spokesmen endeavored to implant the notion that the Government had acted unfairly and even illegally. Neither Social Credit nor Values was really involved; the redistribution battle was part of the continuing war between Labour and National for control of the Government.[23]

The Regulation of Elections

Except in unusual circumstances New Zealand's general elections have been held regularly every third year for the past 100 years.[24] Although successive prime ministers have endeavored to keep the date they have selected a secret for as long as possible, their options are, in reality, extremely limited—so much so that every one of the eight general elections since 1957 has taken place on the last Saturday in November. This predictability has its advantages; while the political

---

[23] One further consequence of the 1977 redistribution, the registration of electors, is considered below, pp. 87-91. See the section on "Incumbents" in Keith Jackson's chapter for another discussion of the problems in particular districts.

[24] The exceptions have occurred in times of national crisis. The term of Parliament was extended during each world war and during the depression of the 1930s, and in 1951 the first National Government called a "snap" election fourteen months ahead of schedule to seek the electorate's approval of its handling of a long drawn-out waterfront strike.

parties tailor their election strategies with this date in mind, the planning for what is one of the state's largest and most complex administrative undertakings is able to proceed in an orderly fashion through a series of clearly delineated stages.[25]

The Registration of Electors. Enrollment as an elector has been compulsory for non-Maoris since 1924 and for Maoris since 1956. The franchise is wide. Apart from a few minor exceptions[26] all persons over the age of eighteen who have lived in New Zealand continuously for at least a year and who are "ordinarily resident" in the country are required to register as electors once they have resided in an electorate for three months. Persons "ordinarily resident in New Zealand" but who are currently living overseas with the intention of returning may retain their registration for up to three years from their date of departure.

A general reenrollment of electors takes place every five years. Until 1972 this was conducted shortly after each electoral redistribution, and the state, through the Electoral Office, took the initiative by forwarding reregistration cards to each household. Between each general reenrollment, however, responsibility for registration rested with individual electors. The electoral rolls thus produced were reasonably accurate, particularly where a general election was held soon after a reregistration had been completed.[27] Certainly, the procedure was widely accepted as fair and equitable, and the overall accuracy of the rolls was seldom questioned.

Nevertheless, at every general election a significant number of votes are disallowed simply because voters have failed to register. Clearly, despite the provision for compulsory enrollment, not all qualified electors are actually registered. Many Labour M.P.s and party activists believed that this situation placed them at a disadvantage, and in 1975 the Labour Government amended the law relating

---

[25] In the 1978 budget just under $2 million was provided for the administration of the general election. In all nearly 15,000 people were employed by the state to ensure its proper conduct, and over 4,150 polling places were established throughout the country.

[26] The exceptions are: (1) persons detained as special or committed patients in a hospital under the Mental Health Act, (2) convicted persons serving prison sentences at the time of the election, and (3) persons who have been convicted of corrupt practices during an election.

[27] Where two successive general elections are held using the same roll, the roll for the second election tends to be rather more inaccurate. This is largely because of the mobility of New Zealanders and the laxity of some in taking steps to reenroll in their new electorate.

85

to registration. Henceforth all those who qualified were to complete reenrollment cards at the time of the quinquennial census.[28]

Advocates of this new procedure claimed that it would both simplify registration and ensure that future rolls would be more complete and accurate than ever before. Its implementation, however, was fraught with difficulties from the outset. The census was taken in March 1976, less than four months after the 1975 election, at a time when public interest in the next general election was negligible and long before the redistribution exercise was (and could have been) commenced.[29] As a result, many electors—perhaps as many as 100,000—failed to complete the reenrollment forms as required.[30] This obvious shortfall in enrollments persuaded the chief electoral officer to include all names from the old (and rather inaccurate) rolls used during the 1975 election on the new rolls. It was anticipated that, with computerization, the elimination of duplicate entries would be a routine matter. This was the case where entries were identical in every respect but not where addresses, occupations, or names had changed in the intervening period. When the main rolls were finally published in the middle of 1978, they were found to contain countless errors and duplications as well as omissions.

Difficulties also arose with the registration of Maori voters. Under the amendment to the Electoral Act passed in 1975, Maoris were required to choose whether they wished to be registered on a Maori or a general roll; having made this decision, they were required to retain this enrollment until the next census. The electoral registration card was not well designed, and a significant number of Maoris who wished to be enrolled on a Maori roll apparently failed to indicate

---

[28] In its 1975 legislation Labour also inserted a clause to permit voters who went to a polling place and found that they were not enrolled to complete a registration card on the spot and have their vote counted as valid. National strenuously opposed this provision. Its view was that it was an elector's responsibility to make sure he was enrolled before election day. If he did not meet this obligation it was right and proper that he should effectively be disfranchised. The provision was one of those repealed after a new National Government took office at the end of 1975.

[29] Whereas in all previous reenrollments electors could be placed in their new electorates immediately, on this occasion the reshuffling could not possibly take place for another fifteen months until after the redistribution had been undertaken.

[30] Despite the legal requirement to enroll, a number of potential electors prefer, for various reasons, not to do so. Although the Electoral Act provides a fine of $20 upon conviction for failing to enroll, this has never been enforced. It should be noted, also, that while census subenumerators had legal authority to insist on the completion of all census papers, they did not have authority to insist that reenrollment forms be completed and returned.

their choice positively in the space provided. As a consequence, they were enrolled in general electorates with no option but to remain there until after the 1981 census.[31]

As public concern began to mount, the Labour opposition launched a vigorous and sustained attack on the state of the electoral rolls. In three private members' bills, two adjournment debates, and a flood of notices of motion and parliamentary questions, it sought to ram home its charge of administrative incompetence against the National Government. National's defense was that all the difficulties were attributable to Labour's own legislation and that the confusion was "being deliberately exploited and carefully fostered by the Labour Party for party political purposes."[32] The minister of justice, David Thompson, publicly expressed his confidence that the rolls would be "accurate and complete" long before election day, and Prime Minister Muldoon also endeavored to allay the electorate's obvious concern by commenting, "I wouldn't get too excited about it. It all comes right on the day."[33]

At the center of the political storm was the chief electoral officer, Jack Wright, who denied repeatedly that the electoral rolls were in the chaotic state alleged by Labour. Nevertheless, his public statements, which were intended to blunt the criticism, frequently had the opposite effect. One statement, that the accuracy of the electoral rolls could not be guaranteed,[34] generated so much consternation that the

[31] In May 1978, Matiu Rata, M.P. for Northern Maori and minister of Maori affairs in the third Labour Government, tried unsuccessfully to persuade the minister of justice, David Thomson, to reopen Maori electoral enrollments for a limited period to permit Maoris who had been inadvertently placed on a general roll to transfer their enrollment to the Maori roll if they so desired. (There is evidence that a number of Maoris who had registered as electors on a Maori roll at the time of the census later reenrolled as electors in a general electorate, contrary to the provisions of the Electoral Act.)

[32] *Parliamentary Debates*, vol. 418, p. 1653.

[33] *Press*, June 20, 1978. Four months later, however, Muldoon was reported as saying that he was far from happy with the state of the electoral rolls. It later transpired that he had applied for registration as an elector in the Western Hutt electorate (a National marginal) where the prime minister's residence is situated but his name was still included on the main Tamaki roll (the Auckland electorate he represents in Parliament). His name was eventually included on the supplementary roll for Western Hutt.

[34] *Press*, September 2, 1978. Wright was reported as saying: "There's no such thing as a completely up-to-date electoral roll. We'll guarantee to make it as accurate as possible. I can't give any more assurance than that. No one can." A few days before the election, Wright stated that errors and omissions in the rolls would not prevent electors from casting a vote. This is true: no one who arrives at a polling place is ever refused a vote. But where a voter's name is not entered on the published roll, he or she is required to cast a "special" vote, the

minister of state services, J. B. "Peter" Gordon, instructed his officials to investigate the procedures being used to compile the rolls. Their report stated that they were satisfied that the Justice Department (of which the Electoral Office is part) was taking all proper steps to ensure that the rolls would be in "as complete a state as is normally achieved" by the time of the election.[35]

Voters whose names had not been included in the main rolls further compounded an already confused situation. In many instances actively aided and abetted by the Labour party,[36] thousands completed new enrollment cards and sent them off to the Electoral Office. Unfortunately, a large number of enrollment cards which had been received by the Electoral Office *after* the date of the census (more than two years earlier) had still to be processed. Thus, when the supplementary rolls finally appeared a fortnight before the election, many electors discovered that they were listed twice—and sometimes as many as three or four times. Despite the many assurances given by both the Government and the Electoral Office, accurate rolls never materialized. The printed rolls indicated that New Zealand had 2,487,494 registered voters, nearly half a million more than the estimated number of people over eighteen living in the country in December 1977—and failed to include thousands of electors who claimed in the days immediately prior to the election that their names were missing even though they had met their obligation to register.[37]

---

validity of which is determined later. This depends entirely on whether the elector in question is registered as a voter. Since the fate of a special vote is never communicated to the elector concerned, the published roll is the only real guarantee a voter has that his or her vote will be adjudged valid.

[35] *Christchurch Star*, September 22, 1978.

[36] Labour provided public booths in many urban centers so that electors could check their enrollment. Where names could not be located, new registration cards were completed and forwarded to the Electoral Office by party officials. The party also maintained a list of electors enrolled in this way, and it was checked against the supplementary rolls when they appeared. Clearly, Labour's objective was to establish itself in the eyes of the electorate as the only political party really concerned with the preservation of democracy. Efforts were also made to make sure that eligible electors currently living overseas were enrolled wherever possible. In October 1978 party leader Bill Rowling paid a flying visit to Sydney to spearhead a drive by the party to enroll eligible New Zealanders living in Australia. This strategy provoked the prime minister to allege that Labour was endeavoring to stack the electoral rolls with the names of people who were no longer eligible to vote in a New Zealand election.

[37] *Press*, November 18, 1978. Despite this huge discrepancy the deputy chief electoral officer was reported as saying that, even though many of the names included on the rolls must be inaccurate, electorate officers would still be able to certify that the rolls were correct. "We can only say that the rolls are correct according to the information we have available," he added. *Press*, November 23, 1978.

The overall effect of this ferment was to partially undermine public confidence in the electoral process. The Labour party exploited this concern to the full in the months leading up to the election. Never before in New Zealand's history had the administrative aspects of a general election come under such fire. Despite the strenuous and repeated efforts of both ministers and electoral officers to minimize the obvious (and for the most part, genuine) concern over the state of the rolls, misgivings about the equity of the impending election persisted. The possibility existed that the election result might not be accepted wholeheartedly by the electorate and that, as a consequence, the legitimacy of the incoming Government might be called into question.[38]

Candidates and Campaign Expenditure. For the past forty years New Zealand's political life has been dominated by the tightly organized, mass-based Labour and National parties. Although Social Credit has contested every election since 1954, it has succeeded in winning only two parliamentary seats in that period, so that the two major parties provide the only realistic channel for entering Parliament. Nevertheless there is never any shortage of parliamentary aspirants. Apart from the ninety-two candidates each nominated by Labour, National, Social Credit, and Values in the last two elections, another sixty-six candidates in 1975 and fifty-one in 1978 were nominated by fringe parties or ran as independents.

As these figures suggest, becoming a candidate in a New Zealand election is a relatively simple matter. Any New Zealand citizen who is a registered elector may be nominated by any two registered electors from the constituency in which he proposes to stand. A deposit of $100[39] must accompany every nomination, but this is returned to the successful candidate and to any unsuccessful candidate polling at least one-quarter as many votes as the winner. Since 1975 parliamentary aspirants have been permitted to run in only one seat, and to prevent indecency, offense, deceit, or deliberate confusion, a "returning officer" has the power to refuse a nomination where he is not satisfied that the

---

[38] Confidence was also undermined to some extent by the large number of inaccuracies found in the *Index of Places and Streets*, a guide for poll clerks which is intended to make sure that special voting papers are issued for the correct electorates. These errors necessitated the hasty publication of an errata sheet, but this was also far from complete. A number of instances of people voting in the wrong electorate as a result of this misinformation were reported. Presumably these votes were recorded as invalid.

[39] Raised from $20 in 1975.

candidate's name, as stated on the nomination form, is the one by which the individual is normally known.[40]

The Electoral Act limits the amount of money a candidate may spend during an election campaign. This provision, which has existed since 1895, is intended to ensure that the possession of wealth does not give one candidate an advantage over another.[41] By the terms of the act no candidate may spend more than $4,000 in promoting his candidacy in his electorate *in the three months immediately prior to the day of the election,* and a return of receipts and expenditure is required within seventy days of the official declaration of the result. Although these declarations of expenditure invariably indicate that candidates have kept within the specified limit, they give virtually no indication of the real costs of an individual candidate's campaign. Enterprising candidates are able to find ways of increasing their level of expenditure without officially breaching the legal limit. In an attempt to close some of the more obvious loopholes, Parliament agreed in 1977 that all advertisements promoting a candidate in a particular electorate must be officially authorized before publication. The aim of this provision was to prevent a practice which had occurred in some previous elections whereby expenditure promoting a candidacy was sometimes incurred and paid for "without the knowledge" of the candidate. This new rule was only partially adhered to in 1978, and it did nothing to stop practices like booking halls and paying the hire fee or preparing, printing, and paying the bills for advertising literature and posters before the three-month time limit came into effect. Nor did it appear to control expenditures incurred by electorate campaign committees in purchasing general policy pamphlets published by their party's central office. Given these loopholes, the $4,000 limit imposed on individual candidates seems rather pointless.[42]

While individual candidates are subject to seemingly rigid financial limits, no similar restriction applies to campaign expenditures incurred by political parties on nationwide or regional advertising and party promotion. Party budgets are usually a closely guarded

---

[40] In 1972 one M. Mouse stood as a candidate in Palmerston North—his policy was to put the "mickey" into Parliament. Also in 1972 a prospective candidate tried to obtain nomination as J. Christ. The right given to returning officers to reject nominations originated with this incident.

[41] *Parliamentary Debates,* vol. 87, p. 329.

[42] The limitation on a candidate's election expenses was originally £200 ($400). This was raised to £500 ($1,000) in 1948, to $1,500 in 1971, and $2,000 in 1975 before being set at its present level in 1977. This latest amendment is one of the few changes made to the Electoral Act in recent years where Labour and National have been in full agreement.

secret—no campaign balance sheets are ever made public and no declaration of campaign expenditures is required of any political party. The National party never discusses its campaign expenditures in public, but various estimates placed its 1978 budget at between $500,000 and $1 million. Labour's general secretary indicated at the end of August that his party was planning to spend between $150,000 and $200,000 on the campaign, while Bruce Beetham drew gasps from assembled delegates at Social Credit's annual conference the same month when he announced that the League had budgeted $120,000 "for a final election campaign."[43] The Values party's budget is unknown, but it is unlikely to have exceeded $20,000. Clearly, the major parties have a decided advantage, if only because their sources of campaign finance are very much more extensive. Election campaigns are expensive and money does play a part in the final outcome. If limitations on expenditure during an election campaign are to have any real meaning, general party expenditure must be rigorously controlled along with the expenses of individual candidates in single electorates.

Election Day—and Beyond. Although voter registration is compulsory, the act of voting is not. Even so, New Zealand's general elections have been traditionally characterized by a very high turnout. When measured against enrollments, the turnout has frequently exceeded 90 percent, although in both 1975 and 1978 it appears to have declined to less than 85 percent. This high turnout can be explained, in part, by the great lengths to which the country goes in its efforts to encourage its citizens to vote.[44] The time and effort expended in ensuring that all qualified persons are registered as voters has already been noted. On the day of the election, a Saturday when comparatively few people are required to work, an extensive network of polling

---

[43] For the Labour party's statement see the *Christchurch Star*, August 30, 1978; for Beetham's statement see the *Press*, August 26, 1978. He also indicated (1) that Social Credit had already spent over $100,000 since December 1975 and (2) that "advertising industry gossip" put National's election campaign at $1 million and Labour's between $250,000 and $500,000. For some estimates of National's proposed campaign expenditures, see the *Christchurch Star*, May 13 and August 30, 1978, and the *Press*, August 26, 1978. It has since been announced by the Labour party that it spent $381,000 on the 1978 election campaign, not including the sum spent by each candidate in his own electorate. The comparable figures for the two previous elections were also released: $125,000 in 1972 and $187,000 in 1975. *Christchurch Star*, July 19, 1979.

[44] Another factor is that New Zealanders may be considered to be habitual voters. In 1969, political scientist Austin Mitchell observed that, in New Zealand, "Voting is a social act, socially conditioned." *Politics and People in New Zealand* (Christchurch: Whitcombe and Tombs, 1969), p. 215. Today, ten years later, this is still basically true.

places is set up in every electorate. In recent years group polling places, where votes can be cast for a number of electorates, have been established at venues where people are likely to congregate—race tracks, Saturday shopping malls, and town halls in the larger cities, for example. Many polling places, particularly in urban electorates, contain two or more booths. The general rule is that no booth should be required to process more than about 200 voters during the course of a day and that no voter should have to wait for any great length of time before receiving a ballot paper.[45]

Any voter who goes to a polling place on the day of the election casts an "ordinary" vote: his name is crossed off the roll as he is handed the ballot paper, and once he has marked it, his paper is deposited in the ballot box. For those who are unable to visit a polling place within their electorate on election day or for whom attendance would be an imposition, "special" votes are available. Strictly speaking, any registered voter living more than two miles from his nearest booth is entitled to apply for and be given a special vote. In practice, however, these are almost invariably confined to electors who are away from their electorate on polling day, are ill, infirm, or hospitalized, have religious objections to voting on a Saturday, or currently live overseas. Special votes may be cast at any time between the closing of nominations and 7 P.M. on election day and must be delivered to the returning officer for the electorate not later than ten days after the election.

Whereas ordinary votes are tallied on the night of the election to give a provisional result, special vote declarations have first to be checked against the electoral rolls: where a special voter's registration is confirmed, the vote is allowed; where no record of prior registration can be found, the vote is disallowed.[46] These checks, and the scrutiny

---

[45] The number of polling places set up in an electorate depends largely on its area. In a compact urban electorate such as Mount Albert (Auckland) the number can be as low as 14, but large rural electorates like Pahiatua and Rangitikei may have nearly 100 polling places. The four Maori electorates each have well over 100 places. One interesting arrangement is the provision, in the Marlborough electorate, of a floating polling place which visits each small settlement in the Marlborough Sounds in the week before polling day.

[46] Special votes account for only about 10 percent of all votes cast, but they provide an overwhelming proportion of the votes declared invalid. While most are discarded because voters have failed to register as electors, a significant number are rejected because the declaration forms have been completed incorrectly. Casting a special vote, therefore, can be something of a hurdle in which functional literacy may be a significant element. Many voters may be unwittingly disfranchised because of their inability to understand the instructions or their failure to complete the declaration form to the satisfaction of the returning officer.

of the marked rolls to identify possible cases of plural voting,[47] must be completed before the official count can begin. During these stages it is normal practice for "scrutineers" from at least the two major parties to be present. Difficulties arose in 1978 because, for the first time ever, all electoral registration cards were held at the Chief Electoral Office in Lower Hutt, outside Wellington, instead of in the headquarters of the local electorate officers. Since in all some 56,000 special votes had to be referred to the Chief Electoral Office for verification, local party scrutineers were unable to verify the decisions given.[48] The Labour party, which was most interested in the fate of special votes, sought permission to place scrutineers in the Chief Electoral Office, but this was refused. Only after the party had sought a court injunction to force the chief electoral officer to give way was a compromise reached in which special votes from a random selection of electorates were examined with scrutineers present.[49] The interparty dissension over the electoral rules that had dominated much of the politics of the previous three years continued to cast a long shadow over the election outcome.[50]

---

[47] Plural voting is a rarity in New Zealand, and the odd instances which are discovered have usually been the result of stupidity or a voter's failure to understand what is involved in casting a vote rather than any deliberate attempt to subvert the electoral system. See Robert Chapman, Keith Jackson, and Austin Mitchell, *New Zealand Politics in Action: The 1960 General Election* (London: Oxford University Press, 1962), p. 8. After the 1978 election the National party's electorate organization in Lyttelton alleged that there had been "several hundred" cases of dual voting in the electorate. Subsequent investigations by the returning officer indicated that clerical errors were responsible and that he had not unearthed "any real case of double voting." See the *Press*, November 30, 1978, and the *Christchurch Star*, November 30, 1978. The clerical errors referred to arose, in the main, from errors and duplication in the electoral roll.

[48] No. M38/79, Supreme Court of New Zealand, Auckland Registry, *Hunua Election Petition: Judgement*, May 11, 1979, pp. 75-89.

[49] *Christchurch Star*, November 23, 1978; *Press*, November 29, 1978.

[50] When New Zealanders go to the polls at a general election they also cast votes in the triennial national referendum on the sale of liquor required under the Licensing Act of 1908. (See the ballot reproduced in Appendix B.) The choice facing voters is a three-way one: National Continuance (that is, maintenance of the status quo), State Purchase and Control, or Prohibition. Since 1922, the referendum has consistently had the effect of ensuring the maintenance of National Continuance by a wide margin, and since 1946 this option has always secured between 60 and 70 percent of the total valid vote, with the balance being split more or less evenly between the other options. This expensive exercise in futility assumed a new importance in 1978 as two opposing single-interest pressure groups attempted to utilize the liquor referendum as a means of demonstrating the degree of public support they commanded: the Abortion Law Reform Association of New Zealand (ALRANZ) urged its supporters to vote "Prohibition"; the Society for the Protection of the Unborn Child (SPUC) called on its members to vote "National Continuance." Provisional results from

Disputed Elections. It is normal in a general election for one or two individual electorate results to be challenged. Where the final count separates the leading contenders by only a small margin, a magisterial recount is frequently, though not invariably, sought by the defeated candidate. During such a recount all votes are again thoroughly scrutinized and tallied. The presiding magistrate, who has all the powers vested in a returning officer, independently determines the validity of all doubtful votes, and he is at liberty to reverse any decision made by the returning officer where he is satisfied that an error of fact has occurred.

Magisterial recounts are concerned solely with determining the accuracy of the declared result. Where a candidate or elector believes that an election result has been influenced by corrupt or illegal practices, or where the validity of some votes is challenged, recourse may be had to the Electoral Court, a special division of the Supreme Court set up ad hoc by the chief justice to try election petitions.[51] The Electoral Act requires the court to "be guided by the substantial merits of the case without regard to legal forms or technicalities."[52] Parliament's intention is that real justice be achieved so that the will of the electorate, as expressed through the ballot box, is upheld. If, however, the court is satisfied that the election was conducted substantially in compliance with the law and that the alleged irregularities or omissions were of a technical nature and did not materially affect the outcome, the petition must be dismissed.

Allegations of bribery, corruption, and misfeasance by returning officers were comparatively frequent during the late nineteenth and early twentieth centuries, but none have come before the Electoral

---

the referendum gave the National Continuance option 62.7 percent of the valid votes (down nearly six percentage points from its share in 1975); Prohibition increased its share from 15.7 percent to 22.3 percent; and State Purchase and Control remained virtually static at 15 percent. Both ALRANZ and the New Zealand Alliance (the temperance organization) claimed considerable satisfaction from the increased prohibition vote. In this way a totally meaningless and irrelevant national referendum on liquor licensing became enmeshed in one of the issues of the 1978 campaign.

[51] The grounds for an election petition are diverse. Corrupt practices include plural voting, bribery, treating, and interfering with or seeking to influence electors on polling day. Illegal practices include payments to electors to display posters and failing to have candidates authorize advertisements before they are published. Technical or administrative transgressions by returning officers or other electoral officials may provide grounds for a petition. The court may also be asked to decide questions relating to whether certain voters were qualified to vote or whether votes had been incorrectly allowed or disallowed by the returning officer or magistrate.

[52] *Statutes of New Zealand*, 1956, No. 107, Section 166 (Electoral Act, 1956).

Court since 1923. Since then, the few election petitions served have focused on defining exactly what constitutes a valid, or "formal," vote. The method to be used when voting is specified in Section 106 of the Electoral Act, which states that the voter must strike out the name of every candidate except the one for whom he wishes to vote. This strict requirement, however, appears to be modified to some extent by a proviso included in Section 115, which states:

> No ballot paper shall be rejected as informal by reason only of some informality in the manner in which it has been dealt with by the voter if it is otherwise regular, and if in the opinion of the Returning Officer the intention of the voter in voting is clearly indicated.

This is usually taken to mean that, as long as a voter's intention is judged by the returning officer to be clear and beyond all doubt, the vote will be treated as valid. Thus, ballot papers marked with the letter "X" (as is normal procedure in many local authority elections) have been accepted as valid votes.[53] On the other hand, papers where a candidate's name has been marked with a tick ($\checkmark$) have normally been rejected—despite general acceptance of a tick as a mark of approbation—unless there was also some other indication of the voter's intention. On rare occasions statements such as "For Labour" or "Who else would I vote for?" have been counted—provided, of course, that the style of handwriting or printing was such that the identity of the voter remained secret.[54]

Between 1880, when the Electoral Court was established, and 1975 a total of forty-three petitions seeking to overturn the declared result in an electoral district were filed with the court. In the past fifty years, however, only five were lodged and none was upheld. Two, the Rangitikei petition of 1932 and the Raglan petition of 1947, were tried by the court, one was withdrawn before the hearing began, and two (Lyttelton, 1955 and Wellington Central, 1973) were both dismissed before any argument of substance was heard because the court ruled that the legal requirements for serving a petition had not been fully complied with.[55] Particularly in these last two instances,

---

[53] Gazette Law Reports, 1926, pp. 141-145 (O'Brien v. Seddon: Westland Election Petition). See also the Press, March 14, 1926 (McCombs v. Lyons: Lyttelton Election Petition). But compare Gazette Law Reports, 1932, p. 555 (Hogan v. Stuart: Rangitikei Election Petition).

[54] New Zealand Law Reports, 1947, pp. 363-367 and 706-708; and 1948, pp. 65-103. (Johnstone v. Baxter: Raglan Election Petition).

[55] In the case of the Lyttelton petition the court's decision was based on the fact that security for costs had not been lodged with the court within the time

there is a strong suggestion that legal considerations far outweigh the fulfillment of "real justice" in spite of the direction Parliament has given the court in the Electoral Act.

In view of the infrequency of election petitions during the past half century the serving of two petitions disputing the 1978 election results in the Hunua and Kapiti electorates must be considered unusual.[56] Indeed, they were the tip of a rather large iceberg of interparty conflict, for, in no fewer than four other electorates, party activists considered challenging the declared result in the Electoral Court. Electoral conflict of this magnitude, which had been unknown for fifty years at least, is a measure of the tensions that have dominated the political arena over the past four to five years. The fact that the 1978 general election continued to be fought for six months after election day is mute testimony to the ill feeling between Labour and National that has its origins in the efforts of both parties to manipulate the electoral rules to their own advantage.

A Crisis of Legitimacy?

The 1978 general election was unusual, not least because the political climate was vastly different from anything many electors had ever encountered before. The provisions of the country's electoral law, which had been accepted by all parties virtually without question during the previous two decades, came under wholesale attack, first as the politicians sought to recast them in terms of partisan advantage and, second, as the electorate endeavored to cope with the consequences of the amendments that were passed. There can be little doubt that the political mood of the electorate in 1978 was shaped in no small measure by the attitudes of the major parties towards the contents of the electoral rules.

There are many reasons why this was so. The polarization of political opinion during the four years prior to the election contributed significantly to the fundamental disagreements that separated the two

---

specified by the Electoral Act. The Wellington Central petition was dismissed after the court had declined to exercise its discretion in favor of the petitioner, who sought to add a number of additional complaints to his original petition—in the court's view he was seeking to submit a new petition out of time. In the 1955 case the court's attitude was succinctly expressed as follows: "An Election Court has no established statutory jurisdiction as have other courts. It does not exist. It is brought into existence *ad hoc*. Its only jurisdiction is such as arises from presentation of a petition properly in order. This Court can say that the Election Court, if brought into existence to hear the present petition, would be a nullity." *New Zealand Law Reports*, 1955, p. 1167.

[56] On the electoral petitions in Kapiti and Hunua see Appendix A.

main political parties. Labour and National were increasingly suspicious of each other's motives whenever proposals to amend the Electoral Act were introduced, and, standing on the sidelines, Social Credit was suspicious of the motives of both. Whenever electoral laws are subjected to political pressure, the whole fabric of the electoral system is likely to be weakened. The election petitions in Hunua and Kapiti and the allegations of hundreds of cases of dual voting in Lyttelton, for example, attest to the strains that have been placed on the electoral system in recent years.

The administrative deficiencies of the Electoral Office, which became increasingly obvious in the months before the election, extended the interparty conflict to the electorate at large. New Zealanders normally show no interest in the details of constitutional or electoral matters, and it took the frustrations of the new electoral registration procedures to shake the electorate from its lethargy. Its reaction, however, was bewilderment and incomprehension rather than knowledge and understanding of exactly what was involved.

Did the strains on the electoral system create a crisis of legitimacy? Without doubt confidence in the electoral system was undermined to some degree by the actions of M.P.s and electoral administrators. By questioning the impartiality of the 1977 redistribution (thus raising doubts about the political neutrality of the six non-party commissioners), and accusing the chief electoral officer of administrative incompetence, the Labour party significantly aggravated the underlying tensions. So, too, did the National Government. Its delight with the new electoral boundaries was ill-concealed and did nothing to moderate the basic disagreements, while its unequivocal support for the chief electoral officer was ultimately seen to be somewhat misplaced, and its credibility, along with that of the electoral system, suffered accordingly. Further, the continuing problems over the registration of electors caused a fair number to ponder whether the electoral system could be relied upon to produce a just result. Many of these anxieties were amplified after National was returned with a clear majority of seats but fewer votes in total than its nearest rival, and the third party, Social Credit, secured only one seat even though it took more than 16 percent of the popular vote (see Table 3–1). In the final analysis the efficacy of an electoral system rests on trust, and where this is compromised the system's viability may be eroded.

Nevertheless, the very real misgivings which remained after the election did not reach crisis proportions. The legitimacy of the National Government elected on November 25, 1978, was acknowledged by the vast majority of electors and its right to govern was not really questioned; criticism was directed more towards the deficiencies inherent in the electoral system that had produced the skewed result, than towards National's continuation in Government. The point was reached, too, where the political parties were beginning to respond to the concerns of the electorate. By February 1979 an ad hoc investigating committee had been established to scrutinize the administrative aspects of the Electoral Act, especially those pertaining to the registration of electors and the preparation of electoral rolls, and in August the Government set up a parliamentary select committee to examine the wider issues of representation. The outcome of this series of deliberations is likely to be the establishment of a new, though precarious, balance between the major parties in time for the 1981 election. But it is highly unlikely that they will heed Social Credit's call for proportional representation. Only if the demands for electoral reform become so strong that the electoral costs of noncompliance are too great to ignore will the major parties be prepared to countenance a thoroughgoing reform of the electoral system. And, since the electorate's interest in electoral reform is minimal, the chances of this happening are virtually nonexistent.

4

Candidate Selection and the 1978 General Election

Keith Jackson

Under the Westminster type of parliamentary system based upon the simple majority vote, modern elections are mainly concerned with deciding which political party will govern. Yet the largely unnoticed process of candidate selection is crucial in determining what type of people will act as representatives. In fact, in at least half the seats at any New Zealand general election the choice of candidate is for all practical purposes the choice of M.P., and the general election merely endorses the party's candidate.

In theory, political party candidates play an important role in shaping the voters' images of the parties as well as in helping to formulate policies. But in addition, in a small-scale democracy such as New Zealand, they can represent a major point of tension between local and national needs. In a nation preoccupied with "roads and bridges" politics, the "good" M.P. is the man who attends assiduously to every local interest, large and small.

At the same time, there is the possibility that a successful candidate will ultimately be called upon to accept national office as a cabinet minister. If an M.P. has spent three years in Parliament and is in the winning party, his chances of being appointed to the New Zealand cabinet are close to one in two, compared with roughly one in twenty in the United Kingdom's Parliament. Only elected M.P.s may serve in a New Zealand cabinet, and in the absence of an upper house like Britain's House of Lords the range of choice is extremely narrow.

Most candidate selection procedures are oligarchical. The selection is frequently made by a limited group in closed, often private, meetings. Decisions may or may not be ratified by a larger body of the party faithful, but in general the role of the bulk of party members is one of docile acquiescence, and mere party supporters (that is, voters) are wholly excluded, having no say at all in the choice of the individuals for whom they are to vote. As Leon Epstein puts it:

> Not only are the ordinary party voters outside the selection process, but so are most of the dues paying members. These members, as many as a few thousand in some units, do not ordinarily exercise a choice between possible candidates. The choice is made for the local members by their local leaders. . . . Candidate selection is meant to be oligarchical.[1]

Although political parties are supposedly democratic bodies soliciting citizens' votes to elect parliamentary representatives, they tend to regard such matters as candidate selection as their private concern. It was not until the mid-1960s in New Zealand, for example, that press and television were granted the "privilege" of witnessing some of the selection procedures, and even today important elements of secrecy persist. There is a marked contrast between the closed nature of the party proceedings and the openness of the formal legal arrangements for the elections themselves.

New Zealand is a nation of highly cohesive parliamentary parties. Both major parties, with their tight caucus organization, emphasize the team approach in politics, and the tendency in the past has been to downgrade the individual candidate in favor of the party. To paraphrase Lord Morrison's remark, people would vote for a sheep if it had the right party label. Worse, it is arguable that in New Zealand, at least in the past, no one would have noticed what the label had behind it. In 1978 this situation was modified by a number of different considerations. On the one hand, the five-yearly electoral boundary revision undertaken the year before had proved unusually disruptive in many areas because of the addition of five new parliamentary seats and the consequent "ripple" effect induced by the narrow electoral tolerance of plus or minus 5 percent. Not only did this disrupt established electorates, but by displacing a number of sitting M.P.s who needed to find new seats, it served also to heighten tensions between central and local interests within the political parties themselves. To this was added the complication of a vigorous pressure group campaign over the issue of abortion, with both the advocates and the opponents of abortion reform urging voters to judge the candidates by their positions on this single issue, ignoring party altogether. In a number of electorates this led to direct intervention by pressure

---

[1] Leon Epstein, *Political Parties in Western Democracies* (New York: Praeger, 1967), p. 220.

groups within the party processes to try to bring about the selection of particular candidates. Both for these and for other reasons the 1978 general election saw a rash of candidates often challenging the official party representatives under closely related labels on a wholly unprecedented scale.[2]

Procedures for Choosing the Candidates

Both Labour and the National party started choosing their candidates midway between the 1975 and 1978 general elections. The National party followed the well-orchestrated plan it had used successfully for the 1975 general election and originally announced at the National party conference in July 1974: first, it would confirm as candidates all incumbents other than those who intended to retire; second, candidates would be selected to replace retiring members; third, candidates would be selected in marginal seats, then in the balance of the electorates. The entire process was to be completed by May 1978. In broad outline this plan was adhered to, although the selection in some hopeless seats was unduly protracted, and in two cases late selections had to be made because of withdrawals. The Labour selections follow a similar pattern but are more affected by geographical considerations as the head office component of the selection panel has to tour the various electorates throughout the country.

Patterns of Central-Local Control. The actual process of selection, which is only semi-public, differs markedly among the main political parties. The National party, the Social Credit Political League, and the Values party all place the emphasis upon local selection, while Labour uses a mixed local-central selection panel. All the central party organizations with the exception of Values, however, retain the right to approve the final candidates.

There are marked variations among the selection procedures adopted by the four major parties in New Zealand, reflecting their different ideologies and the state of their development. The Labour

---

[2] On the other hand the number of independent and minor party candidates has declined slightly: in 1972, there were 147 non-major-party candidates (other than Labour, National, Social Credit, and Values) including 86 New Democrats. The New Democrat party, which resulted from a split in the Social Credit Political League, did not prove lasting. In 1975 there were 66 candidates who were not members of one of the four major parties, and in 1978 only 51. The raising of the deposit required by parliamentary candidates from $20 prior to 1975 to $100 from the 1975 general election onwards does not appear to have had any marked effect upon the number of non-major-party candidates standing for election.

party employs the most centralized system. In each electorate six representatives, three from the central party organization and three from the local organization, choose the candidate. There is a concession to the local electorate in the provision that a straw poll will be taken at the selection meeting, but the results of this are neither binding nor released to the meeting.

The National party uses a more complex, locally oriented system. First the electorate concerned has to receive approval from the Dominion Council to proceed to selection, and then the "nominees"—those competing to become the party's candidate—have to be approved by the council. If there are more than three nominees, a "preselection" committee is formed consisting of the electorate chairman plus four local electorate representatives and four appointees not resident in the electorate, two appointed by the divisional chairman and two by the president. The task of this committee is to reduce the number of nominees to between three and five. This is followed by the selection stage proper. The full selection committee comprises members of the Electorate Committee plus such additional delegates as are needed to ensure an overall ratio of one representative for every twenty branch members in the electorate. These committees sometimes consist of up to 150 delegates; each finalist makes a speech and answers two written questions, one submitted by the leader of the party, the other by the party president. The effect is that although the power of effective choice may be whittled down by the necessity for approval of candidates by the Dominion Council or the work of the preselection committee, the final decision is in the hands of the local organization. Prior to the final selection meeting a series of branch meetings is held at which members and delegates can familiarize themselves with the contenders, both formally and informally. These meetings (although not required by the rules) constitute a valuable part of the selection process. Even so, it is conceivable that carefully selected questions by the party leader and president could play to the strengths of an individual nominee and thus help to influence the local choice.

By contrast the selection systems used by the Social Credit Political League and the Values party are far more rudimentary and locally oriented. The Social Credit Political League chooses its candidates at selection meetings at which all branch members have a vote. The candidate is chosen by a simple majority (in a party that advocates proportional representation for Parliament). If there is only one contender, a selection meeting must still be held, and he or she must receive the support of two-thirds of those attending. The decision of the meeting, however, can be overturned by the league's Regional Council. If an electorate fails to select a candidate, the Regional Council or appropriate dominion councillor in conjunction with the local campaign committee may do so. This rudimentary system makes it extremely difficult for the central party organization to exercise influence over the caliber of candidates selected without precipitating confrontations between the local and central organizations. The Values party has no detailed provisions, placing responsibility for selection solely in the hands of the dues-paying members of the party in the electorate concerned and stipulating that if there are fewer than five such members in the electorate, the responsibility shall fall to the nearest branch or region.

Problems and Changes. A number of difficulties have arisen under the Labour and National selection systems (Social Credit and Values rarely being embarrassed by competition for candidacies). At the level of nomination, for example, certain requirements have to be fulfilled by both nominees and nominators. The Labour party requires that nominees have been bona fide members of the party for at least two years, while National and Social Credit merely require that they be dues-paying members at the time they are selected. The Labour party differed from the other parties too in including for a time an upper age limit of sixty years for candidates other than sitting members of Parliament. This no longer applies, but an upper limit of seventy years for sitting M.P.s has been retained. The National party requires an affirmation of loyalty to the party leader, while Labour requires agreement that the candidate, if elected, will vote on all questions in accord with the decisions of a majority of the members in the parliamentary party caucus. These differences between Labour and National encapsulate the theoretical differences of emphasis between the two parties, with National tending to be more leader-oriented and Labour more policy-oriented.

The Labour party's more restrictive requirements for nominees in the past have often led to practical difficulties and dissatisfaction, particularly over the alleged length of qualifying service. There were allegations in 1972, for example, that one elected Labour party M.P. had been a member of the National party within the two-year qualifying period, and on occasion other promising candidates have been debarred by this provision over a few days' qualifying service. The National party's system is more open to the recruitment of outstanding talent (one successful former cabinet minister told the author that he only formally joined the party at the selection meeting at which he was chosen to be the party's candidate), but it has the disadvantage that it helps to make possible sudden coups by people who have played little or no active part in the party hitherto.

In the case of the Labour party, varying systems of selecting parliamentary candidates have been tried during the party's existence. From 1916 to 1951 candidates were selected by postal ballot conducted in the electorate concerned, and on a number of occasions candidates were appointed by the central party organization. The present system, which dates from 1951, worked with some success until 1969, when, because of heavy competition for safe seats and a dearth of candidates in nearby less attractive electorates, the party moved further away from local control by grouping a number of electorates together in some urban areas and requiring nominations for the area rather than for the individual electorates. That system was not used in 1977, when it may have reduced the mad scramble for seats by M.P.s displaced by boundary changes and former M.P.s unseated in the 1975 general election. Instead, in 1977 the move away from local control appears to have taken another form.

Until this general election, the third head-office nominee on the selection committee had usually been the regional representative,[3] a person who might be assumed to have a foot in both camps. In 1977, however, all head-office representatives clearly came from the central party, and it was left to the locals to decide whether or not to include the regional representative. Although an apparently minor change not detected by many party members, this represented a decisive shift in the balance between central and local representatives on the selection committees. It is not yet clear, however, whether this is intended to be a permanent policy change for it was not used in the Christchurch Central by-election in 1979, and delegates to the 1979 annual Labour party conference voted to change the method of selecting parliamentary candidates from 1980 onwards. In effect, the change represents a modification of the existing system which comprises a panel of six made up of three members appointed by the party's New Zealand Council and three local representatives. In the future local representatives will be strengthened by one additional member when party membership in the electorate reaches 20 percent of the Labour vote in the previous election. When membership is 10 percent, there will continue to be three local representatives, but when it is less than 10 percent there will be only two. The council will continue to name

---

[3] Regional representatives in the Labour party are elected by postal ballot from among the branches and affiliations (that is, trade union members) of the area concerned.

three members of the selection panels but the winning of the hotly disputed presidency of the party by a non-M.P. in 1979 may well produce changes in the attitude and possibly in the role of these representatives.

The effect of these changes is difficult to forecast. They certainly encourage the branches to undertake an active recruitment policy for members, but in the short term at least the changes are more likely to strengthen the council's influence upon candidate selection.

The situation in the Labour party is further complicated by the fact that although the selection machinery is geared to a two-way process, in practice there is often a three-way division involving local branch delegates, trade union representatives, and central party organizations. Thus the crucial factor in Labour party selections may well be the composition of the selection committee itself rather than the performance of nominees at the selection meeting. This has been a major cause of disputes within the party, yet if the local branches almost invariably lose, it is not obvious that there are always clear winners. The central party organization often fares badly in getting its own favored candidates selected or, as happens more frequently, in attempting to exclude a candidate that it does not wish to see selected. The trade union delegates, where united, can usually win, but the defeat of the candidate selected for the "safe" seat of Dunedin North in 1975 showed that there are limits even to this power.[4]

Given the internal politics of political parties there is a tendency for selection to resolve itself into a battle to keep certain nominees out rather than a drive to select the strongest candidate available. This leads to the selection of second-best or compromise candidates. Labour has yet to resolve this problem; National seems to have coped with it successfully by changing its voting system from preferential to progressive voting, under which successive polls are taken with the lowest-polling nominee removed at each stage until one nominee obtains an absolute majority of the votes cast. (Hence the necessity for a preselection procedure.) The effect generally is to reduce the chances of compromise candidates, which the preferential system increases.[5]

---

[4] Trade unionists dominated the local component of the selection panel, effectively excluding all branch representation. After a stormy selection meeting and vigorous branch protests against both the candidate selected and the methods adopted, branch members in effect "withdrew their labor," and what had been a safe Labour seat since 1928 was lost to National at the general election.

[5] Information about candidate selection in Maori electorates in the Labour party is not readily available, but it is clear that a number of different criteria are used. Since an agreement between Wiremu Ratana, the great Maori political prophet, and Michael Savage, the leader of the Labour party, in 1935, all but

In both Labour and the National party an important reserve power is retained by the central party organization through the right of approval. The National party's central organization can intervene at three stages—twice at the preselection level and once after selection. The party, as mentioned earlier, has the right to determine when the local organization can proceed with selection, and after this all nominations must be approved by the Dominion Council of the party. To these safeguards was added a third in 1976 when the central party organization acquired the power to withdraw its endorsement where necessary. This power is vested in the Dominion Executive of the party, and provision is made for a meeting between the executive and the candidate concerned before approval can be withdrawn. The cases in which approval is withdrawn tend to involve such problems as mental instability and sexual or financial indiscretion, although little information is available about specific causes. A candidate was dropped in the North Island in 1975 with some difficulty; another voluntarily withdrew in Christchurch in 1978.

The powers of the New Zealand Council of the Labour party, with its more centralized system of selection, are, as might be expected, more far-reaching. According to the "Constitution and Rules" of the party it has the authority to withdraw the nomination of any candidate who fails to "honour the terms of the pledge" or, rather curiously, whose "incompetence is impairing efficiency" (as if other forms of incompetence were acceptable). The council may request a selection to be held again when the "Constitution has not been followed" or "incompetence has been displayed," and it has the power to appoint in a deadlock or if the selection committee fails to do so. But in general in both parties where nonincumbent candidates present difficulties, the formal powers tend to be held in reserve and the person concerned is usually prevailed upon to resign "for health reasons."

Incumbents

It is an axiom of candidate selection that any incumbent M.P. who wishes to stand again is readopted. Challenges to sitting M.P.s are rare and seldom successful. Challenges have been most frequent in the National party, but here too the parliamentary party tends to regard them as an embarrassment rather than as normal manifestations of democratic competition. Having just displaced the former leader of

one of the Labour party's Maori M.P.s have been members of the Ratana church. All Maori Labour party candidates must be able to speak Maori, and on occasion tribal affiliations may be of significance.

the National party, Robert Muldoon stirred up a hornet's nest at the 1974 National party conference when he asserted: "By and large, the tradition in this party is not to tackle sitting Members."[6] Muldoon appeared to argue that it was good enough for the parliamentary party to change its leader, as it had done two weeks before, but that the electorates were not to be allowed to change their representatives. It is true that National at that time needed every experienced politician possible if it were to have any hope of forming an effective Government after a 1975 general election victory, but to assert that the local party organizations should never challenge incumbents denied them the right to exercise one of the very few powers they retained.

Given the strong cohesion of the parliamentary parties in New Zealand, it would be surprising if tensions did not develop between M.P.s and their local electorate organizations. In general, this seems to apply more to National than to Labour, both because the selection system allows for stronger electorate participation and because the National party, once predominantly rural, has become steadily more urban, with a consequent growth of dissatisfaction in the rural electorates.

Rumors of potential challenges abound among National party supporters before a general election. Up to eleven challenges appeared possible in 1974 at the time of Muldoon's assertion that they were untraditional, but only four materialized and all proved unsuccessful. Whether this was more the result of second thoughts or of party pressures is not clear. But one electorate official at the time left no doubt in the author's mind that party pressure can be a potent factor. He claimed to have been told that, should a successful challenge eventuate, his electorate could expect scant consideration for its needs by the parliamentary party if it became the Government. Although other party officials flatly denied any knowledge of such proceedings past or present, the possibility of this type of influence cannot be discounted. While it is both difficult and dangerous for the central party organization in the National party to influence the initial selection of a candidate for Parliament, the position of an incumbent is much stronger, and the parliamentary party may well feel entitled to try to protect its own.

The problem for the political scientist here is that we are moving in a grey area where hard data are not readily available. An interesting case (from a suppositional point of view) is that of Colin McLachlan, M.P. for the Rakaia electorate. McLachlan, formerly a successful

---

[6] *New Zealand Herald*, July 29, 1974.

divisional chairman of the National party, was the favored candidate for selection for the Ashburton electorate at the 1966 general election (the first selection to be opened to television). To the surprise of everyone—including many at the selection meeting itself—McLachlan was beaten by Robert E. Buick, a local man who had had little in the way of formal connections with the National party organization. In effect, the selection of Buick represented a well-organized coup by largely outside interests. Some months later Buick withdrew "because of circumstances beyond his control," which may or may not have been related to the strong reaction of the party hierarchy to his selection. Meanwhile the M.P. for the nearby Selwyn electorate retired, and since McLachlan—somewhat surprisingly—was the only contender he did not have to face formal selection.

Subsequently, McLachlan was rumored to have played an important role in the replacement of Party Leader Jack Marshall by Muldoon. He was certainly known as a close friend and confidant of the new leader, and on the return of the National Government under Muldoon in 1975 he received cabinet preferment. In both 1974 and 1977 the rumored challenges in his electorate failed to eventuate, and despite widespread criticism both of him within his electorate and more generally of his role as a minister, McLachlan continued to hold his position. This is a somewhat rare example of the power of the parliamentary party and its leaders.

Such power, however, is by no means unlimited. In 1977, when Prime Minister Muldoon took the unprecedented step of publicly threatening to oppose the renomination of one of his most recalcitrant members, Michael Minogue, M.P. for Hamilton, he evoked a firm response from the nonparliamentary president of the party, who made it clear that such matters were simply not the prime minister's business.

In another controversy in 1977 the sitting National party member for Pakuranga, Gavin Downie, was challenged and defeated, to the obvious displeasure of the parliamentary leader. This was the first successful challenge in the National party for twenty years and only the third successful challenge in its forty-year existence.[7] Downie had been one of the incumbents challenged in 1975, having spent only three years in office—again an unprecedented situation. He survived in 1975, to be challenged anew in 1978. The situation was complicated by some indecision on Downie's part as to which electorate he would stand for following the boundary redistribution, but despite this, a

---

[7] The previous successful challenge, in 1957, occurred when the aging John N. Massey proved reluctant to retire; the central party organization can be assumed to have stood aside in the contest.

number of expected strong challenges failed to materialize, possibly once again because of party pressures. At the last minute, however, one challenger was brash enough to enter the lists, and he promptly won. The irony was that, of a particularly strong field of potential challengers, the lone survivor was not necessarily the preferred choice of the electorate; this led to deep divisions not only within the National party in Pakuranga but also between the new official candidate and the party hierarchy. The situation was then further complicated by Downie's decision to stand as an independent against the official National party candidate.

Thus, although it seems likely that the central party organization is not without considerable influence in the readoption of incumbents, this power is by no means unlimited, and when a party leader like Muldoon is rash enough to pronounce publicly on such matters, his influence is likely to be counterproductive.

So-called Alternative National party candidates were an unusual feature of the 1978 general election. These challengers often took little or no part in the original selection proceedings but stood against the official candidates. Some were not even members of the National party; in the South Island, for example, the deputy leader of the party faced competition in the safe seat of Wallace from June Slee, the representative of a dissident farmers' group who highlighted rural discontent in the southern part of the South Island.

In the North Island three Alternative National party candidates stood in the Albany, East Coast Bays, and Eden electorates. Two of these were single-issue candidates who opposed the sitting members' conservative views on abortion; both criticized the National party's selection system, but neither seems to have made a serious attempt to win the party's nomination. The Alternative candidate in the Albany electorate ran specifically on dissatisfaction with the National party's preselection system. In this he may well have been representative of a wider number of party members who were unhappy about the secrecy and possible arbitrariness of the weeding out of the original group of candidates.

In addition, in a number of Auckland seats in particular, strenuous attempts appear to have been made by anti-abortion organizations to sign up new National party members to influence the selection outcomes in favor of their cause. Where National party electorate branches are not particularly strong there is no doubt that the party's method of selection can still be vulnerable to this type of action, although where applicable (that is, where there are three nominees)

109

the preselection system provides a useful counter by quietly weeding out candidates of doubtful acceptability to the party hierarchy.

In the case of the Labour party there is no theoretical division of powers between the parliamentary and the extraparliamentary organizations, so the problems National faced in 1978 did not arise in the same form for Labour. In the past, for example, incumbents have normally been readopted without question other than in the cases where an aged M.P. has been reluctant to retire.[8] The 1977 election, however, did see a growing number of challenges to incumbent Labour M.P.s, many but by no means all resulting from boundary redistributions.

There were a number of other unusual problems too, including a case of refusal of nomination by the central party organization. The New Zealand Council of the Labour party opposed the renomination of the Member of Parliament for the Island Bay electorate, Gerald O'Brien, who had recently been vice-president of the party. This was an exceptional situation following upon unfavorable publicity suffered by O'Brien after the dismissal of an indecent assault charge. The local organization remained resolutely loyal, and eventually the council twice withdrew O'Brien's nomination without giving specific reasons. When his local supporters then succeeded in bringing the selection committee to deadlock, the council appointed a former M.P., Frank O'Flynn, claiming that he had been favored in the straw poll held during the selection proceedings. As a result, for the first time since 1943, the Labour party was faced with the challenge of a serious Independent Labour candidate in an important electorate, and there appeared for a time to be a distinct possibility that the split in the Labour vote would allow the National candidate to take a safe Labour seat. In the event, he failed to do so by some 700 votes.

An equally serious and exceptional problem was narrowly averted when the former deputy-leader of the party and ex-high commissioner in London, Hugh Watt, announced his intention to challenge his successor for his old Auckland seat of Onehunga, which had become a marginal electorate. Such a challenge could well be construed not just as dissatisfaction with the incumbent M.P., Frank Rogers, but as a challenge to the leadership policies of the party itself. Eventually, however, Watt withdrew one day before the selection committee meeting, partly because some party members felt that he was "embarrassing"

---

[8] This was eventually solved by the introduction of a formal retirement age for M.P.s in the party constitution following an embarrassing public fight in New Lynn in 1966, where the stalwart H. G. Rex Mason proved reluctant to retire.

certain Labour colleagues.[9] Rogers, who was clearly favored by the party hierarchy and opposed by local party officials, successfully beat off three remaining challenges and was duly returned for the seat with an increased majority.

Labour also faced a spate of problems in 1977 produced by the extensive Auckland boundary changes, which were compounded by the number of former Labour incumbents who had been defeated in 1975 and were now seeking to return to the House. Once again, the situation was unprecedented, and the party dealt with it ineptly. An undignified scramble for seats ensued, illustrated by the case of Eddie Isbey, M.P. for Grey Lynn from 1969 to 1978. Finding that his seat had simply disappeared with boundary changes, just over 50 percent of it absorbed into neighboring Auckland Central, Isbey sought the nomination for the Te Atatu seat, then withdrew from competition with his former colleague Michael Bassett. Unexpectedly, he failed to win the nomination for the new Waitakere seat and was forced to challenge a younger colleague, the sitting M.P. Richard Prebble, in Auckland Central. Meanwhile the selection committee in nearby Papatoetoe was deadlocked between two former M.P.s, Colin Moyle and Mike Moore, the three central office representatives on the selection committee favoring Moyle and the three local representatives favoring Moore. The central party organization eventually stepped in after much adverse publicity and resolved the deadlock by appointing Isbey as the official candidate despite the fact that he had not offered himself for selection in this electorate. This decision also served to relieve the situation in Auckland Central. The problem of Moyle and Moore in particular, former Labour M.P.s desperately seeking to return to Parliament—led to much criticism of the candidate selection process and gave the unfortunate impression that parliamentary seats were merely vehicles for the ambitions of members of the parliamentary party.

An interesting feature of the problems encountered in the selections for the 1978 general election has been the developing reaction at the local level to the threat of central party influence, whether real or imagined. Challenges in both major parties were more frequent than ever before, and party members have begun to proclaim the principle of the "right to challenge." Interestingly, however, the increased frequency of intervention by the Labour party's New Zealand Council appears to have aroused less overt opposition than might have been expected, partly no doubt because of the obvious reluctance of

---

[9] *Press*, November 19, 1977.

the party to intervene openly except as a last resort. On the other hand, the intemperate intervention of the National party prime minister seems to have occasioned a stronger reaction partly because central influence is officially disavowed by the National party. In both parties, however, it is clear that the long-established tradition of "party loyalty first" is becoming increasingly strained by differences between the needs of the parliamentary parties and those of the local organizations.

The Candidates

Of the 421 candidates who contested the 1978 general election, Labour, National, Social Credit, and Values each fielded a full slate of 92, although Values in particular faced some difficulties in achieving this total and in a number of cases was dependent upon very late selections and self-confessed "token" candidates. Of the remaining 53 candidates, the largest bloc belonged to the Tory party, which fielded 7 candidates (a number that belied both its strength and its seriousness of purpose; the party's leader was known as the Wizard and its grand total was 2C5 votes). There were also 6 independents, 5 Socialist Unity candidates (Soviet-oriented Communists), 4 Socialist Action candidates, 5 single-issue candidates running under the Right-to-Life label, and a variety of others including the National Alternatives and such mavericks as the Garden party. In 1978, what was unusual about the also-rans (who jointly win no more than 1 percent of the total vote in most elections) was that they included two incumbent M.P.s and increased their vote almost sixfold over 1975.

Ignoring the fringe parties and the Maori seats for the purposes of this analysis, the average age of candidates varied little among three of the four main parties, whose candidates were predominantly middle-aged and male (see Table 4–1). Women were clearly under-represented in the National party parliamentary ranks, and the defeat of one of the two National party women M.P.s in Lyttelton by one of Labour's twelve women candidates was a decided setback. (The four main parties all fielded women candidates in this electorate, where five of the six candidates were women. This did not mean that all were in favor of women's rights. The Tory candidate, Suzanne Sadler, claimed to be her leader's slave and encountered difficulties with the Electoral Office when she sought to be registered as Tinkabell). The Values party clearly lived up to its image, that of a younger party active in feminist causes. But overall, the youngest candidates to stand in the campaign were an eighteen-year-old schoolgirl who stood as a

TABLE 4–1

SEX AND AVERAGE AGE OF MAJOR PARTY CANDIDATES,
1978 GENERAL ELECTION

Party	Average Age of Candidates	Number of Women Candidates[a]	
		Total	Winners
National	45.3	7	1
Labour	44.6	12	3
Social Credit	43.2	11	0
Values	35.5	33	0

[a] The National party's winning woman candidate and two of Labour's were incumbents who won reelection. The total number of candidates nominated by each of these four parties was ninety-two.
SOURCE: Compiled by the author from official party biographies of candidates.

Right-to-Life candidate in Eastern Hutt and an eighteen-year-old male who stood for the same cause in Hamilton West. The oldest by far was the Social Credit candidate for Eastern Maori, who was seventy-two. Three sixty-five-year-olds stood in general electorates.

Though the average age of National and Labour candidates as a whole was about the same, there were wide differences among the electorates. In Eden and Pahiatua, for example, the candidates of the two leading parties were the same age, whereas in Waipa the gap between them was thirty-nine years. Of the major parties, Values had the youngest candidate in the campaign, a nineteen-year-old in Tarawera; Social Credit and Labour each ran twenty-two-year-olds, while the youngest National candidate was a twenty-six-year-old incumbent, Marilyn Waring.

Another interesting feature of the 1978 campaign was the number of Maori candidates standing in general electorates. Technically, before 1965, half-blooded Maoris or less had the right to stand in European seats and Europeans were prohibited from standing in Maori seats. This law, based upon a totally unscientific criterion—"the degree of Maori blood"—only appears to have been invoked once, in 1943, when a "full-blooded" Maori was refused permission to stand for a European seat on behalf of the Democratic Labour party. Prior to 1975, only Sir James Carroll, who was elected for both European and Maori seats on successive occasions at the beginning of this century, could be said to have been a Maori elected in a European seat. But the 1975 general election set an important precedent when two Maoris, Rex Austin and Ben Couch, won seats in general electorates.

In 1978, there were no fewer than five Maori candidates standing for the National party in general electorates. Two of these were sitting M.P.s, one in a fairly safe seat, the other in a marginal seat. Two others stood in what were technically a fairly safe and a narrowly marginal National seat, and one stood in a marginal Labour seat. Although only the two incumbent M.P.s were returned, their successes in 1975 and 1978 were clearly an important precedent in this difficult area of race relations. It might be thought that Labour, with its greater degree of central party control of selection, would have been the first to select Maori candidates in safe general seats, but although two Maori Labour candidates stood in non-Maori seats, neither was a serious prospect. On the other hand, the four Maori seats are the safest seats in the country for Labour, having been dominated by that party since the 1940s.

Nonincumbent Winning Candidates in 1978

In all, nine incumbents were defeated (including two ministers), compared with twenty-two incumbents defeated (five of them ministers) in 1975. Even the defeat of nine incumbents (11.39 percent) was high by the standards of the serene politics of the 1960s. In the thirteen years from 1957 to 1969, a total of only four ministers and fifteen other incumbents were defeated—fewer than the total defeated in 1975 alone. Clearly, 1975 was exceptional. In other years, retirements and boundary changes have played a larger role in determining the composition of the House of Representatives than the defeat of incumbents.

Despite the fact that fewer incumbents were defeated in 1978 than in 1975, the number of new members of the House was still substantial (twenty-two in 1978 compared with twenty-nine in 1975; see Table 4–2). The major difference was that only two of the twenty-nine new members in 1975 had previously sat in the House, while in 1978 no fewer than six of the twenty-two new members were former Labour M.P.s who had been defeated in 1975. (These six represented just under half of the former M.P.s standing in 1978.) Of the remainder in 1978, thirteen were standing in their first parliamentary contest, two had stood twice previously but had lost, and one had stood three times unsuccessfully. It would appear then that picking the election with a favorable party swing is more important for candidates than winning their spurs by standing in hopeless electorates before graduat-

TABLE 4–2

Record of Incumbents and Challengers, General Elections, 1957–78

		New Members	
Year	Defeated Incumbents	Total	With previous parliamentary experience
1957	5	12	2
1960	7	16	2
1963	2	10	1
1966	2	12	0
1969	3	17	1
1972	7	21	0
1975	22	29	2
1978	9[a]	22	6

[a] Includes two former party members standing as independents and defeated by the official party candidates, and one incumbent defeated by an incumbent following the redistribution.

Source: *Appendices to the Journals of the House of Representatives*, 1958-1979 (General Election returns H.33 and E.9.)

ing to safer seats. There does, however, appear to be a greater tendency for winning challengers to have previous electoral experience in the Labour party than in National (see Table 4–3).

It is arguable whether being a woman is a disadvantage for a candidate in today's political world, but what is clear is that it is no built-in advantage. If 10.3 percent of the candidates fielded by the

TABLE 4–3

Electoral Experience of New Members, 1978

	National		Labour	
Electoral Experience	No.	%	No.	%
First contest	8	88	5	38
One previous loss	0	—	0	—
Two or more previous losses	1	12	2	15
Former M.P.	0	—	6	46

Source: Official party biographies and *Appendices to the Journals of the House of Representatives*, E.9 and H.33.

115

two major parties were women, only 4.4 percent of the new Parliament consisted of women M.P.s, four out of ninety-two. But with three of these four in the Labour party, it does appear that the chances of selection and subsequent election are greater for women in the Labour party than in the National party.

On the other hand, age appears to make little difference. The average age of the new members was National 40.9 years, Labour 40.6 years. The age distribution of winning challengers was:

	National	Labour
18–29	—	1
30–39	5	8
40–49	4	1
50–59	—	3
60 and over	—	0
Total	9	13

A clear majority of winning challengers in both major parties also illustrated the great importance of local connections for a candidate. Six of the nine successful new National party candidates had strong local connections, while the remaining three had past connections with the electorate or with the general area. There was not a single National party candidate who did not have some real connection with the electorate where he ran prior to gaining nomination. Labour displayed a similar tendency although to a lesser degree than National, perhaps reflecting the difference in emphasis in the parties' selection procedures. Eight of the thirteen successful Labour nonincumbents had clear local connections and a further two had past or geographical connections with their electorates. Only three could be said to have had no real local connections prior to gaining their candidacies. Yet even here, one of the three had gone to live and work in his chosen electorate immediately after his defeat in 1975, and another, Mike Moore, although frequently accused of being a carpetbagger, had worked assiduously for over a year in his chosen electorate before the election. In fact, in Moore's electorate, Papanui, the swing to Labour was considerably greater than elsewhere; clearly, although local connections are desirable, they are by no means indispensable.

Similarly, an advanced education, if not indispensable, appears to be a highly desirable qualification. Six of the nine winning National party nonincumbents and no fewer than nine of their thirteen Labour party counterparts had some form of higher education. A high level of education and to a lesser extent overseas experience appear to be characteristic of new incumbents in the last decade.

116

Conclusion

The process of selecting party candidates represents an important point of tension between the interests of the parliamentary parties and those of the electorates. The parliamentary leadership looks for a combination of potential executive talent, electoral appeal, and the ability to be a good team member; the local people want a person who will pay assiduous attention to their particular, sometimes trivial, needs. Both Labour and National have striven to balance these interests in their selection procedures, but neither has been wholly successful. Indeed it may well be that in a small Parliament such as New Zealand's the need for nearly every M.P. to play a potential executive role as well as nursing his electorate places too heavy a strain upon the system.

At the 1978 general election the National party's system of candidate selection came under fire from a range of members and supporters but also from the prime minister, who said that it was time for the party to have a long hard look at its selection procedures, particularly in the area of challenges to sitting members.[10] Similarly, Labour's deputy-leader, Bob Tizard, was reported to have said that the candidates chosen in some seats were not the best available.[11] On the other hand it could be argued that, given the difficulties faced by both major parties in 1978 in the wake of an extensive boundary redistribution, it is surprising that there were not even more candidate selection problems. It seems clear that the parliamentary parties are wedded to the idea that incumbents shall not be challenged for renomination, but the tendency for local electorate organizations to assert their rights is growing in both major parties.

In these circumstances the candidate selection system adopted by the National party seems better suited to future needs than the Labour party's system. It allows more extensive direct participation by branch delegates and is less divisive and better adapted to encourage branches to recruit new members, although it may arouse suspicions of favoritism at the preselection stage and occasional attempts at stacking at the selection stage.

The Labour party system, in 1977–1978 at least, seemed to lack any effective overall direction, particularly in Auckland where boundary redistributions led to an undignified scramble for seats and the provisions for dealing with the situation were not used. Under Labour's system there is always the suspicion that the composition of the

10 *New Zealand Herald*, December 8, 1978.
11 *Evening Post*, October 4, 1978.

117

selection committee may well prove to be of greater consequence than the merits of the aspirants. The role of the straw vote is also anomalous, and this, combined with the almost total exclusion of most electorate members of the party, means that the system can too easily become a divisive rather than a unifying process. Indeed, it is surprising that the Labour party candidate selection system works as well as it does, for it can all too easily maximize discord. Of the other two parties' systems, that used by Values, though in theory ultra-democratic, is totally without protection from abuse. It is a system suited only to a party whose parliamentary candidates are essentially token representatives with little or no chance of election. The Social Credit Political League too has yet to come to grips effectively with the problems of candidate selection.

It is doubtful, therefore, whether any of New Zealand's political parties are wholly satisfied with their present systems of selection, but they do have at least one particular strength, for financial contributions and sponsorship play no overt part in the selection procedure. Candidates are not asked how much they are prepared to contribute to their campaigns, nor are they officially sponsored, and this is perhaps one of the main merits of emphasizing party rather than the personality or affluence of the candidate.

But if the political parties deserve few accolades for their selection procedures, the same cannot be said of the scores of candidates who stand in election after election in hopeless seats either to show the flag for the party or to represent a deeply held principle with no possibility of reward. These are the unsung heroes of politics.

5

The National Party

Gilbert Antony Wood

The Background

In 1936 the National party was founded and the bases laid for New Zealand's present two-party system. The previous year Labour had swept to power in the aftermath of the Great Depression. It was to combat New Zealand's first Labour Government that the National party was formed from the shattered and demoralized parties that, separately or together, had governed continuously since the 1890s.

The long reign of the Liberals after 1891 had eventually prompted the formation of a rival Reform party, which in turn held power (in coalition with the Liberals during World War I) from 1912 until 1928. Then the erstwhile Liberals, seemingly a dying force, staged a dramatic revival under the name United and with Labour support took office as a minority Government. As the worst of the depression hit New Zealand, in 1931, the United Government adopted harsh retrenching measures which lost it Labour's support but gained it Reform's. Just before the 1931 elections a United-Reform coalition was formed—too late to avoid confusion in those electorates where both coalition parties already had selected candidates. Nevertheless the coalition won the election. In 1935, however, a new right-wing Democrat party (which two sitting M.P.s joined) added to the confusion of the anti-Labour voter. A Government already heading for defeat met total humiliation: its parliamentary membership was slashed from forty-six M.P.s to nineteen in a House of eighty. No Democrats were elected, but they won enough anti-Labour votes to cost the coalition perhaps as many as a dozen seats under New Zealand's first-past-the-post, single-member-district system.

Grateful acknowledgment is made of the assistance and advice of Murray McCully, Ian Stevens, Rosalind Strang, and Richard Mulgan.

If the objective of the founders of the National party was to oust the Labour Government, the immediate and necessary step was to end the confusion and vote splitting that had so disastrously hurt Labour's opponents in 1935. The new National party needed to accommodate the right—a task made easier by the obvious lesson that only a broad antisocialist front could keep Labour out. It also needed to stop interference from its own leaders in party finances and candidate selection which had aroused ill feeling; it needed, too, to obtain the widest possible consensus support in a constituency for the anti-Labour candidate. Where the Labour party evolved from metropolitan committees, the National party drew much of its strength from sprawling rural constituencies: to organize this support a different party structure was needed.

The new National party stood for broad principles but no specific program; an organization independent of the parliamentary wing; local selection of candidates from as wide a membership as possible; and a regional organization grouping country electorates around major urban centers. "Freedom from ideas," A. J. P. Taylor wrote, "was the boast of the most successful Conservative leaders" of twentieth-century Britain; the New Zealand National party took that freedom a step further in dispensing even with an ideological name.[1] Its essential character is that of a mass movement, whose raison d'être is to keep out the Labour party; its values are those of liberalism and the Protestant ethic: "belief in the individual" and in the desirability of encouraging "individual effort and initiative," commitment to "the liberty of the individual" in a "property-owning democracy," "fostering goodwill between all sections" in contrast to the Marxian dialectic, and opposition to statism.[2]

Organization. Although the National party's predecessors, Reform and United, had had extraparliamentary organizations, they had lacked the "large membership, number of active members, widespread sources of finance, [and] consultation of members on policy" of a modern mass party.[3] The National party, however, not only became a mass party comparable to and able to compete with the Labour party—in its membership and its geographic spread, as well as the strength of its organization, it outstripped Labour.

---

[1] *Observer*, January 27, 1979, p. 35

[2] National party pamphlet, *Six Good Reasons for Joining the National Party* [1978]; see also *Constitution and Rules of the New Zealand National Party* (Wellington: National party, 1977), pp. 1-2.

[3] R. S. Milne, *Political Parties in New Zealand* (Oxford: Oxford University Press, 1966), p. 169.

The organization of the former non-Labour parties was dominated by the parliamentary leader—indeed "the Reform Party's central organization seems to have done little more than act as a link between the Leader and the groups and interests supporting the party."[4] To fight the 1935 election the extraparliamentary wings of the Reform and United parties had federated. It was the executive of this federation that took the initiative in creating the National party. It called a conference of M.P.s and over 200 delegates from electorates throughout the country. Two guiding principles of the framers of the new party's constitution were that the organization should "control its own destinies free from Parliamentary control"[5] and that there should be a permanent organization at both the central and the local level. The party organization should control its own funds and select party candidates, then leave National M.P.s to get on with their job in Parliament.

Traditionally at least, the attitude to membership is strikingly different in the two parties. The Labour party is a programmatic party: its members are required to subscribe to the policy of the party; implicitly they can see their party as an organ of change and themselves as participants promoting change and influencing its direction. The National party is for those who like to talk politics; its strategy is to enroll the maximum number of members, however nominal their commitment to the party, on the no doubt correct premise that calling supporters "members" encourages them to turn out and vote every three years. (There is no fixed subscription: members—also called financial members—make a donation, no matter how small, and receive a receipt, not a membership card.) The two parties differ, too, in their attitude to local elections. As the party of reform, Labour regularly contests conservative control of the larger urban councils. National is content to restrict the fight to central politics, "keeping politics out of local government," in tune with its basic principle that there is no place for sectoral and class divisions in a good society. Moreover, the party can comfortably leave to local conservative interests the task of withstanding Labour. It is not seeking to mobilize political action, but to defuse political debate by providing a safety valve in the form of free discussion within its organization.

In staunch Labour territory, in the major cities, the National party organization may be weak, with only a few members under an elec-

---

[4] Ibid.
[5] Alan D. Robinson, "Oligarchy and Democracy, The Distribution of Power in the New Zealand National Party 1936-1949," mimeographed (The Hague: 1959), p. 22.

torate committee. In the wealthier city districts, however, where 3,000–4,000 members may be enrolled, and in rural electorates, the basic unit is the branch. It is on the branches that rests the principal task of canvassing and recruiting. The branches elect the electorate executive, which is responsible for organizing the candidate's campaign.

Tutelage and guidance for the party members are provided by the headquarters and regional offices of the party. The country is divided into five unequal divisions—Auckland, Waikato, and Wellington in the North Island; Canterbury-Westland and Otago-Southland in the South Island. The division is a key unit in the party structure. The divisional chairmen are the principal link between the central organization in Wellington, the party leadership, and the rank and file. It is at the divisional level that a small permanent administrative staff provides the stiffening for the mass, voluntary organization. It is one of the successes of the National party—in contrast to Labour—that its career officials have been prepared to remain organization men rather than using their position as a launching pad for entry into Parliament.[6]

For the local party member the major party gathering is the annual regional conference, formally called the divisional committee, where several scores of delegates from the electorates get together with local M.P.s and divisional officeholders, receive political briefings and inspiration, and spend many hours discussing and voting on a wide range of policy "remits" (proposals, motions). The party considers these meetings of sufficient importance that the president, director-general (general secretary), and leader all put in appearances.

In addition, each year several hundred delegates, spouses, and observers gather for several days in a dominion conference. This nationwide conference is the divisional committee writ large. It is held in a different part of the country each year—an effective publicity exercise. There is further discussion of remits filtered through the divisions, addresses from senior party figures, and discussion groups. The present leader of the party has expressed bluntly (and unchallenged) his view of the function of these conferences: they provide the opportunity for the party's members and M.P.s to exchange views. The conference has little power; it may pass or reject remits, hoping that the M.P.s or, when they are in power, ministers will take note; it elects the president and women's vice president. But party

---

[6] No general or divisional secretary has been elected to Parliament. Even among senior honorary officeholders, movement into Parliament is rare. Of the fifty men who served as president, treasurer, and divisional chairmen between 1936 and 1970, only two, both divisional chairmen, became M.P.s. In addition, Sidney Holland was both M.P. and divisional chairman until elected party leader in 1940. (Incidentally, in 1976 a woman was elected a divisional chairman.)

rules are made by the central executive, comprising delegates from the five divisions. (Strictly speaking, only the conference may alter the "basic constitution," but it is the central executive that decides what is "basic.")

The central executive, then, is the key to the proper functioning of the party and the important point of liaison between M.P.s and the party membership. There is a Dominion Council with fifty-odd members, elected annually by the divisions, and a Dominion Executive of about thirteen members. Dominion councillors are prestige party office-holders. Each division elects one councillor for every four electorates within its boundaries; divisional chairmen and the chairman and deputy chairman of the Young Nationals[7] are ex officio council members, along with the president, women's vice president, chairman of the Maori committee, and party treasurer. In addition the party leader and five other M.P.s are members. None are full-time or paid office-holders. The council, which is the governing body of the party, approves or rejects rules proposed by its rules subcommittee and appoints the party's headquarters staff.

The $4,000 limit on an individual candidate's election expenses leaves to the central committee of a party the key role in promoting the party's election campaign—there being no limit on the amount that a party may spend, nor any requirement that expenditures be made public. Membership subscriptions and local fund raising produce a significant proportion of the party's income: the division lays a quota on the electorates and in turn is answerable to the dominion council, which lays levies on the divisions. At both the divisional and the central level, however, the party also receives donations from businesses and wealthy supporters—although with state provision of radio and television time (the latter worth over $1 million) and the short formal campaign, New Zealand elections are relatively cheap affairs, even for National, the biggest spender. In 1978 National was reputed to have a budget of about $400,000—more than was spent to promote Kentucky Fried Chicken in New Zealand the previous year but rather less than the promotion budget of the state airline.

On the dominion headquarters of the National party rests the responsibility of organizing the election campaign: distributing election material, arranging nationwide advertising, determining priority areas for electioneering, and scheduling appearances for the leading party speakers. Three or four party officers (the president, the full-

---

[7] The party's vigorous youth movement, for persons aged twelve and over, runs its own regional and dominion conferences. In addition Young National representatives are included in electorate delegations to the main party conferences.

time director-general, and the director of publicity) and a staff of two or three, along with the party leader and his deputy, are the key individuals in the running of a campaign.

The parliamentary wing of the party, the caucus, is an autonomous body. It is the caucus that elects the party leader and deputy leader. Although National M.P.s undertake looser obligations than their Labour counterparts—promising only to be loyal to the party's rules and to its chosen leader—in practice the parliamentary party matches the Labour party in the tightness of its discipline. Floor crossing is almost unknown. Even more than in the Labour party the weekly caucus with its various caucus committees works closely with Government ministers (who constitute from a third to half of the caucus membership) under the chairmanship of the leader/prime minister. The caucus and its committees are also involved in the discussion and approval of party election policies.

1936–1975. The National party began its life in 1936 with eighteen European M.P.s[8] representing wealthy city districts in two of the four main centers, a provincial town, and rural areas. As it had begun, so it continued: an alliance of country interests with business and city interests backed by a wide middle-class membership. To a degree it was simply the old Reform party, now converted into a mass organization and absorbing the M.P.s and supporters of the old Liberal/United party. Until 1972 it was led by men who had first entered Parliament as Reform M.P.s: Adam Hamilton, a former cabinet minister, Sidney Holland, and Keith Holyoake. But with its initial small parliamentary team and its readiness to forgive past political differences, by the time it won power in 1949 it was a party largely shaped and recruited in reaction to the Labour Government of 1935–1949.

The party's success in 1949 was reinforced by an unprecedented "snap" election two years later, when Prime Minister Holland, having smashed a major strike, won a crushing victory with 54 percent of the votes and fifty of the eighty seats in the (now) single-chamber Parliament. (Since then, with the advent of Social Credit, no party has won as much as 49 percent of the votes.) In 1954 Holland retained a safe, if reduced, majority of seats over Labour. In 1957, however, under a new leader, Holyoake, National was defeated. Three years later National was back, and Holyoake remained prime minister for nearly

---

[8] One "independent" (a former Reform M.P.) joined the new party. Two of the four Maori seats also were held by National, but after 1943, when the Labour party supported candidates of the politico-religious Maori Ratana movement, National lost its last Maori M.P. Since then, the Maori seats have been solidly and immovably Labour.

twelve years, until his retirement early in 1972. By now the Government was clearly heading for defeat. Attempts to give the party a new look under John Marshall could not save a tired administration. It was reduced to thirty-two M.P.s in a Parliament of eighty-seven: not since the thirties had National fared so badly; not since 1951 had any party fared so well as Labour in 1972.

Nevertheless, National has won all but two of the eleven elections since 1946 and in many respects can be described as the natural party of government, the status quo party. Perhaps because it is accustomed to governing and expects to govern, it reacts with outrage when ousted from power. It is in opposition that the National party recovers its unity and sense of direction, and acquires (or confirms) pugnacious, tough, leaders. In 1973 and 1974 the party organization was revivified. The two key officers retired, and George Chapman became party president, Barrie Leay the new full-time general director. The party acquired a new advertising agency, Colenso Communications. Then in mid-1974, Marshall was ousted from the parliamentary leadership and succeeded by his deputy.[9] Robert Muldoon took over a revived party organization that was ready with an eighteen-month program for regaining power. He vigorously stumped New Zealand, drawing unprecedented crowds, exploiting his image as New Zealand's most provocative and controversial politician and an expert economist,[10] while the Labour Government grappled with economic recession and progressively slipped in the opinion polls. The dramatic National victory of late 1975 was a triumph for Muldoon, but also for the new leaders of the party organization and Colenso's. It had proved staggeringly easy to defeat a demoralized, poorly organized Labour Government. Parliamentary strengths were reversed: now National had fifty-five seats to Labour's thirty-two.

1978

There was no herculean task facing National in 1978. The organization and leadership that had won in 1975 were ready for the next round. Local elections in late 1977 and the victory of the Liberals in Australia confirmed the message of the New Zealand opinion polls: that National would face little difficulty in holding most of its gains of 1975. In February 1978, the third by-election of the 1975–1978 Parliament produced an upset victory by Social Credit; but both Labour

---

[9] See W. Keith Jackson, "Political Leadership and Succession in the New Zealand National Party," *Political Science*, vol. 27 (July-December 1975), pp. 1-24.
[10] Muldoon was finance minister from 1967 to 1972.

and National spokesmen agreed that new electoral boundaries gave an advantage to National, as well as easing its task of recapturing the lost seat in the general election. There was a dip in National's support in May 1978, bringing it to a level with Labour, but thereafter National regained its lead in the polls. Judging by the experience of the sixties, National could expect a movement towards rather than against the Government in the months before polling day.

In keeping with its boasted organizational skills, National had proceeded smoothly in 1977 to rebuild electorate organization on the new boundaries, bringing new blood into the electorate committees. Seminars were held on election organization under guidance from the head office. Through the latter half of 1977 and into mid-1978 candidate selection proceeded more or less according to schedule. From mid-1978 the party began issuing its election pamphlets, sold in bulk to electorates by the head office for a cent or two each. Government policies were adjusted to election year needs—reflation from late 1977, concessions to farmers, tax reductions to become effective shortly before polling day. Candidates went to Wellington for briefing sessions. Party headquarters maintained a stream of information and advice to local officeholders. The party's trump card, Muldoon, started to be played from June 1978, with a series of public meetings.

The final four-week campaign opened in traditional fashion with a public meeting by the prime minister televised and broadcast throughout New Zealand, after which Muldoon dashed around the country, holding nightly meetings, mostly in the vulnerable provincial towns. Audiences were rather more apathetic than in 1975, but attendance was still good, hundreds turning out even in small centers. Colenso Communications produced a series of advertisements skillfully slanted to a modern consumer audience for the party's twenty or so free five-minute evening slots on the two television channels. "We're well ahead," Muldoon telegraphed his candidates halfway through the campaign: "Keep it up."

As expected, National won the election. Rarely, however, can a party have responded so glumly to victory. National's safe majority in the House was no reflection of the votes it had won: in those campaign weeks its support had dropped, and with 39.8 percent of the votes, it had actually fared worse than its major opponent. What went wrong?

A Government that had entered the election campaign riding high in the opinion polls had emerged humbled four weeks later. There could be no excuses based either on a long-term erosion of support or on sudden crisis—or even on a reversion of the electorate to a normal balance between the two major parties after the freak elections of 1972 and 1975. In the "normal" years of the 1960s, National had always polled better than Labour.

Obviously the effectiveness of Labour was crucial, but so was the relative ineffectiveness of National. Political commentators remarked on the impact made by the "new" Rowling and wondered at the lack of impact of a "new" Muldoon. As one cautiously observed, "Mr. Muldoon? Well, it is hard to ignore him, but for the life of me I cannot see that he has gained any ground during the campaign."[11] "His campaign," said another, "has been a curious mixture, but he has never really fired on all cylinders as in 1975. Moreover the National party campaign slogan and back-up campaigning have been substandard."[12]

The Government went to the polls (as had Labour in 1975) both too complacent and too pessimistic. It assumed that victory was assured; it assumed, too, that it could not better its 1975 performance (it had almost captured several traditionally "safe" Labour seats and had actually taken one) or hold its inflated majority. Was there, perhaps, even a fear of being too successful and destroying the Labour party? The National party depends on a continuing and vigorous Labour party for its own mass membership and credibility.

The National Record. A National Government as much as a Labour Government presides over a highly centralized system, with a tradition of state interventionism not only in economic management, but also in the provision of services that in many societies are the concern of local and provincial administration or in which private enterprise has a major role, such as health, education, and housing. In office, National cannot disembarrass itself of the instruments of statism or escape responsibility for the variety of activities traditionally associated with central government in New Zealand. Nor has it been able to dismantle the protective walls built in the 1930s to promote import-substitution. The active and pragmatic Muldoon administration, struggling with recession, could not fail to alienate some of its more ideologically committed party supporters. If a basic purpose underlay the Muldoon policies, it appeared to have been more a determination to reverse specific measures of the previous Labour Government than a pursuit of National objectives.

The National party retains a tenuous link with its Liberal party antecedent; uneasily hovering on the right of the party is a strand of

[11] *Otago Daily Times*, November 18, 1978.
[12] *Evening Star*, November 24, 1978.

constitutionalism and antimajoritarianism, and a certain disquiet at the lack of checks in New Zealand on the power of the executive and of Government-in-Parliament.[13] From its Reform parent comes National's role as the spokesman of country interests. Hence allegations of illiberalism, of disregard for constitutional niceties and legal proprieties, and farmer discontent were particularly damaging to the Government within the ranks of its own supporters.

A catalog of the National Government's sins could begin with what amounted to suspension by executive *diktat* of the Labour Government's Superannuation Act at the start of the administration. (Labour had instituted an income-related universal pension or "superannuation" scheme based on contributions from employers and employees. The new Muldoon Government encouraged people not to pay their contributions months before it called Parliament and changed the law.) The Government broke precedent when it advised the queen to appoint a party politician, former prime minister and cabinet minister Sir Keith Holyoake, to the largely honorific post of governor general. On two highly publicized occasions, the executive dropped court proceedings for political reasons—against protestors who objected to the proposed development of former Maori land, and against freezing workers for infringement of the Government's own tough industrial law (which was subsequently changed). There was the overstayers issue: for a brief period people who appeared to be foreign were stopped by police in the streets. The secret police (the Security Intelligence Service) was given legal power to tap telephones. And there were problems about the methods used to see that solo mothers (unmarried, deserted, divorced, or widowed) receiving state benefits did not have a lover/breadwinner on the sly.

In most cases the Government did not lack arguments for its actions. It could point to such achievements as the establishment of a Human Rights Commission. But it could still be portrayed as illiberal and little inhibited by constitutional convention or legalism. It was also interventionist. The volumes of laws and regulations published annually grew fatter than ever in the Muldoon years. There was considerable farmer resentment when, in early 1978, the Government took the unprecedented step of achieving peace in the freezing works by contributing several million dollars to bridge the gap on back pay between the employers' offer and the employees' demand.

---

[13] "Executive" here refers to the prime minister, who has considerable leeway to act by decree as long as his cabinet colleagues agree. "Government-in-Parliament" refers to the Government acting with the approval of the backbenchers; its law-making power is not subject to any constitutional check.

Policy. "It is years since a political party wooed an electorate as blatantly as the National party courted voters in 1975," wrote a commentator in April 1978. "The success of their seduction surprised even the party's most ardent admirers." "New Zealand the way *you* want it" had been the slogan in 1975, and National's opponents made sure it was not forgotten in 1978. What could National offer this time? Not "political cartoons simplifying issues to the lowest common denominator"[14] or a second-time promise to make New Zealand the perfect country.

Like the Labour party organization, the National party organization demands a say in the framing of the election manifesto. Members at large have only the right to process and forward suggestions. But the policy committee, which makes the final decision, is comprised of equal numbers of M.P.s and organization officers. While this gives an influential voice to the organization, it leaves the party leader in a dominant position. He is chairman of the six-man committee and has a casting as well as a deliberative vote. He has the right to announce policy. If, as in 1978, he delays assembling the policy committee until the last months before the election, the process is held up; if he chooses to have major announcements come as Government decisions rather than party election policy, he can—as in 1978—leave little for inclusion in the manifesto. And he can largely dictate the timing and thrust of the party's campaign.

In the course of 1975, Muldoon had released party policy statements ranging through the various areas of government activity—from agriculture to the post office, from regional development to women. Eventually these were combined in an inch-thick volume of mimeographed foolscap pages containing forty policy statements. Here were set forth National's values and objectives as well as specific election promises. For popular consumption the advertising agents issued a twenty-page illustrated "manifesto"—a boiled-down popularized version of National's policies.

In 1978 National simply issued, after the opening of the campaign, an up-dated version of its 1975 policy statements: fifty-six pages of unrelieved print. Once again the serious student could see attempts to spell out National's objectives and philosophy, combined this time with references to the Government's decisions of the past three years and many a promise to continue the good work. But the document was short on hard commitments: there was a promise to reduce electricity charges to encourage industries in the South Island

---

14 Reg Birchfield, *N.B.R. Outlook, Election Year Special, April 1978* (Wellington: Fourth Estate Newspapers Ltd., 1978), p. 1.

and a handful of specific promises—a sealed airstrip in the Chatham Islands, the appointment of a full-time coordinator of tree crops and a national outdoor education officer, the introduction of FM radio, and so on.

In 1974–1975 an attempt had been made to set goals and express values; 1978 saw essentially a restatement of the results of that exercise. Even the photograph of the leader on the cover of the manifesto was the one used in 1975. National was not so much standing on its record as offering to continue its policy and leadership. It sought to stage a repeat of the 1975 election, with the same players and much the same script. The lame campaign theme and slogan was "We're keeping our word," and four weeks of chorusing on television and radio failed to make it a new hit tune. Labour attempted to emulate its rival of three years before and released many policy promises long before the start of the formal campaign. It also emulated National's concentration on television advertising. The result was a match between slick advertising agencies and a general trivializing of the election. The panache and drama of 1975 were lacking—along with National's anti-Labour crusade, the exploitation of fear and discontent, and Labour's scare campaign against the divisive, authoritarian, dangerous Muldoon.

The Outcome

Like 1975, the 1978 elections showed that a Government that believes both that it is assured of victory and that a loss of seats is unavoidable fights an election half-heartedly. They appeared to show, too, as 1975 had not, that the actual election campaign can change the result. They shook the comfortable assumption, based on New Zealand experience, that National had become the natural governing party, subject only to occasional temporary dismissal after a prolonged period in power. National's superiority in organization likewise was challenged: it had been too easy to boast of mass membership and to assume a weak opponent. It had been easy, too, to assume that a rise in Social Credit support was good for National, causing some inconvenience in a few rural seats but primarily draining votes from Labour.

In 1928 New Zealand's financial wizard and one-time Liberal prime minister, Sir Joseph Ward, had led the United party to its surprise success. Ward died too soon to face the worst of the Great Depression. Less fortunate was the financial wizard of the 1950s, Labour's Walter Nash, whose Government inherited the mild world recession of the late 1950s. In the 1970s New Zealand's financial wizard was Rob Muldoon. Like many previous non-Labour prime ministers, Muldoon acted as his own finance minister, thereby tying his reputation as "economic miracle-worker" to his Government's performance. In 1975 Muldoon's principal theme was that New Zealand's economy was "shattered": to restore it New Zealand needed three years of proper management and effective leadership. But by 1978 the economy was not looking markedly better: inflation was still high, there were record postwar levels of unemployment, a high internal deficit, and continued substantial overseas borrowing. Even before the election there were quips about the miracle worker "turning wine to water."[15]

In three years the Muldoon Government had failed to resolve New Zealand's economic problems or even point to their future resolution. In the aftermath of the election there came louder demands, amply supported by domestic and international economic advisers of the Government, for a restructuring of the economy. The implication was that opportunities had been lost.

"In 1974 and 1975," suggested a senior National party member, "the authoritarian behaviour adopted by our leader was popular, but now it's time for him to back off."[16] From postelection inquests within the party came the message that the Government should take a softer line on humanitarian, social, and environmental issues, pay more attention to the private enterprise elements in the party, and strive for less government intervention and more concern for personal freedoms and the rule of law. Criticism, in short, focused on those features of the Muldoon Government—authoritarianism, economic management, strong government rather than sympathetic government —most associated with Muldoon and his close associates. The man Muldoon had ousted as party leader, Sir John Marshall, exercised his political talents subtly to contrast his own urbane and moderate style with that of his successor; less subtly he called for a return to the party's principles. Sir John emerged from the elections with new stature. On election night, as Muldoon fell Marshall rose: now in the role of commentator, he made what may have been the most effective television appearance of his career.

A generation ago over 40 percent of the National party's vote came from paid-up members. Membership fell in the 1960s, rising again in the 1970s. But if in 1978 National failed to reach its target of 225,000 members (still below its total in 1949), the 200,000 it claimed was more than a quarter of the 676,294 votes National won

---

15 Ibid., p. 16; Ian Templeton, *Guardian Weekly*, September 10, 1978.
16 Quoted by D. Yardley, *Sunday Times*, December 3, 1978.

in the general electorates (that is, all but the four Maori seats). At best, well over a third of National's voters in any electorate are paid-up members. More so than in the Labour party, officeholders in the National party are in a position to represent the views of a membership that constitutes a sizable portion of the party vote and can express them without the inhibitions that come from being aligned more closely with the parliamentary party than with the grass roots. A National party leader also is less secure in his tenure than his Labour counterpart. The Labor leader is subject to triennial reelection by Labour M.P.s, the timing of which he can seek to manipulate in order to win fresh endorsement of his leadership. There is no provision for reendorsement of the National leader. This places an onus on the party organization to monitor the leader's support both within the caucus and in the membership at large, and it can use the monitoring process to put pressure on the leader. A Labour leader can fend off outside pressure by pointing to his reelection by the caucus; a National leader can prove that he has continued caucus support only by conceding that he might have lost it and polling the caucus—as Marshall did, to his cost, in 1974.

Friend and foe alike agree that from the mid-1970s New Zealand politics increasingly centered on the pugnacious, abrasive Muldoon. The first "Muldoon" election was in 1975; the second was in 1978. In both, "leadership" and Muldoon were major issues. The 1978 election gave Muldoon the biggest setback in his political career—and his subsequent responsiveness to party complaints probably reflected not only his political skill but also the weakening of his position within his party.

In the postelection cabinet shuffle, significant changes were made in the Muldoon administration. Muldoon relieved himself of the traditional prime minister's role of leader of the House of Representatives and delegated the task to a man less likely to raise parliamentary tempers. After having frequently boasted of his accessibility to the media, for several months Muldoon retreated into inaccessibility: cabinet decisions were to be expounded and explained by the appropriate minister. There were changes, too, in major spending departments: social welfare, health, and housing. The housing minister was sacked—an almost unprecedented move. In the gentlemanly tradition of New Zealand politics, ministers retire before elections rather than being dismissed after elections. Social welfare and health, both portfolios previously held by close Muldoon associates and men who shared the master's talent for arousing antagonism, were placed under a minister more likely to give a presentable face to National's administration of the welfare state. The effect of the changes was a lower profile for the prime minister and a new image for the administration in politically sensitive areas where ministers had been criticized for their manner, their competence, or both.

The 1978 elections produced greater stress on collective leadership; a decline in the standing of the prime minister and a rise in the assertion of influence by the extraparliamentary wing of the party; pressures for tougher Government measures to restructure the economy, for a more humane approach to social welfare, and for greater sensitivity to civil liberties and the requirements of statutory law. Perhaps, too, some will note the complaint voiced during the campaign that parties should not be sold like hair shampoo. If so, perhaps they will pay greater attention to policy debate in future elections.

6

The Labour Party Campaign

Roderic Alley

Easily the most distinctive feature of Labour's 1978 campaign was its perceived impact. This was remarkable for at least two reasons. First, it shook local electoral folklore, the received wisdom being that the campaign proper is unlikely to have much impact upon voter choice. Second, and perhaps more significant, certainly in the long term, was the effect that it had upon the Labour party itself. By performing better than expected during the campaign, Labour—personified by its forceful leader, Bill Rowling—rebuilt its supporters' confidence that their organization was indeed a serious contender for office.

Yet for most of 1978 this had remained very much in doubt. Barely a month before the election, opinion surveys and analysts alike had shown Labour trailing so badly as to leave it scant hope of recapturing any of the seats lost in the spectacular rout that had driven it from office in 1975. In the end, Labour topped most precampaign predictions, with forty-one seats and a higher share of the total vote than National, 40.4 percent to 39.8 percent or a margin of about 10,000 votes. If doing so proved something of a morale booster, sober reflection soon revealed that Labour's share of the vote had increased by a meager 0.8 percentage points from its post-1945 low, suffered three years earlier. Thus, as it revitalized Labour's hopes for future office, so too did the 1978 campaign and its outcome remind the party of the magnitude of the task of building a wider base of electoral support.

Some Background

Since its formation in 1916, the New Zealand Labour party has been in power for three periods: from 1935 to 1949, when it was led by Michael Joseph Savage (until 1940) and then Peter Fraser; from 1957

134

to 1960 under Walter Nash; and from 1972 to 1975, initially under Norman Kirk, whose untimely death in August 1974 saw the leadership pass to Bill Rowling.

The significant feature of this record has been the party's indifferent performance since 1949: it has won only two elections and as of 1978 has held office for a bare six years. Once in power, it has been handicapped by inexperience and has had the bad luck to hold office during periods of serious economic difficulty. On the whole, its collective management of New Zealand's numerous, often competing, domestic interests has been inadequate. Yet for this analysis a further factor deserves particular emphasis: When Labour has been in power, a large share of its human resources (which are spread thin at the best of times) has been monopolized by the exigencies of governing, rather than by the more mundane tasks connected with maintaining the party's own organization. Unlike its rival, the National party, the postwar Labour party has not had the opportunity to develop the skills and strategies that allow a party to hold on to office as distinct from those that help it win elections. This was apparent in 1972, when Norman Kirk's leadership, more than any real depth of Labour support in the electorate, ousted a National Government tiring visibly from twelve unbroken years in office.

Backed by a seemingly impregnable twenty-three seat majority in the eighty-seven member legislature, the Kirk Labour Government initiated major policy programs, but at a time of massive domestic and international economic flux. So absorbed with office were those who had formerly played key roles within the party's organization that the party was left to stagnate. When the 1975 election suddenly loomed, it was hardly in any shape to fight a campaign. As Labour M.P. Michael Bassett put it: "Anxiously we turned to the party machine to find nothing much there. Scarcely any staff, no publicity and by May 1975 not even a public relations firm contracted as yet. On top of its many commitments, Caucus had to run the campaign as well."[1]

Compounding this problem in the central party was a more deep-seated, long-standing organizational decay, especially at the branch level. Membership was declining, finances were in a parlous state, and internal communication was tangled. The reasons for this slump included the sparse rewards of electoral success; the disillusionment of would-be reformers; generational, regional, ideological, class, and personality strains; and a continuing uneasiness in relations with the

---

[1] Michael Bassett, *The Third Labour Government* (Palmerston North: The Dunmore Press, 1976), p. 303.

trade unions.[2] As Bill Rowling put it in January 1978: "Over a long period when one looks back, we had allowed the membership, the people in the contact situations, to wither. I don't think any of us, myself included, appreciated how much we had allowed this to happen. Our membership [in 1975] was down to 15,000."[3]

The Realities of Opposition. After its drubbing at the polls in 1975, which had left it with only thirty-two seats, Labour faced dismal prospects for recovery. Depleted by the defeat of promising younger M.P.s, the opposition could only sporadically challenge a confident, often brash, Muldoon administration or register with the public as a credible alternative. At the same time, the Government conducted a concerted onslaught upon Labour's record in office, dismantling its policy initiatives in such fields as superannuation, health, broadcasting, local government, and foreign relations and politically discrediting Labour, whose failures in management, the Government claimed, were responsible for the country's continuing economic malaise.

Then in 1976, towards the end of an unusually acrimonious and difficult parliamentary session, the Labour party was worsted with the so-called Moyle affair. A series of heated parliamentary exchanges on November 4 came to a climax when Labour frontbencher Colin Moyle implied that Prime Minister Muldoon's professional accounting firm did "dishonest deals." Muldoon retaliated by claiming that Moyle had been picked up by the police in 1975 for suspected homosexual activities.

In the furor that followed, attention focused on the prime minister's access to police files and documents of the type he threatened to table before Parliament. Following a judicial enquiry, however, the spotlight shifted to Moyle, who had given the police conflicting stories and had been less than straightforward with his party colleagues—in particular Rowling. Moyle resigned from Parliament in December 1976 but signified his intention to continue seeking his party's nomination in the next election. He eventually succeeded, winning nomination (but not a seat) in Whangarei. In the long run this unsavory affair may have done as much to damage Muldoon's public standing as Moyle's, but there can be no doubt that the Labour party was harmed by the impression it gave of vacillation and poor communication, especially within its senior ranks.

---

[2] Barry Gustafson, *Social Change and Party Reorganization: The New Zealand Labour Party since 1945* (London: Sage Publications, 1976), pp. 23-32.
[3] *New Zealand Herald* (Auckland), January 4, 1978.

In 1977, the Labour party suffered further internal strain over the vexed question of party endorsement of candidates. First, and most serious, was the case of Gerald O'Brien, the party's sitting member for the relatively secure Labour constituency of Island Bay in Wellington. Following his involvement in a Christchurch motel fracas, subsequent court appearances, and growing disquiet among colleagues about his parliamentary performance, pressure increased upon O'Brien not to contest the forthcoming election. He refused point-blank, resigned from the party, and ran as an independent, threatening Labour's traditional hold upon the constituency. This episode caused less public concern about the merits or otherwise of O'Brien's continued service than about the spectacle of disarray among senior Labour officials. Many were asking whether the Labour party, seemingly incapable of managing its own affairs, could be expected to run the country.

A further headache for the party was the need to reconcile the conflicting interests of sitting Labour M.P.s, especially in the Auckland area, after sweeping changes in the electoral boundaries. In the musical chairs for nomination that followed, strains were evident between various constituency interests and the party's head office, dominated by President Arthur Faulkner, Vice-President Joe Walding, and Secretary John Wybrow. According to the Labour party's most senior member of Parliament, Warren Freer, Bill Rowling's personal intervention was required to settle some of these candidacy disputes,[4] a task that normally falls to the party president.

Three points should be emphasized, then, about the Labour party's situation as it entered the election year 1978. First, the party was almost continually on the defensive, and as a result many opportunities to attack the Muldoon Government's performance went begging. Second, the party's various internal squabbles and wrangles received substantial, adverse public exposure. This meant that time, effort, and resources that might otherwise have been devoted to strengthening the party's appeal, policies, and links to the electorate were consumed by its internal problems. Third, the fact that the caucus was smaller weakened its traditional dominance within the party at large. This was compounded by the fracturing impact of the abortion issue, on which the differences between Labour M.P.s were as deep as they were potentially divisive. That similar differences existed within the National party's ranks was of little consolation to those seeking unity in an election year.

---

[4] *National Business Review: N.B.R. Outlook* (Wellington), April 1978, p. 4.

Labour's Precampaign Activities. In the first months of 1978, the Labour party conducted six regional conferences. While not providing a platform for policy enunciation or achieving wide national publicity, they nevertheless dealt with themes that were subsequently amplified in the wider Labour campaign. For example, when speaking at the Wellington regional conference, the party's candidate for the Miramar electorate, Bill Jeffries, claimed that public dissatisfaction with Parliament, government bureaucracy, and central political institutions was widespread. "People feel they have little chance to share in the formation and development of their own communities," he said. "The grave danger of this atmosphere of non-participation, because of misunderstanding of our political system, is that centralism can easily occur. Centralist policies aggravate this. A Government-knows-best attitude is the first sign of a process that can lead to the destruction of human rights."[5]

Self-sufficiency in energy, reaffirmation of earlier Labour attempts to promote regional development, an easing of, and more flexible use of, the tax system, and industrial democracy were among the themes to emerge at these regional conferences. Senior M.P. Michael Connolly told the Canterbury conference that Labour would build its election policy around such core appeals as financial and economic credibility, self-reliance at all levels, and regionalism as opposed to centralism.[6] At another conference the party vice-president and candidate for Palmerston North, Joe Walding, warned against promising more than the party could deliver, in particular increased welfare services involving higher taxation. There were no instant political panaceas, he warned.[7]

In addition, the regional conferences convinced the party's leadership (if that was necessary) that the controversial abortion issue would somehow have to be confronted, yet prevented from damaging party unity. Debate at the Wellington regional conference was certainly bitter; a leader of the Society for the Protection of the Unborn Child (SPUC) and sitting Labour member from Porirua, Gerald Wall, clashed fiercely with those campaigning nationally against the restrictive legislation on contraception, sterilization, and abortion passed in December 1977. In fact, the more apparent it became that the party was incapable of formulating an agreed policy, the more Rowling and his colleagues stressed the desirability of holding a nationwide referendum on the issue.

---

[5] *Dominion* (Wellington), February 27, 1978.

[6] *Press* (Christchurch), February 20, 1978.

[7] *Evening Post* (Wellington), February 25, 1978.

The 1978 Annual Conference. The party's five-day annual conference, held in Wellington in May, drew over 800 delegates, a record attendance. This writer attended all sessions as a media commentator. The first point to be made about the conference is that it managed to achieve a sort of consensus on abortion: after a full debate, it passed resolutions supporting repeal of the existing legislation, calling for a referendum on repeal of this legislation, and, for good measure, acknowledging the rights of the fetus. In race track parlance, the party was covering the field by laying a dollar on the issue three ways.

Another feature of the conference was the central role played by women. Figures like Helen Clark (an Auckland delegate), Ann Hercus (the Lyttelton candidate), Helene Ritchie (the Ohariu candidate), Lois Welch (the Hamilton East candidate), Margaret Shields (the Kapiti candidate), and Whetu Tirikatene-Sullivan (sitting member for Southern Maori) conducted an astute floor campaign in favor of the resolution on repeal of the abortion law. In addition to speaking, these women and their supporters pursued mutual-voting-support strategies with trade union delegates,[8] exchanging support in internal party elections for support on the abortion issue. David Lange, the popular Labour M.P. for Mangere, was one candidate for the party executive who lost largely because of his conservatism on the abortion issue.

Third, Rowling projected a far more authoritative presence than ever before. In his keynote speech (rehearsed before a Rotorua audience) Rowling stressed a series of points that were to echo throughout Labour's campaign: New Zealand must return to the path of tolerance, decency, and purpose; its leadership must be a source of pride, not embarrassment; hard work and self-reliance must underlie an economy run in the interests of "real" people, not profiteers.[9] If stronger on emotion and rhetoric than on detail, this call for vision, with its unmistakable anti-Muldoon overtones, effectively rallied the party for a serious electoral effort and strengthened its leadership.

The fourth important feature of the conference was the ambiguous relationship between the floor and the platform, between the rank-and-file and the hierarchy. Many delegates' willingness to work for the party in an election year did not signify endorsement of the methods employed by its headquarters in Wellington. Unofficially,

[8] With the Engineers Union absent and other unions simply failing to send expected delegates, strength from this source was below normal. The fifty-seven unions represented thus held 354 out of a total of 1,225 conference floor votes—barely a quarter. *Auckland Star*, May 13, 1978.

[9] *New Zealand Herald*, May 11, 1978.

the central organization was criticized for being out of touch, for foisting unsatisfactory candidates upon unwilling electorates (for example, Rotorua and Wellington Central), and for lacking any real independence from the party's parliamentary caucus.

Nothing new in the Labour party, this problem failed to obscure a fifth feature of the conference: its vitality. Far more than any other party in 1978, Labour debated a wide policy agenda. Although many of the matters that were discussed failed to find their way into the party's manifestoes, the liveliness and range of the debate left many participants feeling that the conference had been important.

Labour Policy in the 1978 Campaign

Despite New Zealand's mounting problems in 1978 (or perhaps because of their intractability), policy issues did not figure strongly in the election campaign. For Labour this could be partly attributed to the emphasis the party placed upon its midyear showpiece—a revised and comprehensive tax reform program. Arguing for fiscal probity and a "no free lunch" approach to public spending at a time when the ruling party was already ostensibly committed to fiscal conservatism, Labour was left with little scope for policy innovation. New policy directions—certainly for the Labour party—mean heavier public spending, and Labour was already campaigning strongly against oppressive state centralism. Moreover, the party lacked the time, skills, and resources with which to devise more comprehensive, effective, and economical policies. A good illustration of this point is the absence from Labour's 1978 policies of any concept of planning.

Released in late July, barely four months before the election, Labour's tax proposals included basic tax-free-income levels of $50 a week each for parents in a two-income family, $60 a week for a single person, and $70 a week for a married couple with one income; tax rebates for all dependents, including teenagers; a shift towards taxing spending; and revised, simplified scales for income tax and steps toward its indexation. The annual cost of these proposals Labour estimated at $386 million. This would be raised, the party claimed, by increased productivity, employment, purchasing power, sales tax, and, more controversially, a 10 percent surcharge on the use of foreign exchange.

Labour's tax reforms attracted substantial news media coverage, and the party made a major effort to explain the various proposals fully to the public, even establishing a phone-in service. Labour frontbencher Roger Douglas claimed that if the reforms were implemented about 400,000 New Zealanders, including part-time workers, apprentices, and students, could "forget all about income tax."[10] The taunt that the proposals were a massive bribe Bill Rowling dismissed as nonsense, adding, "after all it is the people's own money."[11]

While the tax cuts were an important component of Labour's campaign, they had less impact than they would have had if they had been announced earlier. As the campaign got under way other policy proposals competed for publicity and attention from party spokesmen. Between April and October, the Labour party regularly released statements of policy on specific subjects. Some of this material was printed in booklets—on health, on regional development, and on the environment, energy, and forestry.[12]

Then in late October, the party's thirty-two page manifesto went on sale—a document designed for easy reading and mass consumption.[13] This summarized and compressed, sometimes drastically, the policy statements that had been released over the preceding months. It featured the tax reforms and pledged Labour to removing "useless" penal provisions in the industrial law. On housing there was a pledge to reduce interest rates to the level existing in 1975 and a revival of the formula advocated by Michael Joseph Savage, Labour's first prime minister, for mortgage repayments on public loans for housing: "one day's pay for one week's mortgage repayment."[14] Labour's approach to New Zealand's worsening employment problems was clearly linked to its regional development proposals, which included subsidizing the employment of apprentices in regional development areas; making the whole of the South Island and several areas in the North Island eligible for regional development assistance; buying large blocks of land suitable for diversification, selling them to young farmers, and providing financial assistance and technical advice to small holders; and issuing regional development bonds at attractive interest rates.

Beyond these, the most noteworthy points included in the manifesto were: the intention to make New Zealand self-sufficient in liquid

[10]Ibid., July 27, 1978.

[11] Ibid.

[12] *Help Where and When You Need It—New Zealand Labour Party Health Policy 1978* (Wellington: New Zealand Labour Party, 1978); *Balanced Development* (Wellington: New Zealand Labour Party, 1978); *Environment, Energy, Development: Labour's 1978 Manifesto*, produced and published by R. Prebble, M.P., M. Bassett, and Peter Harris, 1978. In scope, detail, and presentation, this last publication easily outdid that on regional development, which is surprising given the emphasis the party placed upon decentralization during the campaign.

[13] *To Rebuild the Nation: New Zealand Labour Party 1978 Manifesto*, Wellington, 1978.

[14] Rowling specifically mentioned Savage. *Press* (Christchurch), April 14, 1978.

fuel by the year 2000; the passage of a Freedom of Information Act; reform of Parliament and an increase in its membership to 121; revision of the Commerce Act to encourage competition and curb the growth of monopolies; an emphasis upon community health care and negotiations with the medical profession to permit government reimbursement of preschoolers and people over sixty for their consultations; strengthening of preschool facilities and the establishment of a Children's Commission; more police on the beat to deal with violence, as well as a major law enforcement drive against drug trafficking; overhaul of the transportation system, especially coastal and inter-island services; and a tougher international stance against apartheid and the presence of nuclear weapons in the Pacific.

Entitled *To Rebuild the Nation*, Labour's manifesto at once highlighted the need to break down what it called the fences of high taxation, mortgage payments, and government red tape; gave prominence to party leader Bill Rowling ("Statesman, economist, New Zealander—a unique blend of toughness and compassion"), including his campaign itinerary; and called for national dedication, purpose, freedom, and self-reliance. Ironically, the National party's slogan from 1975—"New Zealand the Way You Want It"—would have captured Labour's message well.

The Official Campaign. Bill Rowling completely dominated Labour's official campaign, which he opened on October 31 in a marginal electorate, Palmerston North. In the hectic twenty-four days of the campaign, Rowling delivered more than twenty key addresses. In his opening speech, which was nationally televised, he gave his party a firm and confident start, which contrasted sharply with the prime minister's unexpectedly muted, even casual, performance the preceding evening. Reviewing the country's problems, Rowling presented a stark picture: New Zealanders "required to rot" on the dole; the young and talented voting with their feet by going abroad; the country divided, bitter, and directionless; worsening national indebtedness; surging interest rates, industrial upheaval, and oppressive centralism.[15] "Leadership is not a license to destroy," Rowling said, "to make a fool of your country around the world." In this "moment of decision" the choice was therefore clear: "do we continue to claw and scratch and kick each other, or do we accept the fact that we are all New Zealanders and want to fight for something better?"[16]

---

[15] *Evening Post*, November 1, 1978.
[16] Ibid.

The clear anti-Muldoon sentiments of this speech attracted a strong favorable response, and Rowling's confidence steadily grew as the campaign progressed. Furthermore, the scope for attacking Muldoon seemed as ample as the electoral mileage to be gained in doing so. Rowling cataloged and denounced the Government's failings across a broad front that included the state of the economy, taxation, unemployment, borrowing, industrial relations, transport, housing, the Security Intelligence Service legislation, overseas trade, and foreign relations—and all of his charges implicated the prime minister. The National party tried to construe this as "personality politics" or "playing the man and not the ball," but in fact Muldoon's heavy direct involvement in so many policy areas during the preceding three years made him a legitimate target. Inevitably, in joint television appearances, retaliatory radio reports, and the press, the exchanges between Muldoon and Rowling intensified throughout the campaign. With his light touch and sense of fun, Rowling neatly parried Muldoon's thrusts and scored at the prime minister's expense, sometimes over trivia. He ridiculed Muldoon's personal attacks upon news media representatives at campaign meetings, for example, and made fun of his famous wall charts. At a crowded, enthusiastic meeting in Christchurch, Rowling drew enormous applause by having Papanui candidate Michael Moore hold aloft a large blank chart signifying the Government's record of achievement in the South Island. The Labour leader was undoubtedly helped by his speech writer, Eleanor Roy, an experienced journalist blessed with a sure sense of timing and a way with words.

In planning his campaign strategy, Rowling was clearly anxious to avoid the mistakes of 1975 and pace himself more effectively, steadily building momentum. On the whole he succeeded, despite some voice difficulties, the absence of an evening address in the marginal seat of Hastings, and perhaps too many meetings in the central North Island bunched together early in the campaign. One feature of Rowling's campaign that was markedly absent from his major rival's was plenty of local glad-handing; street-corner, factory, and work-place chats; and informal face-to-face meetings with electors. Again, by comparison with the Muldoon entourage, Rowling's group provided more copy for the traveling news media representatives. Finally, the Rowling campaign was significant not just for its direct appeal to the electorate, but also for the needed boost it gave to the morale of those manning the party's effort at the constituency level.

Campaign Organization. The individual electorate campaigns of Labour's 1978 candidates were striking for their diversity. In Papanui (Michael Moore), Hunua (Malcolm Douglas), and East Coast Bays (Colleen Hicks), candidates had access to computer facilities which they used to identify quickly from the electoral rolls specific targets for propaganda, canvassing, and voter turnout purposes. In marginal Palmerston North, Joe Walding had his electorate workers take on specific areas in which to concentrate their attention. With the largest constituency in New Zealand, as well as a comfortable Labour majority, the Southern Maori representative, Whetu Tirikatene-Sullivan, did not campaign in the conventional sense but spoke in many different constituencies. Some candidates acted as their own campaign managers; others pursued a lengthy build-up through canvassing, cottage meetings, and local news media exposure; and a few hardly campaigned at all.

The reasons for such strong local autonomy are not hard to find. In 1978 the Labour party's national organization was short of money and heavily dependent upon voluntary assistance. Already stretched to meet its budget for advertising, it could offer candidates little assistance. Indeed, if anything the reverse was true: as early as August 1977, party President Arthur Faulkner admitted that funds earmarked for the 1978 election campaign were already being used to run the head office.[17]

Funding—or rather the lack of it—also inflamed traditional tensions between the Auckland region and the head office in Wellington. At the party's 1977 annual conference in Christchurch, it was decided to adopt a new formula for capitation levies to the head office. Under this scheme the electorate organization would pay a twenty-cent registration fee for each member and twenty cents for each Labour vote in that particular electorate in the previous election. In March 1978, a news report claimed that unless certain Auckland electorates surrendered some of their nest eggs to headquarters, they would not be permitted to attend the forthcoming annual conference. The basis of this information was a letter sent by Party Secretary John Wybrow expressing disappointment at the failure of these electorates to meet their financial obligations. Incensed by the news leak, Wybrow said he would do all he could to expose the "disloyal rat" who had passed this information to the media.[18] These electorates seemed to believe, not without justification, that they were getting the worst of both worlds: the need to pay capitation fees to Wellington, yet little tangible

[17] Ibid., August 10, 1977.
[18] *Otago Daily Times* (Dunedin), March 23, 1978.

return for doing so. Indeed, when asked in August, just three months from the election, what the party staff amounted to, Secretary Wybrow said there were only six full-time people at headquarters and "just a handful" in regional offices through the country.[19]

In the wake of Labour's 1975 defeat, Rowling clearly appreciated, and acted upon, the need to revitalize the party organization. Although an improvement was evident, the 1978 campaign revealed Labour to be still a shoe-string organization, critically dependent upon volunteer campaign organizers and clearly distinguishable from National's by its amateurism. Furthermore, the strain on this none too sturdy structure was seriously aggravated by sweeping electoral boundary changes and, even worse, the administrative disarray that followed the drawing up of the electoral rolls.

The advice tendered to all Labour candidates in the party booklet *Organizing to Win* was direct and simple: "get them on the roll, get them to the poll."[20] While candidates were advised on such matters as press relations, advertising, arranging a campaign itinerary, canvassing, and voter enrollment qualifications, the key passage described a system

> to get the maximum number of Labour voters to the poll, to identify National supporters and therefore not encourage or help them to vote. The scope of the system is such that we can tell within any given half an hour of voting whether anybody within the electorate has or has not voted. Therefore, throughout the day our canvassers can concentrate on a smaller and smaller number of more reluctant but important voters.[21]

Less clear was how individual electorates could organize themselves to achieve these objectives. Like some of Labour's other campaign plans, this was implemented only partially and with mixed results. Probably the campaign slogan "Labour and you—together we'll make it," with its message of partnership and cooperation, could have been applied to advantage inside the party.

Advertising and Publicity. The party's national advertising efforts were similarly uneven, though more effective towards the end of the campaign. In April 1978, the party ran half-page newspaper advertisements headed, in large letters, "WAR—you're fighting for your

[19] *Evening Post*, August 16, 1978.
[20] *Organizing to Win* (Wellington: New Zealand Labour Party, 1978), p. 3.
[21] Ibid., p. 21.

145

THE LABOUR PARTY CAMPAIGN

family"; these struck a jarring note, especially since Bill Rowling's key speeches emphasized cooperation, decency, tolerance, unity, and reconstruction. But throughout the campaign, Labour's advertising at least matched National's in both design and appeal, something it could not have claimed in 1975.

Yet there was no ignoring the indifference of the public to much political advertising in 1978. The general attitude seemed to be "a plague on both their houses." This consideration probably affected Labour's thinking on the broader issue of publicity and how to achieve it. On the other hand, its precampaign "demolition squad" was newsworthy. Consisting usually of M.P.s John Kirk, David Lange, Richard Prebble, and Joe Walding, the group conducted meetings using short speeches and visual aids, but achieved the most publicity when they posed in hard hats complete with picks and crowbars courting the working man's vote. Rowling's visit to Sydney, Australia, to help enroll the many expatriate New Zealanders living there through the formation of a party branch also attracted publicity. It was a way of drawing attention to Labour's claim that people were leaving New Zealand because they were unhappy with the National Government's record in office.

Conclusion

What general conclusions can be drawn from Labour's campaign? In the long term this was not a bad election to lose, given the party's general unreadiness to govern. Better by far, it was admitted privately, to have the party recoup as much ground as possible so as to launch a more effective assault next time around. Labour's partial success gave the party an incentive to analyze its overall 1978 campaign performance closely. The following points would appear relevant.

First, if the quality of the candidates has always been important, then for Labour it is doubly so following the 1978 election. Labour's candidates varied widely in their campaign organization, use of publicity, communication skills, and capacity to exploit increasingly significant local and regional issues. Improving on all these factors could well ensure Labour the one-percentage-point swing it would require to win the next general election. In six key seats, Labour had trailed National by no more than 300 votes.[22]

Second, while the 1978 campaign solidified Bill Rowling's leadership and enhanced his national following, other senior and middle-

[22] See Deputy Leader Tizard's statement about being "not totally happy with some of the Labour candidates," *New Zealand Herald*, October 4, 1978.

ranking Labour members of Parliament had too little impact. Labour did not come across to the voters as a strong party well stocked with potential cabinet ministers. Probably the Labour party can count itself fortunate that National did not fight its 1978 campaign along the lines of the Holyoake-Marshall era of 1960 to 1972 when the strength of the team was emphasized.

Third, in an organizational sense Labour's campaign got off the ground, but not by much. Many corners were cut. Policy material was prepared at the last minute by people with competing commitments. Differences between the local offices and national headquarters went unresolved. Cash was scarce and costs an endless obstacle. In this light, the verdict upon Labour's campaign must remain not that the party failed but that it could easily have fared much worse.

147

7
Social Credit and the Values Party

Colin C. James

During the 1970s two parties vied for third-party status: the New Zealand Social Credit Political League and the Values party. The Social Credit Political League, a group committed mainly to monetary reform, had emerged in the 1950s, after more than two decades when no third party had managed to sustain a lasting nationwide presence. Its fortunes varied thereafter, but no serious challenger came along until the early 1970s. Then, when the league's fortunes were at their lowest, the newly formed radical Values party toppled it from third place in the main cities and raised the possibility of total eclipse. The 1978 election was thought likely to resolve, at least temporarily, the third-party conflict.

In addition to the four nationwide parties, fifty-three candidates, ranging from the far left to the far right, stood under a total of twenty-eight party or independent labels. Few of these groupings had contested previous elections, and some candidates stood for whimsical reasons. All together the fringe candidates won only 1.29 percent of the vote, of which four-fifths went to independents in five electorates where special factors applied. The impact of the minor political groupings was negligible.

Social Credit

Origins. The Social Credit Political League traces its origins to a movement formed in the 1930s to discuss and promote the monetary reform ideas of Major Clifford Hugh Douglas, a former British army engineer. Though the movement did not contest elections, the small farmer-dominated Country party was converted to Douglas's credit doctrines, and many Labour party members, including a majority of the Labour members of Parliament, were influenced by the Douglas theories, some adopting them wholeheartedly.[1]

Social Credit theories spread quickly during the depression, which keenly affected New Zealand's little-protected agrarian economy (as it did the agrarian regions of Australia and Canada where Douglas credit also enjoyed some success).[2] In New Zealand in the 1920s nearly half the country's total production and 90 percent of its exports came from pastoral farming—chiefly sheep, cattle, and dairy farming. But between 1928 and 1931 its earnings from pastoral exports fell by 37 percent. Two groups felt this most: small farmers, heavily burdened with debts contracted in the more affluent 1920s; and the larger numbers of unemployed, most of whom had been wage workers.[3]

The urban unemployed look to the Labour party.[4] But the small farmers were susceptible to the Douglas credit message. The phrase "poverty amidst plenty" was much used by Douglas crediters, who diagnosed the problem as a shortage of purchasing power for available goods. Payments made to individuals involved in the process of production—wages, salaries, and dividends, classified as "A" payments—were not sufficient to buy what was produced, the price of which was the sum of A payments and "B" payments, made to other organizations for raw materials, bank charges, and so on. The "gap" was made up by privately created credit, giving banks and financiers

---

[1] Robin Clifton, "Douglas Credit and the Labour Party, 1930-35," (M.A. thesis, Victoria University of Wellington, 1961), chap. 4 and 5.

[2] A Canadian, populist version of the Douglas credit doctrine swept depression-hit Alberta in the early 1930s, and the Social Credit party won a landslide in the provincial election of 1935. The party stayed in power until 1971 but since then has had only a weak presence, with four seats out of seventy-nine in the 1979 state Parliament. In British Columbia Social Credit came to power in 1952 and has remained in power since, with one short break between 1972 and 1975. In both provinces federal restraints have blocked attempts to introduce social credit economic policies and both parties pursued broadly conservative policies, much helped by oil discoveries. In neither province has Social Credit made much impact in federal elections, and currently those provinces send no Social Credit members to the House of Commons. By contrast, the right-wing Créditiste party in Quebec, which has strong separatist tendencies, holds six federal seats but no provincial seats, most of its members supporting in provincial politics the separatist Parti Québecois, which forms the government in the province but is unrepresented at the federal level. In 1979 the English- and French-speaking sections of the Canadian Social Credit movement split.

[3] See Muriel F. Lloyd Pritchard, *An Economic History of New Zealand to 1939* (Auckland and London: Collins, 1970), pp. 350, 289, and 351; and William B. Sutch, *The Quest for Security in New Zealand, 1840 to 1966* (Wellington: Oxford University Press, 1966), p. 139. Sutch estimates peak unemployment, in 1933, at two-fifths of male workers between the ages of sixteen and sixty-five.

[4] Clifton, "Douglas Credit," p. 24.

control over the capitalist system. Douglas proposed the creation of an independent credit authority to make good the "gap" through a system of "just prices" and "national dividends" to be paid to all citizens. The dividends were to enable everybody as of right to enjoy his "cultural heritage," that is, a share in the plentiful supply of the fruits of the earth and of man's ingenuity.[5]

The doctrine appealed at several levels. By identifying the private creators of credit as the root cause of depression, it gave the victims of depression a target for their resentment. It was simple, encouraging converts with limited or no economic training to feel they had unlocked secrets of the economy that had eluded orthodox experts. Converts turned enthusiastic proselytizers. Furthermore, the Douglas credit doctrine transcended the traditional capitalist-socialist debate. To nonsocialist farmers and the middle class (from which the movement drew its most active adherents in the cities) it had the attractions of emphasizing individualism and small private enterprise and offering a solution that did not disturb the existing order. The movement that developed in 1932 and 1933 attracted large numbers of small farmers, particularly in the north, the district of the Auckland Farmers Union. Key members of the union and its political offshoot, the Country party, were recruited by, and then took over, the Douglas credit movement, adapting it to their ends.

On the other hand, there were socialist overtones to the Douglas credit theory of "cultural heritage," and a parallel of sorts between the notion of the "gap" in purchasing power (the much quoted A + B theorem) and the Marxian theory of surplus value. A mildly socialist Labour party looking for means to woo the critical antisocialist vote in the small towns and the countryside could tolerate the use of adapted Douglas credit theory by its candidates and even absorbed two Douglas credit candidates into its own ranks in the Labour landslide of 1935.[6] A limited no-competition deal was struck with the Country party, and outside the areas of Country party strength the Douglas credit movement advised its members, many of them lifelong conservative voters, to support Labour in the hope that it would introduce Douglas credit programs. After the election, however, though the Labour Government introduced a guaranteed price for dairy farmers (shades of the "just price," the subsidy going to the producers) and drastic reductions in mortgage amounts and rates, it

---

[5] A succinct account of the Douglas credit theory may be found in John L. Finlay, *Social Credit—the English Origins* (Montreal: McGill-Queen's University Press, 1972), pp. 106-116.

[6] Clifton, "Douglas Credit," chap. 6, particularly pp. 230-235.

otherwise paid no attention to Douglas crediters. Their numbers dwindled as economic conditions improved, and, though isolated Douglas crediters ran as independents from time to time, the doctrine disappeared from politics until 1953, when the Social Credit Political League was formed.

The League's First Twenty Years. The Social Credit Political League recorded 11.17 percent of the vote in the 1954 election, in which the National Government suffered a severe setback. The following year, prompted by the league's strong performance, the Government set up a Royal Commission of Inquiry into Money, Banking and Credit Systems, just as its conservative counterpart had set up a parliamentary monetary commission when Douglas credit doctrines had been influential in the 1930s. Though a Bankers Association witness stated that banks created credit, a point basic to Social Credit doctrines, the royal commission found no evidence of a "gap" between purchasing power and the value of goods and services.[7] The implementation of Social Credit ideas was therefore left in the league's hands.

In the 1954 election support for the league was scattered. Over the next ten years Social Credit regrouped as an agrarian party. Its strongest support came in the regions where it had been strongest in the 1930s [8]—the Waikato, the western Bay of Plenty, and Northland, all in the northern half of the North Island—and in the small-farmer regions of Taranaki, which for several reasons had resisted the 1930s tide.[9] These areas and, later, neighboring Rangitikei, created a belt of Social Credit strength in the north and west of the North Island. There was also a pocket of support in rural seats in the far south of the South Island.

Support for the league peaked in 1966 when its locally popular leader, Vern Cracknell, an accountant and respected local authority member, won the far north seat of Hobson (see Table 7–1). This was roughly the same seat that had been held in the 1930s by Douglas crediter Captain Harold Rushworth, president of the Country party. Nationally the league polled 14.48 percent, coming second in three seats. This raised hopes of a further advance in 1969, but internal strains deprived the central office of money, contributing to the loss of Hobson and a fall in the national vote. Cracknell was a rather

---

[7] Stuart L. Dickson, "Social Credit as a Parliamentary Party" (M.A. thesis, Victoria University of Wellington, 1972), p. 4.

[8] Clifton, "Douglas Credit," Appendix A.

[9] Ibid., pp. 307-308.

TABLE 7–1
SOCIAL CREDIT'S PERFORMANCE IN NATIONAL ELECTIONS, 1954–78
(in percentages)

Year	Popular Vote	Seats	Seats Where Social Credit Came Second
1954	11.17	0	1.25
1957	7.21	0	0
1960	8.62	0	1.25
1963	7.94[a]	0	1.25
1966	14.48	1.25	3.75
1969	9.07	0	3.57
1972	6.65[b]	0	1.15
1975	7.42	0	2.30
1978	16.07	1.09	11.96

[a] Only seventy-six candidates stood, four short of a full slate, because of an administrative oversight.

[b] The New Democrats won 0.67 percent of the vote. The total Social Credit vote might therefore be said to have been more than 7 percent.

SOURCE: *Appendices to the Journals of the House of Representatives*, papers H.33 for the years 1955, 1958, 1961, 1964, 1967, and 1970; papers E.9 for the years 1973, 1976, and 1979.

diffident man, and his intense respect for the dignity of Parliament led him to make less use of his parliamentary seat than his supporters had hoped for. He was replaced by Deputy Leader John O'Brien, whose faction undermined efforts to centralize electoral strategy between 1966 and 1969. O'Brien, a flamboyant orator given to messianic poses, was more adept at keeping the league in the public eye by a series of stunts than at holding his party's support. In the face of open revolt, he led a small group of supporters, drawn largely from the old guard, out of the league in 1972.[10] They formed a new party, the New Democrats, which quickly perished after the 1972 election. The league, under the new, younger leadership of Bruce Beetham, dropped to its lowest level of support. By the 1975 election it seemed in real danger of losing its third-party status to Values.

The Nature of the League. The birth of the New Zealand Social Credit Political League in 1953 split the movement. A minority continued to stand aloof from politics. The majority concluded that an

[10] Dickson, "Social Credit," pp. 90-103, 122-163. James Eagles and Colin C. James, *The Making of a New Zealand Prime Minister* (Melbourne: Cheshire, 1973), pp. 122-127.

"educational" approach was unproductive and took to the hustings. But the members' strong individualism and a fragmented organizational structure that gave the branches considerable autonomy hindered the development of a coherent national presence. Policies outside the monetary field were uneven. The league was generally considered conservative on most matters and right wing on some. Touches of anti-Semitism in Douglas's writings (an extension of his distaste for money dealers) helped foster this image.

Up to 1972 the league's policies were assembled piecemeal from branch resolutions adopted by the annual conference. Thereafter policy came increasingly to be made by way of coherent position papers put to the annual conference for approval. This change reflected the influence of Beetham, a teachers' college lecturer in history, and of the secretary of the "political executive" (a sort of shadow cabinet), George Bryant, a schoolteacher.

A number of themes run through the league's thinking. One is individuality. Social Crediters believe strongly in private enterprise but intensely disapprove of both big business and big government. They are likely to emphasize "individual enterprise." At the 1978 conference Bryant, by then president, talked of a "property-owning democracy" as the league's ideal, but he was less concerned with the inviolability of property than with the opportunity of as many people as possible to own property. A second theme is democracy, which leads to a concern for decentralization in political decision making and, nowadays, to the inclusion of workers in the business decision-making process. A third theme is Christian morality: Social Crediters, particularly older ones, are more likely than the members of the two major parties to make Christian and religious allusions in speeches and in conversation. This is congruent with the sense of mission that Social Credit adherents exude, their sense of possessing the key to a moral order. This underlies their eagerness to propound Social Credit philosophy to any who will listen. *Policy in Brief*, a pamphlet issued in 1978, stated: "Our basic principle is the establishment of an economic and social order built on the foundations of brotherly love, truth, justice and honest endeavour."[11]

Though there is continuity, there has also been a substantial shift in the league's policy stance since 1972. Where it once stood largely outside the traditional political spectrum, it now occupies a position close to the center. It is characterized by a strong sense of social conscience in its welfare, health, and environment policies;

11 New Zealand Social Credit Political League, *Policy in Brief* (Wellington: NZSCPL, 1978), Principles (a) (no page numbers).

a modern approach to education; a willingness to experiment with cooperativism (which has led some members to complain of "socialism"); a preference for devolving political decision making to smaller political units; and an underpinning belief in the individual. A 1978 pamphlet summarized the league's basic stance as follows:

> Social Credit policies are geared to promote a FAIRER DISTRIBUTION and OWNERSHIP of resources, so that ALL New Zealanders receive a just share of the wealth they produce. . . . The only really free individual is the one who is economically free. . . . Such a truly democratic society may be termed a PROPERTY-OWNING DEMOCRACY, a nation of self-employed owner-operators, cooperative ventures and worker shareholders.[12]

Elements of social democracy mingle with a liberal conservatism. Certainly this is a far cry from a right-wing appeal.

The transition to this moderate position occurred without major defections because most members' overriding concern is the league's monetary philosophy. Older members who may have reservations about some of the new policy directions are able to find solace in the hope that the new leadership offers the best chance since perhaps 1935 that the monetary reform ideas may actually be implemented. What happens in other policy areas is of substantially less concern to older Social Crediters than monetary reform since many believe that monetary reform will of itself bring about a better, more moral world. Newer members tend to look beyond monetary reform.

Yet unanimity on monetary reform has also been elusive. Arguments over points of doctrine have repeatedly wracked the movement; they were woven into the disputes that led to the ousting of Wilfred Owen, the first leader, and of Cracknell. During the 1950s and 1960s most of the disputes were wrangles between "purists" who wanted to keep the doctrine as close as possible to Douglas's theories and those who wanted to adapt Social Credit theory to fit changing economic conditions. The Beetham leadership is of the latter persuasion and has a clear ascendancy over a dwindling number of purists, many of whom have died and some of whom left with O'Brien. Where once the "technical committee," which resolved points of doctrine, occupied an important place in the league's business, in 1978 its one-page report was not even discussed by the conference. The election manifesto, which ran to 55,000 words, mentioned the national dividend only once and the A + B theorem not at all. Instead,

---

[12] New Zealand Social Credit Political League, *What We Stand For* (Wellington: NZSCPL, 1978), p. 3.

the league's other campaign publicity and Beetham's speeches emphasized a range of subsidies and benefits, while referring only in general terms to matching purchasing power to available goods and services to counteract the effect of what they saw as a contracting money supply relative to income. Once the league had talked about cash credits for all; in 1978 it promised to single-income families no tax on the first $100 of weekly income (an offer similar to the Labour party's) and some specific handouts. The "just price" had been fleshed out into a "compensating price" mechanism to ensure farmers the cost of production and a reasonable profit. Once "interest" had been an unmentionable word; in the 1978 policy low-interest loans were proposed for a variety of purposes, a distinction being drawn between the undesirable "rental" element of interest and an acceptable "service" element. The league's differences with the major parties, though fundamental in the eyes of economists (who have never accepted Social Credit doctrine), were less sharp to the ordinary voter.

Organizational Change. The league's political stance had been largely revised by the 1975 election. But organizationally the league remained decentralized and amateurish. The low vote in 1975 convinced Bryant and a group of younger members that changes were necessary. They took to the 1976 conference a background paper entitled "Social Credit: Dead or Alive?" proposing radical change, which Bryant, elected president at the conference, proceeded to put into effect. Compton Associates, a professional fund-raising firm based in Australia, was hired to supplement the league's funds raised through the $5 membership fee and through local electorate efforts like secondhand bookshops and lottery evenings. Social Credit has never had big corporate backers. Paid organizers were appointed in four seats eighteen months before the election to canvass support. Bryant, Nev McConachy, the campaign committee chairman, and Stefan Lipa, the convenor of the Ways and Means Committee, toured league branches convincing them to set membership and fund-raising targets. Seminars were held to train members in canvassing and other basic campaigning and organizational techniques. The membership recording system and collection of fees were centralized, giving headquarters assured access to funds for the first time and permitting an expansion of headquarters staff.[13] A long-term campaign strategy was adopted, pinpointing seats to be won in the 1978,

---

[13] This section is based substantially on an interview with George W. Bryant, president of the New Zealand Social Credit Political League, February 15, 1979.

1981, and 1984 elections and indicating to each electorate targets for membership and votes to be met for each election. The overall target for 1978 was 16 percent of the vote and at least one seat (Rangitikei), rising to 22 percent in 1981 and enough seats to hold the balance of power, and 34 percent and minority government status by 1984.[14]

Along with the internal changes the party undertook a long-term publicity campaign. It hired a new advertising firm, U.S.P. Needham, in early 1977, and a $42,000 newspaper advertising campaign, which ran from September to November 1977, brought 2,000 inquiries and 700 new members (membership had totalled about 5,400 in 1975). The pamphlet sent out in response to inquiries asserted:

> There are three sides to every story . . . listen to ours.
> . . . Social Credit is *not* a bunch of unrealistic idealists
> with strange ideas about finance. It's a strongly united group
> of intelligent people who care enough about their country
> to want to have a say in its future.[15]

The Rangitikei By-election. On Christmas Day 1977, shortly after Social Credit's midterm advertising campaign ended, the speaker of the House of Representatives and National M.P. for Rangitikei, Sir Roy Jack, died. A by-election was set for February 17, 1978. For the league it could not have come at a better time or in a better electorate.

Rangitikei was the sort of electorate in which Social Credit tended to do best: basically rural, with a number of small towns, the biggest of which were Marton (population 4,800) and Taihape (2,800). It was on the edge of the northern belt of Social Credit support. Taihape in the north and the large town of Wanganui, which the electorate surrounded in the south, had forty-five year traditions of Douglas Credit and Social Credit activism. League membership was relatively high.[16] Social Credit had already reached second place in the 1975 election, just 1,756 votes (10.9 percent) behind National, and Labour had come in a distant third with 14.0 percent. Furthermore, the by-election came at a time when the Government's failure to hold down rapidly rising costs and contain strikes in the meat-freezing industry, which processed much of the electorate's agricultural produce, made

---

[14] Campaign committee report to the New Zealand Social Credit Political League annual conference, 1978.

[15] New Zealand Social Credit Political League, *Get to Know Us* (Wellington: NZSCPL, 1978), p. 2.

[16] In an interview with the author on February 8, 1979, Beetham put the Rangitikei membership at the time of the by-election at around 1,000.

the Government majority particularly vulnerable to a protest vote by farmers and farmer-dependent small townspeople.

Social Credit also had the strongest candidate. Beetham was relatively young (forty-two) and ambitious. Leader of the party since 1972, he had joined the league only during the 1969 election campaign. In October 1977, he completed a term as mayor of Hamilton (population 100,000) in the middle of the Waikato region, a Social Credit stronghold. His good looks, infectious smile, and appearance of sincerity, not to mention his accomplished use of television in two national election campaigns, had helped make him a nationally known figure. Both of the country's main opinion polls rated him the most popular political figure after the leaders of the two main parties.[17] He was also locally known, having contested the Rangitikei seat in 1972 and 1975.

The league's campaign centered around Beetham. Posters and advertisements showed a large photograph of Beetham and urged voters simply to "Give him a go." For the first time the league was able to mount a campaign that in numbers, money, and technique surpassed that of the major parties. Since Rangitikei was already the league's top target seat for the 1978 general election, much organizational and publicity groundwork had been done. Party notables were brought in from outside and volunteers came by bus and plane to help.

Beetham won, with 48.0 percent of the vote and a margin of 1,335 votes over the Government candidate, James Bull, a forceful, sometimes tactless, self-made businessman. Labour slipped to 11.4 percent of the vote. Beetham, who in 1976 had proposed an electoral accommodation with Labour, now said Labour would "have to come to us on their bellies."[18]

Election Year. The Rangitikei by-election had two immediate results. Everywhere interest in the league increased dramatically: its public opinion poll rating tripled between December and March to around 20 percent,[19] and membership concurrently increased. Morale within the league also improved. In addition, the by-election provided much free publicity, and Beetham's subsequent much-reported appearances

---

17 The Heylen Research Centre, The Heylen Poll, published monthly in the *Auckland Star*, for example, April 17, 1978; NRB Ltd. poll, published every two months by the *New Zealand Herald*, for example, April 24, 1978.

18 *New Zealand Herald*, March 2, 1978.

19 *National Business Review*, vol. 8, no. 32 (May 24, 1978). Beetham said publicly he thought the poll figures were higher than the league's true support, which he estimated at 16 percent.

in Parliament (where he exploited publicity opportunities more frequently and adeptly than Cracknell had done, receiving procedural assistance from Gerald O'Brien, a Labour M.P. denied renomination for election by his own party) helped keep Social Credit in the news.

Neither a slide in poll ratings during the winter to a little over half their peak nor the short-lived resignation of a spokesman for Auckland candidates, Greg Thomson, over the eclipse of other spokesmen by Beetham, dampened the league's optimism. At the annual conference in August, tightly controlled from the chair, a new campaign target was set: four seats—Rangitikei, Bay of Islands, and Kaipara in the far north, and Hastings, where deputy leader Jeremy Dwyer was standing.

The optimism of the conference seemed vindicated when by the opening of the election campaign proper the poll ratings were once again close to the 16 percent target[20] and membership had climbed to around 15,000.[21] Nevertheless, Social Credit had formidable problems. Substantial boundary changes had been introduced for the election, which meant that Beetham lost the western 40 percent of his old Rangitikei electorate, in return for an area to the east based on Feilding (population 11,000) where Labour had been strong in 1975 and the Social Credit presence had been weak. He also inherited his National opponent—the highly respected education minister, Les Gandar—from the new area where Gandar had sat as M.P. In two of the other seats where Social Credit had hoped to win it had come in a distant second in 1975 with around one-quarter of the vote, and in the third, Hastings, it had recorded only 8.9 percent in 1975.[22] And there was another cloud: fund raising for the campaign had fallen around $100,000 short of the $300,000 target and some projected activities had had to be curtailed.

The Election Campaign. Beetham opened the league's official national campaign on November 1 in Marton in the Rangitikei electorate. He attacked the "soulless" National party, "no longer motivated by any worthwhile, meaningful, or even detectable philosophy," for its handling of the economy and dismissed the Labour party as a spent force, "floundering in a philosophic and policy wilderness." He spent some time explaining how, if the league held the balance of power

---

[20] *Auckland Star*, November 4, 1978; *New Zealand Herald*, November 16, 1978.
[21] Interview with George W. Byrant, February 15, 1979.
[22] All comparisons between the 1975 and 1978 elections in this essay are based on figures in Alan McRobie and Nigel S. Roberts, *Election '78* (Dunedin: John McIndoe, 1978), pp. 60-92.

in Parliament, it would use its influence to avert political instability. Much of the Government's legislation would get Social Credit support, but the Government "would be placed much more on its mettle." "With the prospect of our occasional support," Beetham said, "the Opposition would regain a positive and constructive legislative function which it has progressively lost under the evils of the two-party system." The league would, in general, abstain on votes of confidence. It would enter a coalition only in exceptional circumstances or if there was an absolute guarantee that Social Credit policies would be implemented. The rest of the speech covered a broad range of general topics, introduced two specific promises (no tax on the first $100 of weekly income in a single-income family and a $20,000-a-year company tax exemption) and outlined the league's economic analysis and monetary policies.[23] This formed the basis of his speeches for the rest of the campaign.

Like the two main parties, Social Credit projected its campaign primarily through the leader. In the three and a half weeks after the opening he spoke in seventeen cities and towns outside the Rangitikei electorate and another seventeen in the electorate. Outside the electorate he concentrated on the "northern belt," Hastings, and the far south, the places where Social Credit was thought to have the best chance. He answered questions phoned in by listeners on three radio "talkback" shows and appeared on two hour-long television question-and-answer sessions for the four party leaders. He also was featured in the only television film used by the league in its free slots. Apart from some limited use of Deputy Leader Dwyer and the finance spokesman, Les Hunter, in radio advertisements, there was little attempt to push forward other candidates except in their electorates. Print advertising was left to local electorate campaigns, which also made extensive use of posters. The theme was: "Give Social Credit a go." In Rangitikei this was adapted to "Give him a fair go," appealing to a sense of fair play to extend Beetham's term.

The campaign went smoothly for Social Credit, though Beetham complained that its television coverage should have been more extensive. Beetham achieved a better television rating than the Labour leader, Bill Rowling, for his opening address.[24] Generally, he attracted better crowds than usual for Social Credit leaders, including 1,500 (large by New Zealand standards) in south Auckland. Two incidents drew attention to Social Credit. One was the publication, nine days

---

[23] Typescript of opening address by Bruce C. Beetham.
[24] Ian Templeton, "An unbeatable team—like the All Blacks," *Auckland Star*, November 4, 1978.

before the election, of a National Research Bureau poll taken during the first week of the campaign giving Social Credit 17 percent. The other was Beetham's decision—which set Social Credit apart from the two main parties—to support calls from some public figures and media for a third reopening of the case of a convicted murderer in the light of newly published findings by a British author who had investigated the case. Otherwise attention focused on the major parties.

Under the surface, the campaign was anything but uneventful for Social Credit. Throughout the year the public opinion polls and the league's own canvassers had been reporting greater gains from Labour than from National. But during the campaign Social Credit canvassers reported greater gains from National, precipitated mainly, they said, by Prime Minister Rob Muldoon's abrasive campaign style. A poll by the Heylen Research Centre taken a week before the election and published after voting had ended, found the same shift and a strong corresponding drop in Muldoon's popularity. The same Heylen poll placed support for the league at 19.5 percent.[25]

The Aftermath. Social Credit obtained 16.0 percent of the vote—remarkably close to the target the campaign committee had set in 1976. It held Rangitikei, came second in nine other general electorates and two Maori electorates, and was within 500 votes of second in four more (two general and two Maori). Though leaguists were bitterly disappointed that their 274,756 votes had not brought more seats and called for electoral reform, they had the consolation of clearly ranking as the third party, ahead of Values. In only three seats (Island Bay, Pakuranga, and West Coast) did Social Credit come fourth, and in all three it was displaced not by Values but by strong local independent candidates.

The geographic pattern of success largely followed that of 1966: a main area of strength in the Social Credit belt in the north and west of the North Island and a subsidiary pocket in the far south of the South Island. All of the electorates in which the league came first or second, including the two Maori electorates, were within the belt. Of the thirty-seven electorates in which the Social Credit percentage was above the national average, only four were outside the northern belt or the far south pocket, and three of these were adjacent to one of those areas.

---

[25] *National Business Review*, vol. 8, no. 58 (November 30, 1978), and vol. 8, no. 59 (December 6, 1978).

Social Credit's main base of support continued to be in the countryside and small towns. All but one of the general electorates where the league came first or second were rural electorates previously held by National. (In both of the Labour-held Maori electorates where Social Credit came second, its percentages were very low.) In all but one of the eleven rural electorates in the northern belt Social Credit's percentage was in its upper quartile. The bottom quartile was largely confined to major city electorates, the exceptions being four large-town and rural electorates in the South Island held by Labour.[26]

From its rural base, Social Credit had made inroads in the 1960s into three towns in the northern belt—Tauranga, Wanganui, and Whangarei, all centers of Douglas credit activity in the 1930s—and it did so again in 1978. All three were in the upper quartile of Social Credit outcomes, and Tauranga became the first nonrural electorate in which the league came second. A new development in 1978 was an advance into the National-held fringes of urban Auckland, where four seats fell into the upper quartile. The other nontraditional success was in the large town of Hastings, on the east coast of the North Island. There a 26 percent vote was at least in part attributable to the personality and organizational skill of Dwyer.

Information on who votes Social Credit is sketchy. A number of small-sample single-electorate surveys in the 1960s[27] and those of the Heylen Research Centre and the Fourth Estate group in 1978[28] tend to suggest that support comes mainly from smaller farmers and businessmen and blue-collar workers. Nationwide surveys by Heylen after the 1975 and 1976 elections tended to confirm these findings.[29] Of Heylen interviewees who switched to Social Credit in 1978 one-quarter were skilled or unskilled workers and one-fifth each were in clerical, sales, or service occupations or were housewives. These

---

[26] The term "rural" is used here in the sense adopted in Robert M. Chapman, *Marginals '72* (Auckland: Heinemann Educational Books, 1972), p. 1: "The definition of a rural constituency is taken as being a seat with more than a fifth of its population voting outside towns large and small. It is . . . intended to pick up any considerable farming influence which might affect the character of any electorate."

[27] Dickson, "Social Credit," summarizes all survey work, including Dickson's own, undertaken during the 1960s. Refer particularly to pp. 15-19, 33, 37-38, 59-60, 62-63, 69-72, 75-76. Dickson was research officer of the league from 1967 to 1970.

[28] *National Business Review*, vol. 8, no. 56 (November 15, 1978), and vol. 8, no. 61 (December 20, 1978).

[29] N = 1,000. Data in the author's possession, intended for publication by Fourth Estate Books, Wellington.

figures are similar to the findings for switchers to Labour but reflect a lower occupational status than for switchers to National. According to the Heylen survey, 43 percent of those who switched to Social Credit came from National, 30 percent from Labour, 3 percent from Values, and 24 percent from those who did not or could not vote in 1975.

The core Social Credit vote is low. Except in peak years the vote in elections has hovered between 7 and 9 percent (see Table 7–1). Only 2 percent of the voters interviewed in the 1978 Heylen survey had voted Social Credit in three consecutive elections. A 1972 survey found that Social Credit voters in the Raglan electorate in the Social Credit belt—both those living in the countryside and those living in a small town—were less likely to belong to voluntary organizations, less interested in politics, less well off, and more pessimistic about economic prospects than their major party counterparts.[30] They were also far more likely to be self-employed. Heylen's findings suggest that voters switching to Social Credit in 1978 were more likely to have voted differently in each of the two previous elections than switchers to other parties. They were also more likely to be single and without children.[31] This suggests that Social Credit attracts a less stable and less integrated voter than the other parties. Stuart Dickson and William Mandle found that Social Credit voters in the 1960s were much more likely to give negative than positive reasons for voting for the league.[32] Heylen found that switchers to Social Credit placed less emphasis on policy as a reason for their choice than switchers to National (though the opposite was true among those who had voted for the same party in 1975). There was no significant difference between the proportion of switchers to National and to Social Credit who said that the economy and party philosophy were the elements of policy that had influenced them most.

These findings suggest that, though there is a core of Social Crediters who believe to a greater or lesser extent in the party's monetary reform policies, the bulk of the league's votes at any time are protest votes. The league's propaganda has to some extent recognized this by emphasizing the problem more than the solution (though leaguers are always ready to expound their solution when interest is aroused). It may help explain the apparently paradoxical ability of Social Credit in Rangitikei (and elsewhere) to attract con-

---

[30] Helen Clark, "Political Attitudes in the New Zealand Countryside" (M.A. thesis, Auckland University, 1974), chap. 3 and 4, passim.

[31] Data in the author's possession, intended for publication by Fourth Estate Books, Wellington.

[32] Dickson, "Social Credit," pp. 30-32, 37, 58, 61, 65-67, 75-76.

servative and even right-wing votes with liberal policies—to attract farmers who complained that the Government was too "socialist" and too soft on the unions and at the same time win over nearly all the Labour vote. The league, in other words, is performing a classic third-party role.

According to Pinard's theory of third parties,[33] Social Credit might therefore be expected to do best when economic or social strain accompanies a substantial political imbalance between a strong governing party and a weak major opposition party. Though the National party had been in power for twenty-three of the previous twenty-nine years, these conditions did not apply nationally in 1978, and Social Credit failed to make the hoped for breakthrough. But in the northern belt, the conditions did apply, at least to some extent: in all of the National-held rural, large-town, and Auckland urban fringe electorates of the belt in which Social Credit did best in 1978, Labour had polled close to or below one-third of the vote in 1975 and did so again in 1978. The same was true in the far south.

Social Credit's fortunes therefore appear bound up with Labour's. Though the seats it has most hope of winning are held by the National party and in them Social Credit competes directly with National for votes, to win it has to collapse the Labour vote, as Beetham did in Rangitikei. In Marton, for example, the Labour vote fell from 35.7 percent in 1972 to 7.0 percent in 1978, while the National vote fell from 39.2 percent to 33.5 percent.[34] The league's hopes of doing this on a nationwide scale have so far been fruitless. But the emergence of a region where it seems to have a special appeal gives the league something to work on for the future.

Values

As in other affluent countries, in New Zealand public concern about the environment increased in the late 1960s and early 1970s and a growing minority became preoccupied with alternatives to perpetual economic growth based on technological development. In 1972 this minority found national political expression in the Values party.

Formed by Tony Brunt, a twenty-five-year-old journalist and political science graduate, and Norman Smith, a twenty-nine-year-old public relations director for IBM, the party gained national promi-

---

[33] Maurice Pinard, *The Rise of a Third Party: a Study in Crisis Politics* (Englewood Cliffs, N.J.: Prentice-Hall, 1971), pp. 21-62.
[34] *Appendices to the Journals of the House of Representatives* (Wellington: Government Printer, 1973), paper E.9, p. 65; *Appendices*, 1979, p. 68.

nence through a television current affairs program on its manifesto six weeks before the 1972 election. The program triggered a flood of inquiries, financial contributions, help (including free expert assistance in the production of an imaginative television advertisement),[35] and most of the party's forty-two candidates.[36] In the election it won 1.96 percent of the total vote, ousting Social Credit from third place in thirteen seats. Though Brunt left the leadership in 1973 and the party had difficulty converting enthusiasm into a stable organizational structure, a full slate of candidates achieved a 5.20 percent vote in the 1975 election, taking third place in twenty-nine of the forty-one major city electorates and one large town.

The basic message of Values is the warning that economic and environmental ruin are the inevitable consequences of the existing social and economic order—combined with a call for radical changes in economic, environmental, and social management. Drawing lessons from a study published by the Club of Rome in 1972 entitled *The Limits to Growth*, the Values party seeks a "stable state" or "sustainable" economy. This would mean, in particular, reduced or zero growth in the population and the economy and less wasteful management of (preferably indigenous) resources, particularly energy. This is coupled with a desire for a greater sense of community at the local level through an extension of participatory democracy in the workplace and in decentralized government and through changes in the planning of the urban and rural environment. The party has taken a liberal attitude on moral questions (it was the only party of any significance in 1978 to argue for the woman's right to decide whether to have an abortion) and has become increasingly concerned with civil rights and the rights of minorities. In 1978 it adopted radical policies that would concentrate taxes on wealth and land instead of on income, as well as policies designed to enable the government or employees to convert productive enterprises into cooperatives even against the owners' will. (These last caused some intraparty tension, raising as they did the possibility that the party would be accused of Marxism.)

Despite its limited impact inside New Zealand, the Values party's program as set out in a 65,000-word 1975 election manifesto, *Beyond Tomorrow*, has attracted attention from like-minded individuals and

---

[35] Tony Brunt, "In Search of Values," in Brian Edwards, ed., *Right Out: Labour Victory '72* (Wellington: A. H. and A. W. Reed, 1973), pp. 90-91; Eagles and James, *Making of a New Zealand Prime Minister*, pp. 130, 131.

[36] New Zealand Values Party, *Beyond Tomorrow* (Wellington: New Zealand Values Party, 1975), p. 88.

groups in other countries, including the ecology and green parties of Europe, which were created after Values. The Values party's innovation was less its ideas, many of which derived from overseas thinking, than its role in national politics—to give expression, within the party system, to broad aims shared by various nonsocialists who were dissatisfied with the established order and who were in some cases directly challenging it. These have included "alternative lifestylers" attempting self-sufficiency on the land or partial withdrawal from the economic system in urban communities, groups trying to save native forests from commercial exploitation, and Maori groups seeking the return of land rights, among others. In turn they have drawn the party into pressure group activity, either formally or informally. Values has led national or local campaigns on specific environmental, ecological, liberal, or civil rights issues, most notably one that led indirectly to the shelving of nuclear power proposals. And it has helped a variety of causes by contributing money or professional or technical assistance. At another level, through the network of information and contacts the party provides, members have been encouraged to participate actively in, and sometimes to lead, single-issue campaigns as private individuals to a greater extent and on a wider range of topics than they might otherwise have done.

Values won only 2.41 percent of the vote in 1978. The contrast between national electoral impotence and local influence is reflected in internal strains. Many members considered the party less a potential Government, directing change from the top, than an educative and coordinating organ, influencing attitudes laterally and affecting national policies from below. This tension helped reinforce a tendency towards decentralization within the party, reflected in differences of approach between regions, and an equivocal attitude to national electoral activity. These tendencies have left the central leadership with insufficient resources to maintain a strong national presence. The central campaign effort in 1978 was confined to an opening presentation on television by four leading members on the second Monday of the official campaign, some touring by the leader and deputy leader, four brief television films, some radio spots, and a "kitset" for candidates on organization and policy. Otherwise campaigning was left to local electorate organizations.

Values had hoped to eclipse Social Credit in 1978, but it was clear from its consistent 3 to 4 percent in the public opinion polls that this was out of the question. In the end, it failed to come third in any seat. One contributing reason may have been that the novelty impact of the party's message had worn off, and the major parties (whether coincidentally or as a concession to the threat from Values in the early 1970s) had become more environment and energy conscious. Values leaders themselves saw the drop largely as a result of a determination to "get Muldoon out" by voting Labour.[37] This conclusion is supported by Heylen data, which also suggest that Values's main source of votes in 1975 had been former or potential Labour voters, particularly young professional or skilled people.[38] In addition, however, the data suggest that in both 1972 and 1978 Values drew more support from former National voters than from Labour, indicating either a protest role or an essentially middle-class core vote. In all three elections, the party did best (with two exceptions) in affluent main city seats, coming within 500 votes in 1975 of taking second place from Labour in the richest seat of all, Remuera, in Auckland. One study has concluded that the Values party membership displays the characteristics of the postindustrial "new middle class" radicalism increasingly found in technologically advanced Western societies.[39] Members and candidates tend to be between twenty-five and forty-five, well educated, and of professional and semi-professional background, often well informed in some specialty of direct relevance to the party program. There is also a disproportionately high proportion of creative artists and craftsmen. Turnover of leading members is high: there have been three leaders and deputy leaders in as many elections, and few candidates stood in both 1975 and 1978.

The party ended the 1978 election campaign more than $10,000 in debt. In addition, at the time of writing it was involved in a soul-searching debate on its future direction between the radical left (who seemed likely to drift away and who included the 1978 leader, Tony Kunowski, a recent convert to the socialist cause) and a less doctrinaire majority under the new leader, Margaret Crozier, who ousted Kunowski at the 1979 conference in May. It still maintained a national presence, but whether it would continue to fight national elections on the scale it undertook in 1978 was in doubt.

The 1978 election demonstrated graphically the problems facing minor parties in a first-past-the-post single-member-district electoral

[37] Statements by party "chairer" David Woodhams and party leader Tony Kunowski at a party general delegates meeting at Mangaweka, December 9, 1978.

[38] Data in the author's possession, intended for publication by Fourth Estate Books, Wellington.

[39] Suzanne Mackwell, "Radical Politics and Ideology in the Coming of Post-industrial Society: The Values Party in Perspective" (M.A. thesis, Canterbury University, 1977), pp. 167-178. An analysis of the membership is given on pp. 74-113.

system. Social Credit benefited from disenchantment with both major political parties and won a sixth of the vote yet obtained only one seat. Values probably lost to Labour many potential supporters whose first priority was to oust the Government; and it suffered from the waxing fortunes of its competitor for the protest vote, Social Credit.

8

Polling and the Election

Brian Murphy

History and Methodology of Polling in New Zealand

Until 1968 there was no systematic election polling in New Zealand. The Gallup organization made a brief foray into New Zealand in the early 1960s and did some polling work for the *Auckland Star*, New Zealand's largest circulation evening newspaper, but then withdrew.

In November 1968 the National Research Bureau (NRB), a marketing research company, began preliminary work on election polls, conducting a pilot study in Auckland using street interviews. Additional pilot studies were conducted, again in Auckland in June and July 1969. At this time the NRB attempted to gain newspaper sponsorship of a series of polls leading up to the 1969 election but was unsuccessful. The NRB went it alone and conducted national polls in mid-September and mid-November 1969. In 1970 the NRB instituted a bimonthly national survey (the first in New Zealand) and used this vehicle to conduct national election polls from November 1970 onwards. Since March 1971 the NRB election polls have been published by the *New Zealand Herald*, New Zealand's largest circulation daily newspaper.

The only other election polls in New Zealand are conducted by the Heylen Research Centre, another marketing research company. Heylen began polling in 1972 but did not make its results public until January 1978 when they began to be carried by the *Auckland Star* and TV1, the widest coverage television channel in the country.

Apart from the NRB and Heylen's election polling, little systematic political opinion research is being done in New Zealand. The political parties themselves, which are still very erratic in their use of political opinion research, made virtually no use of it up to 1975.

The National party did nationwide and electorate research through the NRB in 1975 but did little systematic research in 1978. The Labour party did nothing in 1975 but conducted some research in 1978 through McNair, an Australian owned marketing research company. Social Credit and Values have done no political opinion research.

NRB polls are based on nationwide surveys of 2,000 randomly selected eligible voters who are usually interviewed bimonthly in election years and in May and November of nonelection years. A different sample is used for each survey. Each sample is stratified by regional and urban-rural population distribution into the main urban center and surrounding rural county in each of the nineteen "population regions" of New Zealand. In each of the nineteen main urban centers and the surrounding rural county, an appropriate number of clusters of ten personal interviews in their homes are obtained from respondents selected by random procedures in every third house along randomly selected routes. Call-backs are made to secure interviews in houses where no one had been home originally and houses where the selected respondents had been absent, in order to preserve the randomness of the sample. The questions asked to determine voting intentions are:

1. Were you eligible to vote in the last New Zealand General Election?

2. *IF YES TO Q. 1.* Which party, if any, did you vote for?

3. Would you be eligible to vote in a New Zealand General Election now?

4. *IF YES TO Q. 3.* If an election had been held yesterday, which party, if any, would you have voted for?

The results are weighted to ensure sample representativeness in terms of sex, age, and marital status, and also past general election voting behavior by relating the answers to questions 1 and 2 to known election behavior.

Heylen has not made the details of its methodology public, apart from the fact that it conducts personal interviews in their homes with a sample of 1,000 people fifteen years of age and over, in the four main cities (Auckland, Wellington, Christchurch, and Dunedin) and a few smaller provincial cities, monthly in election years and regularly in nonelection years. No rural interviews are included, calls are made at every house in clusters, and no call-backs are made. A question similar to NRB's fourth question is used.

169

The Election Polls

In order to place the 1975–1978 election poll results into proper perspective the full set of NRB's election polls from their beginning in September 1969 through November 1978 are given in Table 8–1. Because Heylen has published so few of its poll results, they have been omitted, but it is worth noting that when Heylen and NRB polls have been conducted around the same date, their findings have generally been similar.

To appreciate what the election polls reveal about changing political attitudes it is instructive to identify from the poll data both the long-term trend and the short-term deviations from it. This analysis has been done for the periods 1969–1972, 1972–1975, and 1975–1978 (see Figure 8–1). Within each period a simple linear time trend has been fitted to data comprising the general election result at the beginning of the period and the findings of subsequent NRB surveys, with the last observation occurring at the beginning of the campaign, about three weeks prior to the new election. This assumes that actual election returns and the subsequent poll findings constitute a logical continuum, revealing the evolution of political attitudes from one election to the next, and implies that the trend line can be used as the basis for projecting the result of the election at the end of each period. In Table 8–2 and Figure 8–1, the data are expressed in terms of the difference between support for National and support for Labour, since even with support for Social Credit growing it is still the margin of support between these two major parties that determines which will govern.

Some tentative conclusions about the relative influence on election results of long-term and short-term movements in political attitudes can be drawn from Figure 8–1. The long-term trend, reflecting the evolution of political attitudes over the Government's three-year term, explains a good deal of the 1972 election result and almost entirely explains the 1975 election result but tells us very little about the 1978 outcome. A short-term influence—namely the intensive three-week election campaign—can be assumed to explain an election result out of line with the long-term trend. In 1972 short-term influences seem to have had moderate impact and in 1975 very slight impact, but in 1978 they appear to have had a strong effect on the outcome.

The 1969–1972 long-term trend in favor of Labour reflected the fact that the National Government, in its fourth successive term in office, was tiring. Late in the day, the mild Sir John Marshall had succeeded the astute, four-time election winner Sir Keith Holyoake

TABLE 8-1

RESULTS OF GENERAL ELECTIONS AND OF NRB VOTING-INTENTION
SURVEYS OF PROBABLE VOTERS, SEPTEMBER 1969–NOVEMBER 1978
(in percentages)

Date	National	Labour	Social Credit	Values	Other
1969, September	48	39	12		1
November	44	44	11		1
Election	*45*	*44*	*9*		*2*
1970, November	37	54	8		1
1971, March	40	50	8		2
May	43	49	7		1
November	40	51	8		1
1972, March	48	46	5		1
May	46	50	3		1
July	48	48	3		1
September	46	49	3		2
November	44	45	8		3
Election	*42*	*48*	*7*		*3*
1973, May	39	51	5	5[a]	—
November	44	47	6	3[a]	—
1974, May	44	44	5	5	1
September	40	50	5	4	1
November	44	44	7	4	1
1975, March	46	42	6	6	—
May	46	43	5	6	—
July	51	40	5	4	—
September	52	39	5	4	—
November	46	44	6	4	—
Election	*48*	*40*	*7*	*5*	—
1976, May	44	41	8	7	—
November	46	40	9	5	—
1977, May	42	42	9	6	1
November	48	37	9	5	1
1978, January	45	37	13	5	—
March	41	31	22	5	1
May	40	37	19	4	—
July	47	36	14	3	—
September	44	35	16	4	1
November	44	35	17	3	1
Election	*40*	*40*	*16*	*3*	*1*

[a] Includes "Other."
SOURCE: NRB Election Polls.

TABLE 8–2

NATIONAL'S LEAD OVER LABOUR, GENERAL ELECTIONS AND
VOTING INTENTION SURVEYS OF PROBABLE VOTERS, 1969–78
(in percentage points)

Date	National's Lead over Labour
1969 Election	1
1970, November	−17
1971, March	−10
May	− 6
November	−11
1972, March	2
May	− 4
July	0
September	− 3
November	− 1
Trend Prediction	− 3
Election	− 6
1973, May	−12
November	− 3
1974, May	0
September	−10
November	0
1975, March	4
May	3
July	11
September	13
November	2
Trend Prediction	7
Election	8
1976, May	3
November	6
1977, May	0
November	11
1978, January	8
March	10
May	3
July	11
September	9
November	9
Trend Prediction	9
Election	0

SOURCE: NRB Election Polls.

172

FIGURE 8–1
TRENDS IN MAJOR PARTY SUPPORT, 1969–1978

National's Lead over Labour (N–L) in NRB's Bimonthly Voting-Intention
Surveys of Probable Voters and in Parliamentary Elections, Expressed in
Percentage Points

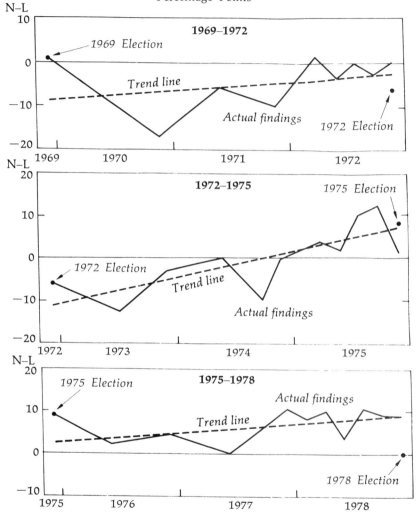

(subsequently governor general of New Zealand), just as National was
being challenged by a vigorous Labour opposition led by the forthright Norman Kirk. A significant feature of the election year was the
electorate's growing concern about social problems. In November
1971 the NRB added to its voting-intention survey questions measur-

173

ing New Zealand's most important problem as seen by the voters. In the months leading up to the 1972 election, an average of 54 percent of the voters were most concerned about social problems and 46 percent about economic problems. Three weeks before the election the figure for social problems was 60 percent, for economic problems 40 percent. The Labour campaign, which emphasized social issues, no doubt contributed to a short-term movement in Labour's favor that accentuated an already favorable long-term trend.

In 1972–1975 the long-term trend in favor of National similarly reflected political developments. After a promising start, the Labour administration weakened as the prime minister's health deteriorated. It enjoyed a wave of sympathy support after Kirk's death in 1974 but then faltered under the new leadership of the mild Bill Rowling. At the same time, the National opposition became more vigorous. Robert Muldoon, who had succeeded Sir John Marshall, was an aggressive leader. A cost accountant by profession, he made the most of New Zealand's worsening economic situation between 1973 and 1975, when the overseas account went from a small surplus to a record deficit. Imports doubled and the terms of trade halved. Overseas borrowing and inflation soared. During this period, an average of 59 percent of the voters expressed concern about economic problems and 41 percent about social problems, a complete reversal of the situation between 1969 and 1972. In the November polls three weeks before the election 62 percent expressed most concern about economic problems and 38 percent about social problems. The National opposition stressed economic issues right through 1975, then staged a spectacular campaign spearheaded by Muldoon, who traveled all over the country addressing public meetings. The "Muldoon roadshow" reinforced the effect of the long-term activity that underpinned National's favorable long-term trend.

In contrast with the two previous periods the 1975–1978 period reveals a curious paradox: the long-term trend was clearly in favor of National, but the election campaign just as clearly favored Labour. That the long-term trend favored National was due more to the default of a dispirited Labour opposition under Rowling's uninspiring leadership than to effective government by the National administration. An aggressive, often abrasive Muldoon practiced stop-go economic management, deflating the economy for two years, reflating it in election years, and antagonized most sections of New Zealand society at one time or another. Thus, through no great efforts of its own the National party was poised for a comfortable win when the election campaign began.

TABLE 8–3

VOTE SWITCHING, 1975–78
(in percentages of eligible voters, November 1978)

Recalled Vote, 1975	Party Preference, November 1978						Total Sample, 1975 Vote
	National	Labour	Social Credit	Values	Other	Un-committed	
National	27.6	0.9	2.6	0.3	—	3.6	35.0
Labour	1.2	20.8	2.9	0.3	0.1	3.7	29.0
Social Credit	0.2	0.6	4.0	0.1	—	0.5	5.4
Values	0.4	0.8	0.6	1.0	—	1.0	3.8
Other	—	—	—	—	0.2	—	0.2
Abstained	2.3	1.7	1.3	0.4	0.2	9.7	15.6
Ineligible	2.9	2.8	1.6	0.5	—	3.2	11.0
Total sample, 1978 intended vote	34.6	27.6	13.0	2.6	0.5	21.7	100.0

SOURCE: NRB Election Poll, November 1978.

The voting-intention survey taken three weeks before election day forecast no unexpected decline in National's support (see Table 8–3). National had the highest proportion of loyal supporters of the four parties and the figure had grown in 1978. National was losing fewer voters to Labour than it was gaining, and it was also picking up about as many new voters as Labour. There was a hint of trouble in the 2.4 percentage point net loss from National to Social Credit, but Labour was incurring much the same net loss. The uncommitted group was high at 22 percent, compared with 19 percent in the 1975 preelection survey, but this was more indicative of a high level of abstention (17 percent in the 1975 election) than of a high proportion of swinging voters on whom the election result would depend. The uncommitted group in any case comprised roughly equal numbers of former National and Labour supporters.

On election day, an estimated 20 percent of eligible voters did not vote (down 1.7 percentage points from the November poll figure), 32 percent voted National (down 2.6 percentage points), 32 percent voted Labour (up 4.4 percentage points), 13 percent voted Social Credit (no change), 2 percent voted Values (down 0.6 percentage points), and 1 percent voted for all other parties (up 0.5 percentage points).*

*EDITOR'S NOTE: All of these election return percentages are based on an estimate of the number of eligible voters.

The November 1978 voting-intention poll data were broken down by sex and age (see Table 8–4). They show that National supporters were representative of all eligible voters in terms of sex distribution, while Labour and particularly Social Credit attracted higher than average proportions of men (perhaps to National's ultimate disadvantage). National attracted a lower than average component of eighteen-to-thirty-four-year-olds, who were relatively strong supporters of Social Credit and Values, but derived some compensation from its above average component of voters fifty-five and over, who made up one-third of its support. This age group, once strong Labour supporters, became National's most loyal supporters after the National Government introduced a generous superannuation scheme in 1976.

But neither its supporters' age nor their sex explains the short-term movement away from National. Instead it is in the voters' relative concern about economic and social problems between 1975 and 1978 that a potential for the subsequent erosion in National support becomes apparent. During this period the overseas account deficit was cut in half and the inflation rate dropped, but unemployment rose to the highest level since the depression of the 1930s, and the voters were just as concerned about economic problems as they had been

TABLE 8–4

SEX AND AGE OF ELIGIBLE VOTERS, BY INTENDED VOTE, NOVEMBER 1978
(in percentages)

	Total Sample	Party Preference, November 1978				
		National	Labour	Social Credit	Values	Uncommitted
Sex						
Women	51	51	49	45	57	56
Men	49	49	51	55	43	44
Age						
18–24	20	15	19	20	37	27
25–34	21	19	23	25	28	20
35–44	16	17	15	14	22	16
45–54	16	16	17	16	9	16
55 and over	27	33	26	25	4	21

NOTE: The columns add to 100 percent separately for sex and age profiles.
SOURCE: NRB Poll, November 1978.

between 1972 and 1975: again, an average of 59 percent were most concerned about economic problems, while 41 percent were most concerned about social problems. In the November preelection poll 60 percent of voters expressed concern about economic problems (compared with 62 percent in November 1975 and 40 percent in November 1972), with the remaining 40 percent expressing concern about social problems (38 percent in November 1975 and 60 percent in November 1972).

The fact that concern about economic problems just before the 1978 election was lower than it had been in 1975 was reflected in growing economic confidence as measured by the NRB Confidence Index. This index is compiled by the NRB from bimonthly surveys of 2,200 randomly selected New Zealanders fifteen years of age and over who are questioned on their feelings about their present and future personal economic situation and about present and future social and environmental conditions in New Zealand. Index values of 0 to 49 reflect public pessimism, values of 51 to 100 reflect public optimism.

In November 1978, after five and a half years of varying degrees of pessimism (an average index of 45), the New Zealand public actually felt optimistic about their current and future personal economic situation (index of 51, compared with 50 in November 1975), a feeling no doubt attributable to the National Government's pump priming and election year largesse. The tax cuts announced in the May 1978 budget would take effect in October, just in time to remind voters of the Government's benevolence. But this confidence was premature. The country faced serious economic difficulties, and all the Government had done was paper over the cracks. The public's hope evaporated quickly when the overseas account deficit failed to drop further, unemployment remained at a record level, and the prospect of higher inflation loomed. By May 1979 economic confidence had plummeted to the lowest level in four years (index of 39).

Even so, shortly before the election voters were sufficiently confident about the economy to give some of their attention to social concerns. The NRB Confidence Index showed the public to be considerably more pessimistic about present and future social and environmental conditions in New Zealand in November 1978 (index of 40) than in November 1975 (index of 44), and this may have worked to Labour's advantage. In 1972 a much higher level of concern with social questions seems to have favored Labour, while increased concern about the economy in 1975 seems to have favored National. Thus, the rise in social concern in November 1978 just before the election was a favorable portent for Labour, which had emphasized social problems in its campaign. Even economic issues had been given a social slant: the need for greater productivity had been portrayed as a need to heal divisions, to pull together, shoulder to the wheel, to get New Zealand working again, and so on. Labour's emotional appeal contrasted vividly with National's cool, bland logic. Faintly reminiscent of its successful 1972 campaign, which had also centered on social issues, Labour's effort undoubtedly contributed greatly to a short-term movement from National to Labour during the three weeks before the election simply because National's steps to allay the voters' economic fears had left social issues a fertile ground in which to cultivate voter support. The polls indicate that Social Credit played no part in this final movement from National to Labour in the preelection survey; Social Credit took as much as 17 percent on the basis of the long-term trend alone.

A final factor that probably contributed to the short-term swing from National to Labour is the relative impact of the two main party leaders during the campaign. In the November poll Muldoon was rated well ahead of his colleagues as the most impressive National politician, while Rowling was a long way behind Beetham, leader of the Social Credit party, and even behind David Lange, a Labour backbencher, in the category of most impressive non-Government politician. But a politician can be impressive without being liked, and many National supporters expressed distaste for Muldoon's aggressive, abrasive manner, preferring the more gentlemanly style of Rowling or of Muldoon's predecessor, Sir John Marshall. However, during the election campaign Rowling surprised his critics with his vigor, enhancing his party's support. By contrast, Muldoon's supporters, expecting a replay of the 1975 "Muldoon roadshow," were disappointed by the prime minister's uninspiring performance, which may have cost his party some support.

The polls suggest that in three weeks a rejuvenated Rowling and a vigorous, emotional, socially oriented Labour campaign sufficiently overshadowed Muldoon's insipid, cerebral campaign focused on economics to erode completely National's nine percentage point long-term trend margin and bring National and Labour to parity in the popular vote; but this short-term influence had insufficient impetus to bring about a change of Government.

Implications for Political Strategy

Election polls have taken a long time to be accepted by political strategists in New Zealand. When NRB introduced them in 1969,

Labour spokesmen accused the polls of being misleading, and even now the Labour party publicly denies their usefulness although it uses them privately. This was also true of National before Muldoon became leader; since then National has publicly and privately acknowledged that opinion polls are useful in shaping political strategy. Most surprising of all, until the beginning of 1978 the Heylen polling organization itself opposed the publication of election polls as not in the public interest, deeming them to have an adverse influence on the democratic process. Ironically the Labour party accused Heylen of attempting to mislead the public by *not* publishing a poll taken one week before the 1978 election showing National and Labour neck and neck; Heylen had intended to release its findings after the election, but Labour party officials leaked them to the media on the eve of the election.

The foregoing long-term and short-term analysis of political attitudes provides useful insights into political strategy in New Zealand. A long-term conservative trend in New Zealand politics is evident from 1969 to 1978. Labour won the 1972 election, but its support was already slipping towards the end of 1972; if the election had been held six months later, National might well have been re-elected. The setback National suffered in November 1978 can be attributed more to poor strategy than to a significant structural shift in political attitudes, while the increase for Social Credit reflected the deeper conservative trend. The parties of the right (National and Social Credit) now have the support of 56 percent of the voters, (compared with 55 percent in 1975, 49 percent in 1972, and 54 percent in 1969), while the parties of the left (Labour, Values, and others) have 44 percent (compared with 45 percent in 1975, 51 percent in 1972, and 46 percent in 1969). And National has won nine of the eleven general elections since 1949. This too suggests that the Labour administrations of 1957–1960 and 1972–1975 were deviations from a long-term postwar conservative trend. This conclusion is hardly surprising, considering that, despite economic difficulties, New Zealand is now a relatively affluent, home-owning, middle-class society—not the struggling, working-class society it was in the 1930s when the party was strong.

A favorable three-year interelection trend can be a crucial ingredient of electoral success; it helped Labour win in 1972, and it helped National win in 1975 and avoid defeat in 1978. Social Credit's highest ever support at the 1978 election can also be attributed to a favorable long-term trend. On the other hand, a favorable long-term trend is no guarantee of victory: a party that means to win must also be ready to exert a reinforcing short-term influence just before the election. Labour did this successfully in 1972, as did National in 1975, but in 1978 National, resting on its laurels, ran a weak campaign and almost lost the election. Social Credit, thanks to a solid campaign, retained virtually all its long-term support. Labour, meanwhile, demonstrated the power of short-term influences when it almost succeeded in turning around a very unfavorable long-term trend.

The fact that Labour failed in 1978 points to the importance of timing. In 1969, 1972, and 1975, the party leading in the September preelection poll had seen its lead over its major opponent cut to almost nothing by the November poll as a result of the opponent's activity but had been able to withstand the challenge, draw back into the lead during the campaign, and win the election. But Labour in 1978, perhaps conscious that the September underdog in the last three elections had started to push too early and had run out of steam before the election, erred in starting its major effort too late.

What the election polls have to teach political strategists is that both long-term activity throughout the three-year parliamentary term and short-term reinforcement sustained through a period of up to six weeks before the election are required in order to influence political attitudes in a manner conducive to winning elections.

9

The Mass Media

Les Cleveland

Whatever deficiencies New Zealand's electoral process might have, lack of mass media coverage of campaigns is not one of them. A remarkable amount of space and time is devoted to reporting the details of campaign organization, to publicizing the utterances of party leaders and candidates, and to analyzing the progress of events as election day approaches—to the point where citizens can hardly avoid being exposed to campaign material either in the press or in broadcasts on radio and television. Whether this enhances the electorate's democratic enlightenment or refines its judgment may be questioned, but certainly the voters have convenient access to an abundance of basic political information. The extent of this coverage owes much to the organization and working practices of the New Zealand news media.

The New Zealand Media

The Daily Press. The New Zealand newspaper industry has remained entirely in the hands of the private business sector of the economy and is highly conscious of itself as a defender of the values of competitive economic enterprise. Not that the newspapers themselves must compete fiercely to survive. In 1979 the country boasted thirty-five daily papers for a population of only 3.1 million people, but the majority of these were provincial publications with small circulations based in rural districts and minor population centers. The eight major papers, the metropolitan dailies, are published in the country's four main cities.

All these papers subscribe to the New Zealand Press Association (NZPA), a wire agency which distributes a basic New Zealand news service (to which all its members are obligated to contribute) as well as a world news service which it derives from the Reuter organization. The costs of running the NZPA are borne by the members on the basis of their size, so that the larger papers bear the greatest share of the cost and indirectly subsidize the operations of the smaller ones by making a supply of cheap news available to them. This is no minor advantage; up to 50 percent of the news in a typical provincial paper is likely to be derived from the NZPA service. To the small provincial daily with only one or two reporters on its staff this service could make the difference between profit and loss. A further consequence is that a degree of standardization is imparted to the contents of the entire New Zealand daily press, with individual papers tending to reproduce substantially the same core of NZPA material. This situation is not without its advantages, but it can discourage innovation and diversity.

Apart from this news sharing through NZPA, another factor that has enabled the New Zealand press to retain a certain artificial equilibrium is its immunity from direct foreign competition. The New Zealand newspaper market is hardly large enough to attract ambitious foreign investors, but when the Canadian newspaper magnate Lord Thomson was contemplating a takeover of a New Zealand metropolitan daily, the government passed legislation to prevent overseas interests from obtaining a majority holding in any New Zealand news media company.

The Government still has the power to prevent foreign takeover of commercial enterprises and the New Zealand press has enjoyed the advantages that flow from this restraint on competition. In many respects—and especially in each metropolitan center—the newspapers may be considered "rivals in conformity," faithful to a tacit agreement not to pursue sensationalism for its own sake and hence able to deal conservatively with sex, crime, and the seamy side of life, politics included. In this they are regulated by the laws on obscenity and defamation as well as by a Press Council (set up in 1972 along the lines of the English one) to maintain standards and consider complaints about either the conduct of the press or the conduct of persons and organizations towards it. They have also faced local competition, particularly for advertising, from broadcasting services.

Radio and Television. Unlike the press, the electronic media in New Zealand (with the exception of a small number of radio stations) are publicly owned enterprises under various degrees of government control and nominally pursuing public service goals. They have been beset since their infancy with political conflicts over the appropriate degree of government control and with continual disagreements over the most desirable method of administrative organization. Proposals to reorganize broadcasting have been a regular component of the election campaigns of the last decade, and employees in the industry have had to endure a great deal of uncertainty and disruption as successive Governments have tried to implement policies that have not always been either workable or wise. Under the latest of these upheavals the Broadcasting Corporation of New Zealand (BCNZ) was established to operate a public broadcasting system, which at the time of writing included a radio network (Radio New Zealand) and two television networks (TV1 and TV2). The corporation is responsible to Parliament through the minister of broadcasting, who appoints a corporation board to operate the various services "in the public interest." The board, the three services, and the various officials with administrative responsibilities in the operations of the corporation are directed by principles laid down in the 1976 Broadcasting Act. These establish the corporation's accountability to Parliament "as a trustee of the national interest" and require it to ensure that programs are produced and presented "with due regard to the need for good taste, balance, accuracy, and impartiality, and the privacy of individuals." Under the provisions of the act the corporation is also placed firmly under the broad financial control of the minister of broadcasting and the cabinet. This is more than sufficient to ensure that corporation officials observe a certain caution, if not deference, in their dealings with the Government generally, but the act also states that the corporation "shall have regard to general Government policy in relation to broadcasting and shall comply with any directions given by the minister to the corporation by notice in writing pursuant to that policy." A copy of any directive issued under this procedure has to be laid before Parliament. This machinery has not been used since the legislation was passed in 1976, but it is available should the corporation or its board at any time prove fractious.

The act is also concerned with programming, which must "be generally acceptable in the community" and cater "in a balanced way" to the interests of different groups, observe standards of "good taste and decency," and attend to "the accurate and impartial gathering and presentation of news in the public interest according to recognized standards of objective journalism."

As if all these specifications were not enough to keep broadcasting firmly under public control, a Broadcasting Tribunal was also set up to exert licensing powers, to approve program rules, to advise the minister, and to deal with complaints about programs. The complaints procedure obliges the corporation to receive and consider formal complaints about its programs "where the complainant alleges that a program has presented inaccurate information, or has misrepresented material facts, or has demonstrated bias, or is a breach of acceptable community standards, or has infringed the privacy of any individual." If it fails to take action on a justifiable complaint, a complainant may refer the case to the tribunal. This legislation encountered strong criticism from broadcasters, who claimed that it completely destroyed their autonomy, opened the way to direct governmental interference in all levels of the service, and would precipitate a great deal of interference from moralists in the community. Not only would a producer have to cultivate the approval of his immediate superiors, they said, but he must nervously comply with "community standards" as well as with the views of the politically appointed corporation board, the minister, and finally the Government. This, it was argued, would keep broadcasting timid and subservient.

Under the 1976 legislation broadcasting remained a commercially oriented, publicly owned service, but how it would operate within these limitations would depend upon how well professional broadcasters in fact managed to stand up to political pressure and what they thought the purposes of a publicly owned electronic media system really were. By 1979 there were signs of increasing strain. The broadcasting corporation wanted to increase license fees to offset financial losses, but the Government refused to allow it. Prime Minister Muldoon criticized specific broadcasters and attacked television in a series of articles he wrote for *Truth*, a weekly newspaper, claiming that current affairs programs were biased against the Government. He also demanded, and got, time on both television channels, as well as on Radio New Zealand, to make a broadcast about economic policy, though what he had to say could easily have been handled as routine news. The broadcasting corporation, rather than retaliate under these provocations, nervously rearranged its programming and the management of its two channels with the object of getting more revenue from advertising.

None of New Zealand's attempts to organize broadcasting have seriously faced up to the need to guarantee the autonomy of broadcasting; instead they have concentrated on problems of profitability, administration, and accountability. Policy making in broadcasting, as in most other policy areas, has been incremental; it has lurched from one financial crisis to another, and from one election campaign to the next. This is of special importance in New Zealand where television has a highly attentive mass audience.

Operational Characteristics. The electronic media are required by law to operate their news services and public affairs programs in accordance with public service ideals. The newspapers have more freedom of choice in devising appropriate modes of operation, but in general they also subscribe to professional standards of fairness, impartiality, and objectivity and are under a degree of surveillance from the Press Council as to how they apply these standards. The major daily papers function as newspapers of record, publishing a high proportion of news stories in which some identifiable or publicly accessible organization, person, or authority has been cited as a source. This convention gives much New Zealand journalism a conveyer-belt quality, the journalist merely acting as a transmitter of views and information; on the other hand, it has the advantage of allowing the reader to scan a daily paper and extract from it a concise but surprisingly broad survey of the day's news, both national and international.

The style of reporting is conservative by comparison with the exuberance and sensationalism of the tabloid press of Australia or the United Kingdom. It tends to be deferential towards public officials and personalities out of respect for the law of defamation, which bears heavily on the news media and inhibits them in their functions as critics of government and watchdogs of the public interest. Supreme Court juries in the past have not hesitated to award punitive damages against newspapers stepping outside the boundaries of what they consider permissible, and this has limited the papers' readiness to pursue crusades and expose deficiencies. The need to cite reliable sources for all provocative or potentially damaging statements, of course, has reinforced the tendency towards conveyer-belt journalism. This has been accompanied by a marked degree of deference towards central government, which is an important generator of news. In addition, politicians and journalists in Wellington are, in a sense, close working associates. The major New Zealand news media keep correspondents stationed in a Press Gallery with offices in the Parliament buildings from which the journalists can maintain daily contact with ministers and senior officials of the state services. The volume of news output from central government sources owes much to the fact that New Zealand is a welfare state with a comprehensive system of state-supervised social services and a mixed economy; many of the major productive enterprises and most of the public services are either owned and operated or extensively regulated by the state. In the case of the electronic media the relationship with government is further complicated by the fact that they are not allowed to express editorial opinions and must operate within financial boundaries laid down by

185

particular administrations. As a result the electronic media are extremely sensitive to the sources of political power.

The Campaign

Election campaigns are taken very seriously by the news media in New Zealand. They are regarded not only as a convenient source of ready-made news, but also as an opportunity for the media to demonstrate a sense of public responsibility. Newspapers have traditionally made generous allocations of space for reporting the utterances and campaign activities of the major political parties, while radio and television have allocated extensive free time for party political broadcasting in addition to covering politics in the normal news and public affairs programs.

The custom has been for New Zealand political parties to begin intensive campaigning three to four weeks before the general election. During this period they issue manifestoes and pamphlets, canvass voters in their homes, hold public meetings, advertise extensively in the mass media, and above all generate a flow of news and information that they hope will win them coverage by the press. An impressive amount of space is devoted to this material by the daily press. Each paper goes to considerable pains to cover the activities of the local candidates on a day-to-day basis. A number of meetings are reported in detail, and after that, candidates are invited to contribute statements, comments, and excerpts from election addresses. In earlier years, extraordinary steps were taken to see that this publicity was distributed as equitably as possible. Editors were sometimes seen measuring the column inches devoted to a particular party's campaign to make sure its share had not been exceeded and accusations of calculated bias could not be substantiated.

At one time the daily press offered almost unanimous editorial support to the National party, and there was more than a dark suspicion that this allegiance sometimes insinuated itself into the news columns. However, in the 1970s, impartiality in the treatment of election news became much more evident. The newspapers have always relied on a fundamental distinction between editorial opinion (expressed in the regular editorial columns or in signed articles) and objective, impartial reporting of the news. For various reasons, editorial opinion itself has now become more flexible and less dependent on the views of management. Newspaper editors now frequently offer criticism of the policies and accomplishments of Governments, regardless of their party label. In the 1972 general election campaign, editorial opinion was often critical and by no means unanimous, and it remained so in subsequent campaigns. Some papers sat on the fence, summing up the attractions and deficiencies of the major parties; others invited readers to make their own decisions; a few continued to support National and warned of the dangers of "a return to socialism"; but for the first time, two papers came out in open support of Labour.

In 1978 there was no direct intervention of this kind, but there was a good deal of editorial criticism of both major parties, with newspapers like the *Press* in Christchurch describing the Labour opposition as "muddled and poorly led" and the National Government as needing to improve its performance. Most of the daily press also expressed concern about the style of leadership adopted by the prime minister and its effects both on New Zealand politics in general and on the electoral prospects of the National party.

One reason for this welcome growth of editorial independence has been the increasing lack of sharp ideological distinctions between the parties as well as their increasing concern with management of the economy inside the framework of the welfare state. Television, in its painful struggle to fulfill its duty to the public by maintaining editorial and political impartiality, may also have offered an example, but the greatest encouragement to editorial autonomy has come from structural changes within the newspapers themselves. The daily press, as in other countries, has been passing into fewer hands as managements have sought to reduce production costs by plant amalgamation and the rationalization of resources. As newspaper units have become larger they have taken on a more impersonal character, managements have become more distant, and editors have been able to cultivate a little more political autonomy. The strain towards greater efficiency in management has brought with it a heightened sense of the possibilities of editorial independence.

When accused of bias in its political reporting, the press points to such examples of editorial versatility and argues that if any distortions occur in the presentation of party views and achievements they are more likely to be due to either the nature of the events described or the inability of the parties themselves to make the fullest use of the extensive facilities that are open to them, rather than to prejudice on the part of the press. This observation is generally reinforced with a reminder that in determining how much prominence to give any particular news item editors are obliged to consider its relative newsworthiness rather than its merits as party propaganda.

During an election campaign the daily press follows the cut and thrust of local political conflict among candidates on the hustings, but it also prints a flow of material from national sources. This consists of the statements released by the respective party leaderships and accounts of their progress along the campaign trail. New Zealand elections since the advent of television in the 1960s have increasingly taken on the style of American presidential campaigns in which rival leaders and their teams tour the country and vie for maximum mass media exposure. The party leaders usually announce their election policies at the beginning of this campaign. Since 1972 the party manifestoes have been designed with increasing care by the advertising agencies hired by the parties to manage their campaigns. Increasingly they have shifted towards a glossy, visual presentation of party objectives and leaders along with an emphasis on campaign slogans like National's 1975 winner, "New Zealand the Way You Want It," and the 1978 refrains—"We're Keeping Our Word," "Years of Lightning," and "Into the 1980s" (National); "To Rebuild the Nation," "Labour and You: Together We'll Make It" (Labour); "Give Social Credit a Go"; and "New Zealanders Are Angry" (Values). The parties try to distribute their campaign literature as widely as possible and attempt to offset the considerable expense of its publication by putting their manifestoes on sale at bookstalls and at party branches. In addition, National and Labour (which have the greatest financial resources) reinforce the slogans and imagery of their manifestoes with full-page advertisements in the daily newspapers.

Against this background, teams of competing press, radio, and television journalists follow the party leaders as they barnstorm the main population centers of the country. The demands of television coverage have taught them to warm up their audiences with musical entertainment and stack the front seats at meetings with smiling party supporters whose enthusiasm will impress the national audience. Any disruption of such obviously stage-managed occasions, of course, is welcomed by the media. In 1978 there was widespread coverage of angry scenes outside National party meetings in Wellington and Dunedin where hostile crowds of young demonstrators fought with police as the prime minister and his wife were leaving. Such occasions, however, were not necessarily a liability for the prime minister, an aggressive leader who is quick to seize on any display of audience emotion. His success in the 1975 election had owed much to his assiduous canvassing of the entire electorate with a kind of traveling road show. Nightly, at meeting after meeting, he had denounced the incompetence of the Labour Government's economic policies with the aid of charts expounding such mysteries as inflation, the balance of overseas payments, and the rate of government expenditure.

But in 1978 the situation was reversed. Muldoon found himself on the defensive, putting a brave construction on his Government's record while his chief opponent, Bill Rowling, vigorously assailed it. In this defensive posture, Muldoon was not able to project the image of a strong-armed savior of the national well-being. In 1975 he had proclaimed boldly: "trust National with power and we will rectify our opponent's mistakes and set the economy right," but in 1978 he was obliged to mumble a refrain to the effect that National's performance had been more credible than Labour's and that the Government therefore deserved continued support.

When circumstances force a contender into a weak, defensive position, the classic strategy is to mount a diversionary attack in some unexpected quarter. Accordingly Muldoon claimed that the Labour party was behind a series of bomb hoaxes at his meetings and complained to the police that film scripts being prepared for National party political broadcasts had been removed from the office of a film production company in Wellington, photocopied, and replaced, then circulated to journalists at one of the television channels and leaked to Labour party officials. This drew attention to the whole question of the National party's television advertising.

A notable piece of National party propaganda in the 1975 campaign had been a televised cartoon which suggested that the Labour movement was dominated by Communist-inspired trade union agitators and that Labour would take over all companies and farms in order to introduce Russian-style communism. The socialist bogey, of course, had been a traditional figure in National party campaigns since the 1930s. The scripts that were copied and leaked in 1978 dealt with industrial relations and depicted a hairy arm flexing powerful muscles in a wrestling contest with "a strong clean arm," presumably that of a National party Government putting down industrial disorders.

In order to grasp the significance of these crude images, the hold that New Zealand's two television networks have over the ordinary New Zealand household has to be appreciated. Full-scale research on the effects of political television in New Zealand has not been carried out, but the prime-time audience is very large, the more so since there are only two channels to select from. A 1975 survey of a Christchurch electorate indicated that 91 percent of those sampled had seen one or more political broadcasts, with 60 percent getting most of their political information from television. Four percent said TV had changed their political preference, 60 percent that it had confirmed their preference, and only 26 percent that it had not affected them. A shift on the order of 4 percent of the electorate in favor of one or the other of the major parties is enough to have a decisive effect on the outcome of a close election. The free television time the parties receive is therefore a crucial component of their campaigns.

In 1978 the parties received a total of eight and a half hours free time on the two television channels. They were free within the framework of normal program standards to use their time as they thought fit. National and Labour each received 31 percent of the total time, while Social Credit was given 20 percent and Values 18 percent. The party leaders' television appearances are especially important because they can influence voters who might not be inclined to take much notice of campaign material in the media, extensive though it is. In 1978 Radio New Zealand gave the campaign wide coverage, and local stations broadcast detailed electorate-by-electorate analyses of issues and conflicts at the local level during the three weeks preceding the election. Radio and both television channels went to almost absurd lengths to provide continuous coverage of the poll, with reports of the returns beginning at 7 P.M. Indeed election night has become an established social occasion, and people expect to build their parties around the television coverage. In 1978 the channels attempted to make the occasion more bearable for the frivolous minded by interpolating light entertainment spots in the analysis of the returns. For many viewers the general election coverage on television must seem more like a variety show and an excuse for an evening's drinking than a solemn ritual of democracy.

If the media are so important to the parties it might be thought that they would be at some pains to keep on good terms with journalists and their editors, but this has not always been the case. At one time or another every New Zealand political party has complained that the media were not presenting its point of view with sufficient dedication and enthusiasm. Accusations of bias continued to be frequent. In 1978, the National party, as part of its diversionary strategy, claimed that by concentrating on the behavior and stylistics of party leaders, the media were giving insufficient attention to the party's philosophy and attainments in office. Therefore, the argument ran, if the electorate was not receiving National's message and the National Government was faltering in the eyes of many voters, this was the fault of the media, not of the party or its leadership. This complaint raised some important questions about the National party's conduct of the election campaign, the style of its leadership, and the prime minister's relationship with the media.

The Prime Minister. The National party's allegations that the media were devoting too much attention to the party leaders and their campaign styles contained a degree of truth. The personal characteristics of political leaders, had, in fact, been a prominent consideration on the hustings since 1972. The election that year was dominated by the personality of Norman E. Kirk, a powerful, shirtsleeves style Labour leader who assiduously courted public support with the help of a sophisticated advertising campaign orchestrated around the slogan: "It's Time for a Change." Kirk became prime minister but died in office. National's success in the 1975 election owed much to the energies and drive of Muldoon, who had risen to the leadership of the National party by demonstrating not only that he had a firm grasp of the economic issues that are central to all the major policy-making problems of New Zealand Governments, but also that he was able to project himself on television and in the press as an aggressive and successful personality. One of the secrets of his success was shrewd analysis of the news media's coverage of his statements and actions.

Muldoon was the first New Zealand politician to fully adapt to the requirements of television reporting, and he succeeded so well that his television image was almost irresistible. He seized every opportunity for media exposure, established himself as the star of a one-man soap opera in which enemies were put down, critics discomfited or shown to be hopelessly wrong, and interviewers rebuked, contradicted, or discredited.

Muldoon's performances were always newsworthy, especially if they were accompanied by expressions of anger and the spectacle of somebody being ignominiously demolished. Muldoon describes himself as a "counter puncher" who always hit back when attacked. The fact that this made good copy for journalists and sometimes generated scandalous exchanges of insults was not seen as necessarily disadvantageous until ten days before the 1978 poll, when Muldoon accused the news media of allowing trivia to obscure the substance of his election addresses. This charge was followed after the election by the National party's criticism already referred to and by the formal complaints Muldoon lodged against specific newspapers and both television channels. He claimed that the news media were the biggest single factor in the party's election setback, and he accused the *Evening Post*, a Wellington daily, of directing the minds of the public away from "the real issues of the campaign." Describing it as the worst of the daily press, he said its editorials showed "an unbounded arrogance."[1] The newspaper defended itself by pointing out that the editorials Muldoon had complained of reflected the concern of a large number of people and had simply asked the party leaders to offer the voters some serious discussion of the major problems facing the country. "Whether Mr. Muldoon likes it or not," the paper observed, "his style of leadership is an item which is of public concern and which the *Post* believes had a significant bearing on the election results."[2]

The broadcast media also defended themselves stoutly against the prime minister's formal complaints. The BCNZ conducted a review of all election news and current affairs programs and concluded that its radio and television coverage had given satisfactory service to the country and had "fairly reflected the substance and style of the campaign."[3] The political parties and their leaders undoubtedly had had sufficient access to radio and television on terms and under conditions that had allowed them to put their case to the electors as they saw fit to present it. They alone in dealing with the issues facing the country had been the authors of their fate at the polls.

The corporation noted that the different styles of the two major party leaders (Muldoon and Rowling) and the very different atmospheres of their meetings in terms of audience reaction and heckling had gone a long way towards shaping the television images that had emerged. (Muldoon's meetings had been turbulent, Rowling's tranquil.) Looking to the future, the corporation wondered whether the presidential style of campaign pursued by the party organizations and all the media adequately represented the workings of New Zealand parliamentary democracy and successfully defined for the voters just what they were being asked to decide when they got to the polls. In the future, the broadcast media would have to conduct their election coverage across a much broader range of political campaigning and discussion of issues than was possible when they concentrated on the party leaders.

Whether future election campaigns are sober exercises in the art of democratic discussion or continue to be verbal mud-slinging matches depends partly on how seriously the BCNZ takes its responsibility to serve the public and partly on the images projected by the party leaders themselves. In this respect the 1978 election results could be interpreted not only as a warning to the major political parties but as a cry of alarm from the electorate.

[1] "The PM Says," *Evening Post*, December 9, 1978, p. 1.
[2] Ibid.
[3] "Broadcasting 'Happy' With Election Coverage," *Evening Post*, December 20, 1978, p. 1.

Leadership Images. In the post-mortems that followed the election, the National party's decline in support was thought by many observers to reflect a current of anti-Muldoon sentiment rather than any sudden enthusiasm for either Labour or Social Credit. Indeed, this view was publicly confirmed by no less a figure than Sir John Marshall, a former National party prime minister, who described the leadership style as "undoubtedly an adverse factor" and Muldoon as a dominant and dominating man who had come to be regarded by the public as personifying the Government. He argued that the cabinet should be seen to be working as a team, with individual ministers taking more responsibility for their own portfolios.[4]

This criticism typified the alarm of the National party executive, which was faced with the problem of mending its fences in preparation for the next general election in 1981. It put pressure on the prime minister to adopt a less visible and aggressive posture, but he complied awkwardly. He stopped holding the usual news conferences after cabinet meetings and obliged journalists to conduct their own inquiries among the nineteen cabinet ministers. This was a direct response not only to internal party apprehensions but also to an editorial in the *Press* expressing the hope that ministers, who had too often relied on the prime minister, might be encouraged to take more public responsibility for their portfolios.

Most journalists regarded Muldoon's abrupt termination of a practice that had been part of the regular procedure of government for twenty-five years as an act of spite, carried out in a characteristically provocative manner. "Profile Is Definitely Negative," was the *Auckland Star*'s headline over a story that reported a series of questions its parliamentary team had put to the prime minister in writing about a number of serious topics for cabinet discussion. Four out of five had been answered with an uninformative "No," and the fifth had been dismissed in six words. By 1979, Muldoon's attempts to repair his image had made him, if anything, more vulnerable to media criticism.

In an important sense, every New Zealand prime minister is largely a creation of the mass media and can be destroyed as easily as he can be nurtured by them. In 1978, this was dramatically true for Muldoon, whose image shifted in the course of a single television program at the height of the campaign. This was an interview with four party leaders: Bruce B. Beetham, representing Social Credit, grave and low-voiced; Tony Kunowski, for Values, quietly humorous;

---

[4] Sir John Marshall, "Lessons of the Election," *Evening Post*, December 21, 1978, p. 4.

Rowling his usual soft-spoken self; and Muldoon, gravel-voiced and somber, with occasional ironic smiles. Muldoon began by projecting himself as the country's toiling savior. Gradually, however, the tone changed. While Rowling spoke, Muldoon repeatedly contradicted him, but Rowling firmly ignored these interruptions, and his polite refusal to be talked down left Muldoon seeming more and more the incompetent blusterer.

This rare failure of Muldoon's browbeating approach to opponents also signaled an evolution in the capabilities of Rowling, whose media performances before the 1978 campaign had been lacking in vigor and self-confidence. Rowling's rather belated emergence in a more assertive role was one of the unspectacular but significant features of the 1978 campaign. Rowling had become prime minister and assumed the leadership of the Labour party following the death of Norman Kirk in 1975. He had found himself with a cabinet of mediocrities trying to deal with the severe and prolonged economic crisis into which the country had been allowed to drift. From Muldoon and the National party opposition he had received derisive criticism. Throughout the 1975 election campaign Rowling had combined an air of calculating coolness with a habit of diffident, modest understatement, which had enabled Muldoon and the National party cartoonists to satirize him as an ineffectual mouse at the head of "the failure Government." Yet Rowling had always been a smooth speaker with a feel for timing and an unpretentious sense of humor. This did not always emerge in the media coverage.

The parliamentary news-gathering system relies heavily on handouts; Press Gallery journalists receive a flood of xeroxed material from the party information machines and from cabinet ministers. Their reliance on documentation has tended to work against Rowling, who generally performs best in live situations, working from rough notes rather than from scripts. But journalists do not always bother to cover informal speeches.

The team of journalists following Rowling on the campaign trail in 1978 were surprised to discover a more resolute, more forthright candidate than they had expected, one much more capable of standing up to his opponent's attacks. Whether because he had changed or merely because he was more sensitively perceived by the media than in the past, Rowling seemed to speak forcefully and imaginatively about the need for cohesion among those working for the country's good. He said he had a vision of a Government that could make New Zealand "a decent country once more," where those in need of security could be helped and where people could speak out without fear of criticism.

For many voters, then, the election was a contest between rival leaders who symbolized two opposing modes of conduct and styles of performance as well as two differing philosophies. Both men tried to conform to egalitarian notions of leadership, with Muldoon appealing to the sensibilities of the "ordinary decent Kiwi" and Rowling describing himself as "just plain Bill, and your friend." But Muldoon's way of asserting himself was characteristically divisive: he would select a suitable target, perhaps a political opponent, or a journalist, sometimes the Communist bogey in the trade unions, sometimes the "trendy lefties" in the universities, and attack it until he triumphed. Rowling presented himself as a less abrasive and more liberal-minded person, sincere and likable.

The problem of New Zealand politics in the late 1970s was to find some combination of leadership talents that could provide the skill and cohesion to overcome the nation's economic and social problems. Unwittingly the 1978 election-eve telecasts provided a very exact commentary on this problem. In between election announcements, two retired politicians conversed amiably about the significance of the results and of the election generally. They were Sir John Marshall (National) and Martyn Finlay (Labour). The discussion, though ideologically charged, was urbane and amusing, a lesson in the art of political debate without recourse to the vulgar abuse of opponents or the scoring of points for the sake of effect. This, however, may have been a fortuitous interlude rather than a sign of any sudden infusion of decorum and restraint into New Zealand electioneering. On the contrary, the effects of inflation and other economic disorders on the New Zealand voter were likely to intensify political conflict.

Here it should also be noted that leadership conflicts and presidential style politics are not simply by-products of the television era. They are to some extent derived from the limitations of New Zealand political life, particularly the lack of talent in the aging upper echelons of the parties, their unimaginative recruitment, and the smallness of the legislature. In the absence of an array of talent or distinction, the parties lend themselves to capture by a few dominating personalities and become one-man bands by default. The passivity of the news media encourages this—and their lack of sensationalism and preference for the documentary, objective treatment of events mean that political parties and their leaders are likely to be that much more sensitive even to very subdued criticism.

Perhaps in the long term the corrective to this tendency towards the inflation of leadership and of campaign styles resides in the democratic sensibilities of the voters themselves. In the 1978 campaign anonymous anti-National party posters appeared in the streets of Wellington drawing attention to the alleged sexual misdemeanors of M.P.s and cabinet ministers, and a devastating graffiti proclaimed: "I'd rather eat wetas than vote National!" A weta is a large, repellant, indigenous insect, prized by the Maoris in more primitive times as a delicacy but now considered a very lowly item of diet indeed.

10

Women in New Zealand Politics

Judith Aitken

The place of women in society has been an important public issue in two periods of New Zealand's history. The first public debate took place in the late nineteenth century. Feminists recognized that the social and economic reforms for which they had been pressing during the 1870s and 1880s were unlikely to be implemented while women remained excluded from the political process. They concentrated their attention on the electoral system and in 1893 won the right for women to vote in general elections.[1] Some eighty years later it was apparent, however, that if the ability to influence the action of legislators and political parties through their vote had helped women promote the development of the welfare state, neither the right to vote nor the right to run for Parliament (acquired in 1916) had significantly changed the position of women in society or in electoral politics.

A second wave of feminism began in New Zealand in the late 1960s. It has been moderate in tone and reformist in intent. On the one hand, politically active women lobbied powerful men for legal and other changes in favor of women; on the other hand, some feminists argued that change was unlikely to occur unless women were in a position to make the necessary political decisions themselves. By the mid-1970s women had had some success in expanding their role as advisors to the Government and to political parties.[2] As parlia-

---

[1] Patricia Grimshaw, *Women's Suffrage in New Zealand* (Auckland: Auckland University Press and Oxford University Press, 1972); William B. Sutch, *Women with a Cause* (Wellington: New Zealand University Press, 1972).

[2] For example, since 1970 the Government has been advised by a permanent body, the Committee on Women, which complements the advisory work of other official agencies such as the National Advisory Council on the Employment of Women (1967), the Women's Advisory Committee of the Vocational Training

mentary lobbyists, feminists secured some useful concessions for women, such as matrimonial law reform and equal pay in the private sector;[3] they also suffered some critical failures, for example in their fight for the legalization of abortion and the provision of public child care facilities. But the main thrust of this reforming movement has not been toward participation in electoral politics at the national level. The general election of 1978 demonstrates, to some extent, why this has been so.

Women in Politics

Candidates for Parliament. In 1975—International Women's Year— forty-six women stood as general election candidates for the National, Labour, Social Credit, and Values parties, almost twice as many as had been nominated by these parties three years before. Only four were elected to the eighty-seven-seat Parliament. The number of women candidates for the four main parties rose to sixty-one in the 1978 general election, but again only four were returned to office. In the slightly enlarged House of ninety-two seats this outcome meant that the female membership remained under 5 percent, a typically low level of participation by New Zealand women.[4]

Only sixteen women have ever been returned to the New Zealand House of Representatives, and although the number of women candidates for the main political parties has grown slowly since the Second World War, the proportion of women in Parliament has never exceeded 6.3 percent. Only three women have ever

---

Council (1976), and the Committee on Women and Education (1976). The Labour and National parties both have advisory women's councils, and most of the employees in the Labour party's parliamentary Research Unit are women who have been active in feminist organizations such as the Society for Research on Women (founded in 1966).

[3] Equal pay for women was introduced in the public service (civil service) in 1960 and in the p ivate sector in the Equal Pay Act, 1972 (to be fully implemented by 1977). The Matrimonial Property Act, 1976, provides for an equal distribution of assets acquired during a marriage on its dissolution. The Human Rights Act, 1978, made discrimination on the grounds of sex (among other things) illegal. It is not, however, overriding legislation. Under the Juries Amendment Act, 1974, women are equally liable with men for jury service.

[4] Roberta Hill, "A Woman's Place—in the Home not the House: an Analysis of Proportions of Female Candidates and Elected MPs in Nine New Zealand General Elections" (project submitted for M.A. degree, University of Canterbury, Christchurch, New Zealand, 1978). For international comparisons see, inter alia, Anne Elysee, "Women in Party Politics," Australian Quarterly, vol. 49, no. 3 (1977); Jorgen S. Rasmussen, "The Role of Women in British Parliamentary Elections," Journal of Politics, vol. 30, no. 4 (November 1977); Ruth B. Dixon, "Measuring Equality between the Sexes," Journal of Social Issues, vol. 32, no. 3 (1976).

served as cabinet ministers,[5] and in the 1975–1978 National administration not a single woman held a ministerial portfolio, although the Government did appoint its two women backbenchers to important parliamentary select committees, on public expenditure and statutes revision.[6]

Historically, women have run for Parliament much less frequently than men. One analysis of electoral data for nine postwar elections shows that between 1946 and 1975 nearly 93 percent of all general election candidates were men.[7] Over the same period, however, there has been a modest trend towards the recruitment and nomination of women by the parties.[8] In 1946 only 2.5 percent of all Labour and National candidates were women. By the mid-1950s, when Social Credit first entered a general election, the proportion of women running for major and third parties rose to 5.4 percent. Over the following twenty years this increased slowly, to 13.2 percent in 1975 and almost 17 percent in 1978. In 1946 National and Labour nominated only two women each, and although by 1975 the number of Labour women had risen to six (or just under 7 percent of the party's team), this nearly doubled in 1978, when women made up almost 12 percent of Labour's ticket. National, the dominant party, has increased its female component even more slowly. From 1946 to 1975 the percentage of women candidates running for National rose fitfully from 2.5 to 5.7 percent. In 1978 women constituted 7.6 percent of all National candidates (see Table 10–1)—an increase over the previous election of only 1.9 percentage points, compared with Labour's 5 percentage point increase in the same three-year period.

Third parties, which in New Zealand have significantly less chance than either National or Labour of winning a parliamentary

---

[5] Mabel Howard (Labour), minister of health (1947-1949) and minister of social security (1957-1960); Dame Hilda Ross (National), minister without portfolio (1949-1957) and minister of social security (1957); and Whetu Tirikatene-Sullivan (Labour) minister of tourism and associate minister for social welfare (1972-1973) and minister of tourism and minister of environment (1973-1975).

[6] Marilyn Waring served as a member of the Public Expenditure Committee from 1976 to 1977 and again in 1979 as the chairperson of that committee. Colleen Dewe served as a member of the same committee from 1976 to 1978. Waring served on the Statutes Revision Committee from 1976 to 1978.

[7] Hill, "A Woman's Place," p. 12. See also Ann M. Burgin, "Women in Public Life and Politics in New Zealand" (M.A. thesis, Political Science, Victoria University of Wellington, 1968); Sonja Davies, "Women in New Zealand," *Spirit of an Age; New Zealand in the Seventies, Essays in Honour of W. B. Sutch*, John L. Robson and Jack Shallcrass, eds. (Wellington: Reed, 1975).

[8] The following data for the period 1946-1975 are based on Hill, "A Woman's Place." No equally comprehensive survey of electoral data, analyzed in terms of women's participation in electoral politics, is available as yet in New Zealand.

TABLE 10–1

PERFORMANCE OF THE MAJOR PARTIES' WOMEN CANDIDATES,
1978 HOUSE ELECTION

	National	Labour	Social Credit	Values
Candidates				
Total	92	92	92	92
Women				
Number	7	11	11	32
% of total	7.6	11.9	11.9	34.8
Winners				
Total	51	40	1	0
Women				
Number	1	3	0	0
% of party's candidates	1.1	3.3	—	—
% of party's winners	2.0	7.5	—	—
% of party's women candidates	14.3	27.3	—	—

SOURCE: *The General Election, 1978,* report presented to the House of Representatives, Wellington, New Zealand, 1979.

seat, have been more likely than the two leading parties to place women on their party ticket. Social Credit nominated six women in 1957 (7.5 percent) and this number had more than doubled, to thirteen (14.9 percent), by 1975. However, in the run-up to the 1978 general election, when Social Credit was confident of winning second place from National and Labour in several electorates,[9] its support for women candidates dropped slightly to under 12 percent. Values, on the other hand, which had almost no expectation of winning first or second place, has been consistently more inclined to nominate women since it first contested an election in 1972. That year, over 9 percent of its nominees were women, and this proportion rose from 25 to nearly 35 percent between 1975 and 1978.

Successful women candidates have generally belonged to the Labour party, which has consistently had more women in Parliament than National since 1949. This is a consequence of the fact that Labour has been more inclined to place its few women nominees in safe seats. Labour women have thus been more successful than

[9] Alan McRobie and Nigel S. Roberts, *Election '78, The 1977 Electoral Redistribution and the 1978 General Election in New Zealand* (Dunedin: John McIndoe, 1978).

other female candidates. Indeed, Robert Hill has suggested that a woman's chance of being elected, if she is nominated by Labour, is substantially greater than that of a male candidate, while a woman running for National generally has less chance of winning her seat than her male colleagues.[10] Almost half of Labour's eleven women candidates were nominated for "winnable" seats in 1978, and three of these were successful—Mary Batchelor (Avon), Whetu Tirikatene-Sullivan (Southern Maori), and Ann Hercus, who won the Lyttelton seat in a unique four-way, all-woman contest.[11] Four of National's seven women stood in seats that were technically winnable, but only one of these was classified by political analysts as safe for National.[12] This rural seat (Waipa) was retained by Marilyn Waring, a young M.P. who had entered Parliament in 1975.[13]

Incumbency has overwhelming significance in New Zealand's male-dominated electoral system, where sitting M.P.s not only are more likely to be nominated than newcomers but also have a stronger claim to winnable seats[14] when these become available, for example, through electoral boundary changes. This makes it very difficult for women to gain party nomination or have any real likelihood of winning. Although the contribution of third parties, particularly Values, has increased both the numbers and the proportion of women candidates in each election since 1972, the electoral dominance of National and Labour severely reduces the chance of any payoff for a woman candidate aiming to enter Parliament through anything other than the political mainstream.

Evidence from several countries suggests that voters themselves do not necessarily discriminate against women candidates in elective

---

[10] Hill, "A Woman's Place," p. 19. Hill calculated the Rasmussen Success Index (Rasmussen, Role of Women, p. 1047) over all nine postwar elections studied, for all parties, in conjunction with an analysis based on the use of "swing" (McRobie and Roberts, Election '78).

[11] In 1975, Colleen Dewe (National) won the Lyttelton seat from Labour, and in 1978 each of the four main parties nominated a woman for this electorate. Ann Hercus, in her first attempt to enter Parliament, won the seat for Labour.

[12] McRobie and Roberts, Election '78.

[13] Waring had been nominated by National in a surprise selection in Waipa in 1975, when she was a twenty-two-year-old research student. She survived a public debate over her alleged homosexuality and has been a consistent advocate of women's rights, particularly abortion, since winning her first election.

[14] Keith Jackson, New Zealand Politics of Change (Wellington: Reed Education, 1973), pp. 48-50. See also John Halligan and Paul Harris, "Local Elections and Democracy," Politics in New Zealand: A Reader, Stephen Levine, ed., (Sydney: George Allen and Unwin, 1978), pp. 247-249, for a discussion of incumbency in local government politics; McRobie and Roberts, Election '78, pp. 33-37.

contests,[15] and this is borne out in New Zealand when women stand for the party preferred by the electorate.[16] But the limited and uneven nature of major-party support for women leaves them little opportunity to benefit from the relative neutrality of voters as to the candidate's sex. The third parties' willingness to nominate women must be measured against the fact that the voters tend not to choose these parties, in particular Values, the party most likely to run women candidates. Thus it seems that in both their recruitment and their nomination processes, the major political parties offer a significant obstacle for women wishing to enter Parliament. This would compound other difficulties many women face, such as lack of relevant political experience and the constraints of domestic life.

An interesting sidelight on women's access to Parliament has been noted by Stephen Levine,[17] who points out that by-elections have been a significant point of entry for women interested in electoral politics. Seven of the women to reach Parliament in the past sixty years were initially elected in by-elections. Five were Labour candidates, two of whom later became cabinet ministers, and two were National candidates, one of whom also acquired a ministerial portfolio in later years.[18] Levine observes, however, that—like Mrs. Ghandi in India and Mrs. Bandaranaike in Sri Lanka, who entered politics as replacements for successful male relatives—most New Zealand women elected in by-elections replaced a husband or father M.P. A similar "substitution factor" has been observed in New Zealand local government elections, where women whose husbands or fathers were members of Parliament or were prominent in local affairs have gained election to local councils.[19] In recent years fewer women M.P.s have been directly associated in the public mind with

---

[15] Malcolm MacKerras, "Do Women Candidates Lose Votes?" *The Australian Quarterly*, vol. 49, no. 3 (September 1977); Naomi Lynn, "Women in American Politics: An Overview," *Women: A Feminist Perspective*, Jo Freeman, ed. (California: Mayfield Publishing Co., 1975); John Halligan and Paul Harris, "Women's Participation in New Zealand Local Body Elections," *Political Science*, vol. 29, no. 2 (December 1977).

[16] Hill, "A Woman's Place," p. 10.

[17] Stephen Levine, *The New Zealand Political System* (Sydney: George Allen and Unwin, 1979), pp. 104-108.

[18] The women elected in by-elections were Elizabeth McCombs (Labour), Mary Dreaver (Labour), Mary Grigg (National), Mabel Howard (Labour), Hilda Ross (National), and Whetu Tirikatene-Sullivan (Labour). Each of the last three became a cabinet minister. Women M.P.s elected in general elections include Iriaka Ratana (Labour), Esme Tombleson (National), Rona Stevenson (National), Dorothy Jelicich (Labour), Marilyn Waring (National), Colleen Dewe (National), and Ann Hercus (Labour).

[19] Halligan and Harris, "Women's Participation," p. 107.

prominent male relatives, though women probably still need the patronage of powerful men to succeed in gaining a nomination for either Labour or National.[20]

An examination of the geographic distribution of the female candidates selected in 1978 by the four main parties points to another aspect of the politicization of New Zealand women. In 1978 all the general seats contested by Labour women were in large metropolitan centers. No Labour woman ran in a rural electorate, and only three sought election in the South Island.[21] Four of the seven National women candidates were selected for urban seats, and four electorates where National placed women were in the North Island.[22] All but four of the twenty-six general electorates where a woman stood for National, Labour, or Social Credit were in large urban centers—mainly Auckland, Wellington, and Christchurch.

This concentration of women candidates tends to reinforce other evidence that women are more active politically in urban than in rural areas.[23] Country women have long been associated with organizations such as the Country Women's Institute and the Women's Division of Federated Farmers (WDFF), rural-based women's groups aimed at improving the general standard of living in farming districts. But they have not tended to produce political party activists. Of the four women returned to Parliament in 1978, only Waring (Waipa, National) was elected in a predominately rural seat.

---

[20] Whetu Tirikatene entered Parliament in a by-election in 1967. She was selected to replace her father, Eruera Tirikatene, and was approved as a Maori candidate for Southern Maori by the powerful male Maori elders only after they discovered that their preferred male candidate could not speak Maori, in which Miss Tirikatene was a fluent speaker and writer. (Reported by Whetu Tirikatene-Sullivan at Victoria University of Wellington, 1979). In recalling her preselection experiences, Marilyn Waring places some emphasis on the fact that the National party leader (Robert Muldoon, now prime minister) nominated housing as the topic for her selection night speech. This area was one in which Muldoon knew Waring was well versed, largely through her work as a researcher in the National party parliamentary Research Unit.

[21] In Avon, Lyttelton, and Southern Maori. The latter extends from roughly halfway down the North Island to the south of Stewart Island (the southernmost point of New Zealand). The electoral boundaries of Southern Maori have not altered since 1954.

[22] Lyttelton, New Lynn, Auckland Central, and Christchurch Central were contested by National party women—they are all metropolitan electorates. The only South Island seats contested by National women candidates were Tasman (rural) and Lyttelton and Christchurch Central (both urban). The urban-North Island concentration of women, of course, also reflects the greater number of seats in the more heavily populated North Island. McRobie and Roberts, *Election '78*, pp. 33–39.

[23] Halligan and Harris, "Women's Participation"; McRobie and Roberts, *Election '78*.

One implication of this finding is that, since rural voters have generally supported National, the party's mediocre record in selecting women candidates, especially outside major cities, may mean a double disadvantage for rural women. But whether women are discriminated against in the selection process in rural seats or they are perceived as unacceptable to conservative rural electorates, urban life appears more likely to offer the initial stimulation, group support, and selector sympathy necessary to allow women to come through as candidates for electoral office.

The outcome of recent local elections in one rural district suggests an interesting variation on this pattern. In 1977 the Wairarapa branch of the feminist Women's Electoral Lobby (WEL) took a strong interest in the local elections.[24] The Wairarapa is a farming district in the North Island which includes a chain of small towns and villages. WEL actively recruited, publicly endorsed, and energetically campaigned for twenty women candidates in various local authorities —and sixteen of these women were elected.[25]

Candidates for Local Office. Local elections outside the main metropolitan centers are generally not run on party lines, and the Wairarapa experience suggests that where party influence is weak and parties do not control the nomination process, women find it easier to enter. Second, where strong feminist support is extended to women as candidates, they may have an improved chance of success at the polls. Although this particular phenomenon has not yet been shown to have occurred elsewhere in New Zealand, women's involvement in local elections is significant.

Several aspects of women's participation in local government follow patterns similar to those observed in general elections. Until 1968 the numbers of women who ran for election to territorial authorities (city, borough, and county councils) were very small; moreover, they had remained almost static through the 1960s. In 1968 only 4 percent of all candidates for territorial bodies were women. John Halligan and Paul Harris found, however, that from 1968 to 1971 there was an increase of almost 50 percent in the proportion of

---

24 The Women's Electoral Lobby was founded in Auckland and Wellington in March 1975 by Albertje Gurley, Marijke Robinson, and Judy Zavos. See also, Marie Keir, "Women and Political Activism: The Women's Electoral Lobby, 1975," *Politics in New Zealand*, Stephen Levine, ed. (Sydney: George Allen and Unwin, 1978); Judith Aitken, "Women as Candidates for Local Government Office" (research paper for M.P.P. degree, Victoria University of Wellington, 1978).

25 Aitken, "Women as Candidates," Appendix H.

women candidates for local office, and between 1968 and 1974 the proportion running in boroughs and cities almost doubled.[26] In their initial findings from the 1977 local elections, these researchers tentatively report that in cities and boroughs the proportion of women candidates rose from 14.3 percent in 1974 to nearly 18 percent in 1977—a rise of over 10 percent in nearly ten years.[27] This increase in women's willingness to seek local office during the 1970s, when the women's rights movement was active in New Zealand, parallels the trend already noted in general elections.

Candidates for local bodies in large centers of population are almost invariably affiliated with one party ticket or another. As at the national level, parties are an important source of recruitment for women candidates, but in the same way, party support for women is uneven. In 1974, for example, women constituted 44 percent of Values candidates for territorial local bodies, but less than a quarter of those running on the Citizens ticket (which corresponds to the National ticket in national politics). Labour's support for women was slightly stronger than Citizens's: 32 percent of its nominees were female in the same elections.[28] Citizens selectors have admitted that they make no attempt to recruit women for their ticket (although one study shows that the type of woman candidate accepted by Citizens is highly specific).[29] Nevertheless, unlike the women selected by National as candidates, women nominated by Citizens tend to share in the party's general ability to win elections.[30] Halligan and Harris concluded from their survey that women candidates are not

---

[26] Halligan and Harris, "Women's Participation." See also, R. H. Brookes, ed. *Betts on Wellington: A City and Its Politics* (Wellington: Reed, 1970).

[27] Halligan and Harris, "Women's Participation," pp. 112-113.

[28] Ibid., p. 107.

[29] Aitken, "Women as Candidates." This study showed that the typical Citizens woman candidate seeking office for the first time is white, married, and over fifty, with no dependents living at home. She is engaged in a wide range of voluntary organizations but is not employed, full or part-time, in paid work at the time of her selection. Her husband has a professional, managerial, or commercial occupation. She has received no formal tertiary education and has no educational qualification higher than the university entrance qualification. In contrast, a typical Labour woman seeking local government office is white, about thirty-eight years old, not necessarily married, either at the time of her selection or earlier, and engaged in voluntary organizations, trade unions, or political party activities. She has at least one university degree. If she is, or has been, married, she seeks election while she still has preschool and school-aged dependents living at home. If she is not, or never has been, married, she is not responsible for any dependent care. See also, Halligan and Harris, "Local Elections," p. 248.

[30] Halligan and Harris, "Local Elections," p. 247. See also R. H. Brookes, "Electing Wellington's City Council," *Political Science*, vol. 12, no. 1 (1960), p. 6.

handicapped by any sexist prejudice among voters. Where parties contest seats in local government the problem for women is not to overcome discriminatory attitudes on the part of the local ratepayers, but to increase their acceptability to Citizens, the party that does best at the polls.[31] The problem faced by women in relation to the National party in general elections seems to have its parallel in local politics.

Women at the Polls

Few data are available on the voting behavior of New Zealand women. The interest in women shown by recent students of electoral politics illustrates a general change in social attitudes, but their studies are, on the whole, a limited source of information on women's voting behavior. Specific reference to women voters was almost entirely absent from a seminal analysis of New Zealand politics published in 1962,[32] although it presented and analyzed data on most of the other significant factors in voting behavior. "The man" was the interesting voter, and the clear presumption was that "his family" would go along with him. Wherever the male led, the household would follow.

In 1969, Austin Mitchell, one of the co-authors of the 1962 study, published a further analysis of New Zealand politics.[33] By this time, sex-specific data were available, and Mitchell found that they showed women to be more likely than men to vote National, while men were more likely than women to vote Labour. The reasons he offered were tentative:

> Perhaps women are more conservative or the more anxious for stability. . . . Probably women are more status conscious, but a more important fact seems to be that they are also more isolated from all those contacts of job, shopfloor, union, club and pub, which sustain Labour opinions, and they are more likely to form their impressions from the mass media. . . . Almost certainly another element of the explanation is less dramatic. Women live longer and there are more of them in the older age group, which mainly votes for National.[34]

---

[31] Brookes, "Electing," p. 6.

[32] R. M. Chapman, W. K. Jackson, and A. Mitchell, *New Zealand Politics in Action, The 1960 General Election* (London: Oxford University Press, 1962).

[33] Austin Mitchell, *Politics and People in New Zealand* (Christchurch, Whitcombe and Tombs, 1969).

[34] Ibid., p. 206.

Speculating about the identity of the "floating-voter" group in New Zealand, Mitchell suggested that it might include a majority of females, "if only because [women are] more fickle," but he could find no evidence to this effect and concluded, somewhat regretfully, that "apparently no sex has a monopoly."[35]

This study also included information on how often voters stayed away from the polls. Mitchell cited one city survey that showed women more likely to abstain than men; in most other places where electoral rolls had been analyzed, he found that women voters, particularly working women, were less likely to vote than men, the only exception being married women, "a dutiful section of society."[36] It should be pointed out, however, that in the 1960s *most* New Zealand women over twenty years of age were married, which suggests that the rate of abstention among women in general was probably modest.

Stephen Levine and Alan Robinson carried out a nationwide survey of voters in 1975, immediately after the general election.[37] Like Mitchell, they found that women were more inclined to support National than Labour: nearly 53 percent of all female respondents reported having voted for National, but only 28.1 percent preferred Labour to any other party. By this time Values had entered the lists, but Levine and Robinson found that slightly more men than women gave Values their support, and in any case the preference of both sexes for the major parties was overwhelming.[38]

Public debate on the question of liberalizing the abortion laws has been intense during the 1970s. M.P.s on both sides of the issue had attempted to introduce legislation either reinforcing or modifying a legal situation that most feminists found intolerable. The legislation passed in 1978 threw up new obstacles to women seeking abortions and was definitely seen as a step backward by the advocates of reform. Safe, accessible, legal abortions were not available in New Zealand, and for most women the expense of flying to Australia was prohibitive. During the 1978 campaign the Women's Electoral Lobby attempted to encourage voters, particularly women, to use their votes in the parliamentary election and the triennial referendum on liquor to demonstrate their support for repeal of the

---

[35] Ibid., p. 218.

[36] Ibid., p. 223.

[37] Stephen Levine and Alan Robinson, *The New Zealand Voter: A Survey of Public Opinion and Electoral Behavior* (Wellington: Price Milburn for New Zealand University Press, 1976).

[38] Ibid., p. 132.

abortion law.[39] And independently of WEL, Eric Geiringer, a well-known medical doctor and campaigner on the abortion issue, published an analysis of electoral data which showed voters how they could cast their votes most effectively in order to return only those candidates who supported liberalization.[40] He urged voters to avoid the general conclusion that a vote for Values (the only party to advocate "a woman's right to choose") was necessarily a vote for reform and pointed out that in at least twenty-four electorates support for Values or any other nonmajor party could in fact guarantee the the return of a conservative M.P. This meant ignoring party preference, confining one's options to Labour and National, and supporting whichever of these two parties' candidates had the more liberal record on abortion. While the proportion of liberal M.P.s returned to the House did rise slightly in 1978, there is no conclusive evidence that the efforts of WEL and Geiringer to capture the uncommitted and the single-issue voter were successful, that they weaned women away from other parties, or that they appealed more to women than to men.

The 1978 election results did show, very generally, that the voters did not automatically reject women candidates with feminist sympathies. All four of the women who were elected had emphasized women's rights in a wide range of fields, including abortion, during the campaign. What is not known is whether women voters are more likely than men to support candidates of their own sex when they have the chance to do so. Further, although more women politicians align themselves with Values than with Labour or National, the same cannot be said for New Zealand women at large, since in the past three general elections Values has never taken more than 5.2 percent of the total vote. Indeed, in 1978, it took only 2.4 percent of the vote nationally and lost ground in every district.

Forces Shaping Women's Participation in Electoral Politics

The New Mood of the 1970s. In the 1970s more women were candidates in general elections than at any time since the end of the Second World War. This can be explained in a number of ways. First, it is striking that the increase in the numbers and proportions of women in the parties' candidate lists has coincided with the

---

[39] On the use of the liquor referendum to highlight the abortion issue in 1978, see Chapter 3, footnote 50.
[40] Eric Geiringer, *Spuc 'Em All: Abortion Politics 1978* (Waiura, Martinborough: Alister Taylor, 1978).

development of the women's rights movement. Feminist activity in New Zealand intensified in the late 1960s,[41] and since 1973 four massive national conferences of women have been organized by feminists aiming to provide a forum for an accurate public account of the social and economic circumstances of women's lives and to activate women as political advocates for the feminist cause. Studies of the social background of the women attending each of these United Women's Conventions suggest that a desire to reform, if not to restructure, New Zealand society is widespread among New Zealand women. In a number of other national conferences, regional seminars, and ad hoc meetings of women discussing women's concerns, the need for more direct participation by women in the electoral process has always been an important agenda item, though usually overshadowed by matters such as the provision of child care facilities, abortion law reform, and legal protection from marital violence.[42]

Feminist organizations like the National Organization of Women (NOW) and WEL were very active during the 1975 general election campaign. Their aims were to increase the number of women M.P.s and to educate politicians on women's concerns. They lobbied all candidates, and WEL's survey of candidate opinion on matters such as abortion was widely publicized. WEL even became a target for unfavorable comment by the prime minister, whose public criticism of the organization and its methods ensured that the news media

[41] See, inter alia, Stephen Levine, ed., New Zealand Politics: A Reader (Melbourne: Cheshire, 1975); Marie Keir, Women's Electoral Lobby, 1975; Phillida Bunkle, Stephen Levine, and Christopher Wainwright, eds., Learning about Sexism in New Zealand (Wellington: Learmonth Publications, 1976); Judith Aitken, A Woman's Place: A Study of the Changing Role of Women in New Zealand (Auckland: Heinemann Educational Books, 1975); K. Goodger, A Strategy for Women's Liberation (Wellington: Pilot Books, 1974); Broadsheet, New Zealand's Feminist Magazine, Auckland; Raewun Stone, "Group Struggle in the Value Field: The Comparative Performance of New Zealand Pressure Groups on the Question of Abortion, 1970-1975," Political Science, vol. 29, no. 2 (December 1977); Women Workers in New Zealand, Mary Sinclair, ed., New Zealand Working Women's Council, Wellington, 1977; The Role of Women in New Zealand Society, Report of the Select Committee on Women's Rights, June 1975; Government Printer, Wellington, New Zealand; Society for Research on Women, inter alia, Urban Women, Dunedin, 1972; United Women's Convention 1973 Report, Sandra Coney, ed., Auckland, 1973; United Women's Convention 1975 Report, Phoebe Meikle, ed., Wellington, 1976; United Women's Convention 1977 Report, Joy Browne, ed., Christchurch, 1978.
[42] United Women's Convention Reports, 1973, 1976, 1978; Committee on Women, Women in Social and Economic Development, Background papers and report, Wellington, 1976; Penny Fenwick, Liz Griffiths, and Christine Tremewan, A Guide to Getting ON: A booklet to assist the appointment of women to boards, committees, tribunals, etc., Christchurch, 1977.

would turn to activists in WEL for comment on the numerous issues relating to women and give extensive coverage to any activities their group had arranged or sponsored. WEL was very active in the local election campaigns in 1977 and continued its campaign work up to the 1978 general election. Also in 1978, a new women's political party was formed.[43] Although its founder did not gain sufficient support from women to field any candidates (probably because by then politically active women were already committed to one of the established parties or were working through groups like WEL), the novelty of the event suggested that women were more serious than in the past about entering politics. Aggressive pressure groups such as those supporting or opposing reform of the laws on abortion and homosexuality or lobbying for equal rights for women over matrimonial property charted policy options for candidates across the political spectrum.[44] Taken as a whole, developments such as these undoubtedly stimulated women to enter the political fray in 1978.

Second, by the late 1970s the influence of several important changes in the lifestyle of New Zealand women was freeing women from the largely domestic, private world they had always inhabited. It has been suggested that women lack the training, skills, and experience that are essential for candidates in an electoral contest.[45] Certainly citizens who have not had access to money and other resources, individually or as a group, are unlikely to enter public life with ease. By the late 1960s women had begun to take advantage of their relative freedom from childbearing and prolonged child care to move out into the paid work force in increasing numbers.[46]

Third, the abortion movement, which has been sharply focused on the national legislature, had highlighted the need for political leadership among women. Historically, New Zealand women leaders have tended to rise from organizations that are female-intensive and specifically or purportedly apolitical, such as the National Council of Women, the WDFF, the Maori Women's Welfare League, and the

---

[43] *Evening Post* (Wellington), March 2, 1978. The founder was Jackie Wilkinson.

[44] See Stone, *Group Struggle*; and Levine, *New Zealand Politics*, p. 235.

[45] See, *inter alia*, Marcia Manning Lee, "Why Few Women Hold Public Office; Democracy and Sexual Roles," *Political Science Quarterly*, vol. 91, no. 2 (Summer 1976), p. 304; Rod Wise, "The Role of Women in the ACP as Policy Makers and Candidates," *Australian Quarterly* (September 1977), p. 32.

[46] See *New Zealand at the Turning Point*, report of the task force on economic and social planning, December 1976, Wellington; *Planning Perspectives 1978-1983*, New Zealand Planning Council, March 1978; *New Zealand Official Yearbook*, Department of Statistics, Wellington, New Zealand.

New Zealand Plunket Society.[47] Women who have acquired some public reputation have often done so in low-status occupations like nursing or teaching and have concentrated their political energies largely on matters relating to their own profession or on general social reforms affecting women through children.[48] The occasional female maverick has appeared in the trade union movement: women like Mary Batchelor, M.P., and Sonja Davies[49] have attracted the attention of political party recruitment agents. But women labor leaders have generally not had sufficient support in the industrial wing of the Labour party to gain legislative office. Women leaders, on the whole, have continued to promote general social and economic improvements, and few have used their power base among women to cross over into electoral politics. Those who have done so, particularly in local government, have usually felt isolated by their male colleagues.[50]

It was only in the 1970s that a need for female role models and effective women's leadership in the decision-making systems of government became widely apparent. In 1975 and 1978, when general elections were held, several women candidates made it clear that among their intentions in running for office was to provide a focus and a role model for other women.[51] All but one of the women M.P.s elected in 1975 and all four elected in 1978 had taken at least a moderate feminist line and had supported the feminists on abortion. After both elections, the women M.P.s became the subject of intense interest to feminist groups, who either saw among them an individual leader (such as Marilyn Waring) or looked forward to the forma-

---

[47] The Society for Promoting the Health of Women and Children (known as the Plunket Society after its first patron, Lady Plunket) was formed in 1907. See Eric Olssen and Andree Levesque, "Towards a History of the European Family in New Zealand," Peggy Koopman-Boyden, *Families in New Zealand Society* (Wellington: Methuen, 1978).

[48] The New Zealand Post Primary Teachers Association and the New Zealand Educational Institute (primary teachers), which are the professional associations of state school teachers in New Zealand, have both elected women as their presidents in recent years.

[49] Sonja Davies, a prominent feminist, is industrial relations officer of the New Zealand Shop Employees union. She was elected to the Executive of the Federation of Labour in 1978, the first woman to hold such a position. She has sought election as a Labour party candidate in Hastings (1966) and was an unsuccessful contender for the Labour party's nomination in 1966 (Rotorua) and 1976 (Nelson).

[50] Reported by women councilors of several years' experience in Auckland and Wellington. See Aitken, "Women as Candidates."

[51] In the National and Labour parties, Marilyn Waring (National), Ruth Richardson (National), Margaret Shields (Labour), Lois Welch (Labour), and Ann Hercus (Labour) were among those who declared a strong feminist position, with a specific interest in political leadership.

tion of a feminist cell in Parliament. Either way, they were expected to provide much-needed political leadership for New Zealand women.

In addition to such factors as these, which have encouraged women to seek entry to electoral politics, it is apparent that the established political parties, particularly National and Labour, have themselves become slightly more prepared to accommodate women. The Values party's capacity to win votes in 1975 had alarmed both National and Labour.[52] Although Values's main effect was to alert these parties to the need to formulate some kind of policy on the environment and other quality-of-life questions, its emphasis on women's participation and women's issues was not lost on the party leaders. While publicly rejecting WEL's tactics (especially the uncomfortable publicity it gave to individual politicians' records on women's issues) and the feminists' criticism of Parliament as a male bastion, the major parties apparently recognized some electoral force in the feminist argument and quietly modified their recruitment policies. The Labour party, in office from 1972 to 1975, had set up a select committee of inquiry into women's role and status in New Zealand;[53] its findings, published in 1975 and widely circulated, had made it clear that the major cause of inequality between the sexes in public life was not legal discrimination but the conservative and increasingly inappropriate attitudes of those in influential positions. The slight increase in the female proportion of Labour's candidates in 1978 suggests that if National was fairly unresponsive to this message, the party that had commissioned the report was less so.

Obstacles and Handicaps. Nevertheless, any account of the progress women are making in New Zealand elective politics must be qualified. First, while women have been involved in political party activities at the branch level, they do not, on the whole, hold any major party office. The exception is in the Values party, which had a woman deputy leader, Cathy Wilson, at its inception in 1972 and elected a woman leader in 1979, when Margaret Crozier became the first woman to head a significant political party in New Zealand. Women have not yet confronted National, Labour, or Social Credit with any serious challenge for a leadership position. In recent party conferences, women have become both more active and more vocal,

---

[52] In 1975, Values took 5.2 percent of the total vote, a considerable increase over its showing in 1972 (2.0 percent). The party polled better than Social Credit in city seats, and Values candidates came in third in twenty-eight of the forty electorates in the four main cities. See McRobie and Roberts, *Election '78.*
[53] *The Role of Women,* 1975.

but in the three main parties, party management and policy determination remain the virtually unchallenged domain of males.[54]

Second, the recent history of the abortion movement demonstrates a further complication. Organizations like the Society for the Protection of the Unborn Child (SPUC) and Feminists for Life, which adamantly oppose any liberalization of the current abortion law, include many politically active women. SPUCKsters (as they are colloquially known) are justifiably confident that with a male majority, the House of Representatives is unlikely to promote the interests of the abortion lobby. Thus their considerable political energies are directed towards supporting conservative male politicians rather than recruiting women as parliamentary candidates, since all of the women in the House, even those who are otherwise conservative, have supported a liberal approach on abortion over the past few years. Anti-abortionists are among the best-known women in all of the major parties excluding Values, and conflict on this single issue has prevented activists, in National and Labour particularly, from uniting behind a strategy to produce women M.P.s from among their own ranks. On the other hand, the abortion issue has scarcely penetrated local politics, and its relative absence may have encouraged women politicians to prefer this arena.

Third, general elections may attract as few women as they do in relation to women's numbers in the population (over 50 percent at the 1976 census) because Parliament itself is not attractive to women. Since the first United Women's Convention in 1973, and most strikingly during the contentious debate over abortion that has taken place since then, women have publicly expressed the view that there are too many items on the agenda of central government. In 1977, women candidates for local bodies strongly contended that it was at the local level, rather than in the national legislature, that effective decisions concerning communities—and the women in them—should be made.[55]

In 1978, feminist groups like WEL reported having some difficulty in persuading their members to give direct financial and personal support to women party candidates—although in 1975 they had done so and in 1977 WEL members had worked hard for independent and affiliated women candidates in the local government elections.[56] In

---

[54] In 1974 the National party established the office of Women's vice president, which has been held by Helen Sinclair, Julie Cameron, and Sue Wood. The Women's vice president has no ex officio access to the National party Policy Committee; however, in 1980 Wood was elected to serve on the Policy Committee in her own right.

[55] *United Women's Convention Reports*, 1973, 1976, 1978; Aitken, "Women Candidates."

[56] Interview with Marijke Robinson, cofounder of WEL, October 1978.

1978, women with financial resources which they had previously drawn on to support affiliated women candidates apparently donated these to feminist organizations like COACTION and Sisters Overseas Service, which arranged for women to fly to Australia for the abortions denied them by New Zealand law. By the late 1970s some feminists, at least, were apparently unwilling to donate personal time or money to nationally organized, male-dominated political parties. While this attitude may not have been widespread, it does suggest a pessimistic climate of opinion among women. Moreover, the feminists' disenchantment has implications for the major political parties, since in the past such women have provided important services as party workers and propagandists.

If politically motivated New Zealand women are disinclined to promote the positions they support through Parliament, and if they do not regard this central institution as an effective forum for the satisfaction of their needs, then they may also be unwilling to stand as candidates for the party-bound legislature. To look for a significant increase in the numbers of women running for Parliament in the future may be to look in the wrong place. The reservations women have expressed about the efficacy of the elected legislature reflects a general and growing concern in the New Zealand electorate as a whole about the unequal relationship between the legislature and the executive and the relative impotence of the House.[57] It is possible that in the late 1970s women generally do not see Parliament as either the most effective or the most important agency through which or in which to work. In the future, the more interesting trend to follow may be the participation of women in local government and community politics.

Finally, it should be remembered that by 1978 New Zealand was suffering a major economic depression, with unemployment at an unprecedented postwar level and chronic difficulties in trade relationships with overseas countries. Although women now constitute over one-third of the labor force, they are still clustered at the lower occupational levels and are experiencing considerable difficulty in holding jobs as the labor market shrinks. Whatever opportunities and encouragement women have had to enter electoral politics, the reality is that even politically motivated women are unlikely to do so while they are preoccupied with a lack of job opportunities, a lack of child care facilities, reduced social services, and a hostile economic environment.

---

[57] See, inter alia, Les Cleveland, The Politics of Utopia: New Zealand and its Government (Wellington: Methuen, 1979); Geoffrey Palmer, Unbridled Power: An Interpretation of New Zealand's Constitution and Government (Wellington: Oxford University Press, 1979); Levine, New Zealand Political System, 1979.

11
The Outcome

Nigel S. Roberts

The results of the 1978 general election in New Zealand are immediately noteworthy for four reasons. First, the turbulence that had characterized the first two elections of the decade did not disappear: the swing away from the Government was the second largest since 1935. Second, for the first time since the advent of the modern political party system in New Zealand, the official opposition won more votes than the Government. Third, the Social Credit Political League won its largest share of the poll in the quarter-of-a-century it has contested general elections in New Zealand. And, fourth, both the basis of the election and its outcome were more hotly disputed than in any poll in New Zealand since the 1919 prohibition referendum on the one hand and the 1946 general election on the other.

Since the advent of the modern two-party political system in the 1930s, New Zealand's electoral history has been a near perfect example of pendulum politics. Once in office, Governments have seen their electoral strength ceaselessly erode.[1] Table 11–1 sets forth the votes won by the political parties in New Zealand from 1946 through 1978, as well as the proportions of the seats in the House of Representatives held by the political parties, the voter turnout, and the overall swing against the Government. Only in 1951—in New Zealand's sole snap election in the twentieth century—did an incumbent Government increase its share of the major party (or two-party) vote. All the other elections have supported the contention of the authors of *The American Voter* that "a majority party, once it is in office, will not continue to accrue electoral strength."[2]

---

[1] Parts of this section are based on Alan McRobie and Nigel S. Roberts, *Election '78: The 1977 Electoral Redistribution and the 1978 General Election in New Zealand* (Dunedin: John McIndoe, 1978), p. 15.

[2] Angus Campbell, Philip E. Converse, Warren E. Miller, and Donald E. Stokes, *The American Voter* (New York: John Wiley, 1960), p. 554.

TABLE 11–1

RESULTS OF NEW ZEALAND GENERAL ELECTIONS, 1946–78

Year and Party	Popular Vote	% of Vote	Seats	% of Seats	Turnout	Swing[a]
1946						
Labour	536,994	51.3	42	52.5	92.5	−1.5
National	507,139	48.4	38	47.5		
Other	3,072	0.3	0			
1949						
Labour	506,100	47.2	34	42.5	93.5	−3.8
National	556,805	51.9	46	57.5		
Other	10,276	0.9	0			
1951						
Labour	490,143	45.8	30	37.5	88.8	+1.7
National	577,630	54.0	50	62.5		
Other	2,018	0.2	0			
1954						
Labour	484,082	44.1	35	43.7	91.3	−4.0
National	485,630	44.3	45	56.3		
Social Credit	122,068	11.1	0			
Other	5,113	0.5	0			
1957						
Labour	559,096	48.3	41	51.3	92.9	−2.3
National	511,699	44.2	39	48.7		
Social Credit	83,498	7.2	0			
Other	3,072	0.3	0			
1960						
Labour	508,179	43.4	34	42.5	89.8	−4.5
National	557,046	47.6	46	57.5		
Social Credit	100,905	8.6	0			
Other	4,373	0.4	0			
1963						
Labour	524,066	43.7	35	43.8	90.5	−0.5
National	563,875	47.1	45	56.2		
Social Credit	95,176	7.9	0			
Other	14,928	1.3	0			
1966						
Labour	499,392	41.4	35	43.8	86.0	−0.5
National	525,945	43.6	44	55.0		
Social Credit	174,515	14.5	1	1.2		
Other	5,243	0.4	0			
1969						
Labour	592,055	44.2	39	46.4	88.9	−0.7
National	605,960	45.2	45	53.6		

TABLE 11–1 (continued)

Year and Party	Popular Vote	% of Vote	Seats	% of Seats	Turnout	Swing[a]
Social Credit	121,576	9.1	0			
Other	20,577	1.5	0			
1972						
Labour	677,669	48.4	55	63.2	89.1	−4.4
National	581,422	41.5	32	36.8		
Social Credit	93,231	6.6	0			
Values	27,467	2.0	0			
Other	21,364	1.5	0			
1975						
Labour	634,453	39.6	32	36.8	83.1	−8.4
National	763,136	47.6	55	63.2		
Social Credit	119,147	7.4	0			
Values	83,241	5.2	0			
Other	3,756	0.2	0			
1978						
Labour	691,076	40.4	40	43.5	68.4[b]	−5.0
National	680,991	39.8	51	55.4		
Social Credit	274,756	16.1	1	1.1		
Values	41,220	2.4	0			
Other	22,130	1.3	0			

[a] Percentage-point swing to (+) or against (−) the incumbent Government.
[b] For a discussion of the turnout figure for 1978, see the last section of this chapter.
SOURCE: For 1946 through 1954, Stephen Levine, The New Zealand Political System (Sydney: George Allen and Unwin, 1979), pp. 193-195; for 1957 through 1978, official returns, found in the Appendices to the Journals of the House of Representatives (Wellington: Government Printer), in 1958, 1961, 1964, 1967, and 1970 as Appendix H. 33, and in 1973, 1976, and 1979 as Appendix E. 9.

Throughout the 1960s in particular, the proportion of the two-party vote going to the National party declined slowly but steadily. Small swings to Labour in 1963, 1966, and 1969 all served to strengthen the electoral position of the Labour party vis-à-vis the incumbent National party and to diminish the National party's share of the seats in the House of Representatives. In *Political Parties in New Zealand*, R. S. Milne noted in 1966 that "after a Government has been in office for some time enough electors believe it is 'time for a change' for the Government to be turned out."[3] His argument was

[3] R. S. Milne, *Political Parties in New Zealand* (Oxford: Clarendon Press, 1966), p. 96.

supported dramatically six years later when there was a 4.4 percentage point swing to the Labour party, which had specifically based its 1972 election campaign on the slogan "It's time. For Labour."

After twelve years in office and four election victories in a row, the National party had been unceremoniously dumped from office by the second largest two-party swing in New Zealand in more than a quarter of a century. However, just three years later, in November 1975, the swing back to National was bigger than any since 1935. Throughout New Zealand, the overall two-party swing in 1975 was 8.4 percentage points. In all but two of the eighty-seven electorates there was a swing to National, and the average was 8.2 percentage points.

Seen in this light, the 1978 general election posed several crucial questions. In a preelection study of the effects of the 1977 electoral redistribution in New Zealand, Alan McRobie summarized them:

> Will the behavior of the New Zealand electorate continue to be volatile and unpredictable? Will the large swing in 1972 and the even larger swing in 1975 set the pattern for this year's election? Or will New Zealand voters take a leaf from their Australian counterparts in December 1977 and endorse the present Government's performance with only a small swing to Labour? Will New Zealand return to an era of electoral stability like that of the 1960s?[4]

The 1978 Results

Those four questions were quickly answered on election night 1978, when the National party's share of the poll dropped by nearly 8 percentage points compared with 1975, and on an interim election-night count, the Government lost thirteen seats—twelve to the Labour party and, on paper at least, one to Social Credit. A magisterial re-count and a Supreme Court petition enabled the National party to "recapture" two of its "lost" seats, Kapiti and Hunua, from Labour, and when the composition of New Zealand's thirty-ninth Parliament was finally determined, nearly six months to the day after the 1978 general election, National's overall majority (over Labour and Social Credit combined) was ten. In 1975, by way of contrast, National had won a twenty-three seat majority in the House of Representatives; and after the 1977 electoral boundary revisions, the party's paper majority had been calculated to be thirty-two seats. An overall comparison between the 1975 and 1978 elections is provided in Table 11–2.

---

[4] McRobie and Roberts, *Election '78*, p. 19.

TABLE 11-2
ELECTION RESULTS FOR 1975 AND 1978 COMPARED

Party	Popular Vote		Share of Total Vote (in percentages)		Two-Party Swing (in percentage points)		Seats Lost	
	1975	1978	1975	1978	1975	1978	1975	1978
Labour	634,453	691,076	39.6	40.4	—	+5.0	23	0
National	763,136	680,991	47.6	39.8	+8.4	—	0	11
Social Credit	119,147	274,756	7.4	16.1	—	—	0	0
Values	83,241	41,220	5.2	2.4	—	—	—	—
Other	3,756	22,130	0.2	1.3	—	—	—	—
Total	1,603,733	1,710,173	100.0	100.0	—	—	—	—

SOURCE: Official returns, appropriate years.

National's Losses, Labour's Gains. National lost the following ten seats to Labour: Dunedin North, Hastings, Lyttelton, Manurewa, Palmerston North, Papanui, Papatoetoe, Taupo, Western Hutt, and Yaldhurst. However, it should be noted that although three of these seats—Manurewa, Papatoetoe, and Yaldhurst—would have elected National candidates in 1975 if the 1977 boundaries had then applied, none of the three was actually held by a National party member of Parliament. All three seats were, in fact, contested by Labour incumbents: Roger Douglas, M.P. for the former Manukau electorate,[5] was the Labour candidate in Manurewa; Eddie Isbey, M.P. for the former Grey Lynn seat, was the Labour candidate in Papatoetoe; and Mick Connolly, M.P. for the former Wigram electorate, was Labour's candidate in Yaldhurst.

Only six sitting National party M.P.s, five of them first-term members, were actually defeated in races against Labour candidates: Richard Walls (Dunedin North), Robert Fenton (Hastings), John Lithgow (Palmerston North), Brian Lambert (Western Hutt), and Colleen Dewe (Lyttelton). The sixth casualty in the battle with Labour was Bert Walker, M.P. for Papanui and minister of social welfare in Robert Muldoon's first Government. Walker had been in Parliament for eighteen years. The member for Taupo, Ramon La Varis, retired from Parliament because of ill-health after just one term and thus avoided a personal defeat when his seat was recaptured by Jack Ridley, who had held the electorate for Labour from 1972 to 1975.

As Keith Jackson has pointed out in his chapter on candidate selection, Labour's victors included six nonincumbent candidates with previous parliamentary experience. In addition to Ridley, they included Joe Walding, who recaptured Palmerston North, the seat he had held for Labour from 1967 until 1975; and Mike Moore, who had been Labour M.P. for Eden (in the city of Auckland) from 1972 to 1975. Despite allegations of carpetbagging, he won the Christchurch seat of Papanui (in the South Island—about 600 miles from Auckland) with ease. The other Labour "returnees," however, were all adopted as Labour candidates in seats that Labour would have won in 1975 had that election been fought in the 1977 boundaries. Kerry Burke (M.P. for Rangiora from 1972 to 1975) moved over the Southern Alps after his 1975 defeat to teach in Greymouth and was adopted as the Labour party's candidate for the West Coast electorate after the incumbent Labour M.P., Paddy Blanchfield, announced his retirement

---

[5] The term "former" electorate refers to electorates that were in existence for the 1972 and 1975 general elections but not for the 1978 general election.

from Parliament. Frank O'Flynn (M.P. for Kapiti from 1972 to 1975) was installed as Labour's candidate in Island Bay by the New Zealand Council of the Labour party after the council refused to readopt sitting Labour M.P. Gerald O'Brien, and O'Flynn held the seat for Labour despite a two-party swing of 2.2 percentage points to National. Michael Bassett (M.P. for Waitemata from 1972 to 1975) secured the Labour nomination for the new Te Atatu electorate after its creation by the Representation Commission in 1977 and after Martyn Finlay, Labour M.P. for the former Henderson electorate (from which Te Atatu had been largely created), announced his decision to retire from Parliament. It has been calculated that the area encompassed by Te Atatu would have had a Labour majority of 746 on 1975 voting figures,[6] and Bassett held the seat for Labour in 1978.

Rangitikei: Social Credit's Victory. The eleventh seat lost by National was Rangitikei. The leader of the Social Credit Political League, Bruce Beetham, had captured the old, unredistributed Rangitikei from the National party in a by-election in February 1978 after the death of Sir Roy Jack, the speaker of the New Zealand House of Representatives in 1976 and 1977. But the 1977 electoral redistribution substantially altered the seat's boundaries, and a redrawn Rangitikei not only was technically a safe National seat on 1975 voting figures, but also was contested for National by the incumbent minister of education, Les Gandar. (Gandar's home base for two elections, Ruahine, was abolished by the 1977 electoral redistribution and divided between the new Manawatu and Rangitikei electorates on a 60:40 basis.) Rangitikei was thus unique in 1978 in being contested by two sitting M.P.s.

Table 11–3 gives the 1975 general election results in the old Rangitikei electorate and the results of the February 1978 by-election held within the same boundaries, as well as the actual results in Rangitikei in the 1978 general election. Table 11–3 also includes an assessment of what the results in the new Rangitikei electorate would have been had the 1975 general election been held under the redrawn boundaries.

The reason why Rangitikei should be counted as a loss for the National party will be clear. Prime Minister Muldoon, certainly regarded the result in Rangitikei as a defeat for National: Les Gandar "was beaten by his own National people," Muldoon argued after the election, and he added that Gandar's defeat made "a mockery of the

---

6 McRobie and Roberts, *Election '78*, p. 133.

TABLE 11-3

Results in the Old and New Rangitikei Electorates, 1975–78

| | Old Rangitikei | | | | New Rangitikei | | | |
| | November 1975 general election | | February 1978 by-election | | 1975 election results in redrawn boundaries | | November 1978 general election | |
Party	Vote	%	Vote	%	Vote	%	Vote	%
Labour	2,263	14.0	1,614	11.4	4,317	23.4	1,490	7.4
National	7,631	47.3	5,469	38.6	8,865	48.1	7,716	38.4
Social Credit	5,875	36.4	6,804	48.0	4,799	26.0	10,569	52.7
Values	253	1.6	264	1.9	469	2.5	291	1.5
Other	119	0.7	13	0.1				

Source: Alan McRobie and Nigel S. Roberts, *Election '78: The 1977 Electoral Redistribution and the 1978 General Election in New Zealand* (Dunedin: John McIndoe, 1978), p. 119; and official returns, 1975 and 1978.

idea you have to get better men into Parliament."[7] On election night, Muldoon was even less charitable: he complained that the electors had thrown out "a man who would make three of Beetham any day."[8]

Gandar believed that a report during the campaign that he might succeed Sir Douglas Carter as New Zealand's high commissioner in London "had done him some harm. Rumours had been rife that if he was elected he would resign and take the London post."[9] Gandar did not win, so the rumors could not be put directly to the test; but less than five months after the general election Muldoon announced Gandar's appointment to London. As for the other cabinet minister defeated in the general election, Bert Walker, he was appointed an accident compensation commissioner early in 1979. Apparently cabinet ministers, like generals, can take comfort in the adage "to the loser the spoils."

Swings and Roundabouts

The Labour party's concrete gains in terms of seats in the general election were at the expense of the National party, but they were the result of a nationwide movement to the Social Credit Political League. Although the Labour party's overall share of the poll rose by less than one percentage point compared with 1975, the net effect of the sharp drop in National's share of the vote and the fact that Social Credit more than doubled its vote was, as we have seen, an overall five percentage point swing to Labour.

The average of the individual swings to Labour in the ninety-two electorates, however, was 4.3 percentage points. As Michael Steed has argued with respect to Britain, "Any swing calculated by combining votes cast in different constituencies is in danger of . . . distortion if turnout is changing. The average of the individual swings is almost always the more significant figure."[10] It certainly was in New Zealand in 1978.

Figure 11–1 shows the 1978 New Zealand "electoral pendulum" I designed with Alan McRobie. It illustrates (by way of shading) the National party's losses in 1978 to both Labour and Social Credit. According to the pendulum, an average swing to Labour of 4.3 percent-

---

[7] *Christchurch Star*, November 28, 1978; and *Press* (Christchurch), November 28, 1978.

[8] *Christchurch Star*, November 27, 1978.

[9] *Press* (Christchurch), November 28, 1978.

[10] Michael Steed, "An Analysis of the Results," in David Butler and Anthony King, *The British General Election of 1964* (London: Macmillan, 1965), p. 339.

TABLE 11–4
1978 Election Results, by Region

Region	Votes (in percentages)[a]			Seats Won		
	Labour	National	Social Credit	Labour	National	Social Credit
Northern North Island	26.3	45.2	26.4	0	12	0
Auckland	41.0	39.3	14.6	11	10	0
East Coast North Island	37.6	44.4	16.2	2	5	0
West & Central North Island	33.3	42.6	21.9	3	9	1
Wellington	44.9	38.0	10.5	6	4	0
West Coast & Northern South Island	44.0	40.1	11.7	4	4	0
Christchurch	53.1	34.6	8.9	7	1	0
Dunedin	49.1	33.5	12.7	3	0	0
Southern South Island	33.7	45.5	17.7	0	6	0
Maori Seats	78.3	10.0	10.5	4	0	0
New Zealand	40.4	39.8	16.1	40	51	1

[a] Excludes votes for the Values party and other candidates.
Source: Official returns, 1978.

age points would have resulted in a ten-seat majority for National. This is, of course, what occurred. All ten National seats susceptible to a swing of 4 percentage points fell to Labour, but Gisborne— which required a swing of 4.1 percentage points to fall—stayed National. (The swing to Labour in Gisborne was only 3.3 percentage points.) Above the 4.3 percentage point marker, the only seat that National lost was Rangitikei (which, as we have seen, fell to Social Credit).

Nevertheless, it must be admitted that the concept of two-party swing can cause some oddities in an analysis of the results of the 1978 general election in New Zealand. A careless reader, impressed by the 16.5 percentage point two-party swing to National in Rangitikei, for example, might not notice that National actually lost the seat! But the two-party swing in Rangitikei is *not* meaningless—it indicates, of course, that a greater proportion of Labour supporters deserted their party in favor of Social Credit in Rangitikei than did National supporters.[11] In addition, it is extremely interesting to note that—on a two-party basis—there were swings to National in a mere eight electorates. Apart from Rangitikei, five of the eight were seats where Social Credit came second, again indicating that Social Credit took more support away from Labour than from National. Another was Island Bay, where the incumbent Labour M.P. was not renominated by his party and stood against the official nominee, garnering more than 3,500 votes in an unsuccessful bid to hold the seat as an independent Labour candidate. The eighth seat, Birkenhead, is distinguished by the fact that its M.P., Jim McLay, was the only National party candidate in the entire country to benefit from a genuine swing to National in a straight two-party fight. McLay was rewarded for his efforts: in December 1978, after just one term in Parliament, he was made a cabinet minister at the age of thirty-three.

The range of the swing is illustrated by Figure 11–2. Both for the sake of greater knowledge and by way of contrast, three additional figures illustrate the range of the change in the Labour vote, the National vote, and the Social Credit vote from 1975 to 1978. Several points stand out. National's share of the poll dropped in every electorate (see Figure 11–4). It dropped least (1.6 percentage points) in McLay's electorate. At the other extreme, it dropped most in Wallace (13.8 percentage points), West Coast (20.8 percentage points), East Coast Bays (22.2 percentage points), and Pakuranga (22.7 percentage points). In each of these four electorates, an independent

---

11 This was also true in the February 1978 by-election in Rangitikei. *Dominion* (Wellington), February 20, 1978.

FIGURE 11–1

NEW ZEALAND ELECTORAL PENDULUM, 1978

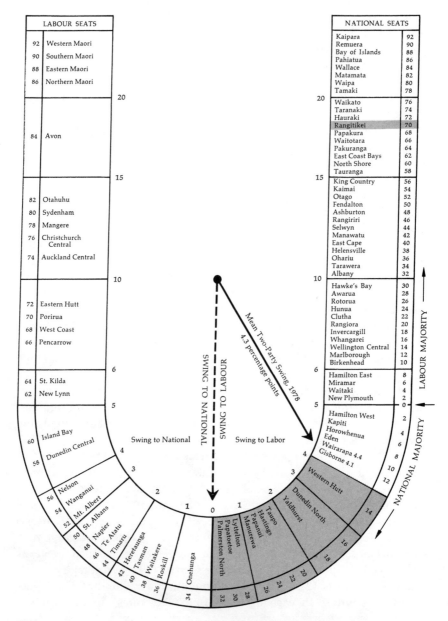

Seats changing hands in 1978. (All were lost by the National party; all fell to Labour except Rangitikei which was captured by Social Credit.

NOTE: This figure shows the distribution of seats in 1978. The seats are listed in order of safeness before the election, from Labour's safest seat at the top left, to National's safest at the top right, with both parties' marginal seats at the bottom of the pendulum. The two-party swing that would cause a given seat to change hands is shown on the inside perimeter of the pendulum; it is largest, of course, for the safest seats, smallest for the most marginal ones. The figures on the outside perimeter indicate the majority in Parliament that would result from the corresponding swing if it were uniform across districts. Thus, a uniform five percentage point swing to Labour in 1978 would have left the parties tied in Parliament. A *mean* swing of the same magnitude would have been likely to produce this result.

When the pendulum is "at rest" and the arrow points straight down, it indicates the situation before the 1978 election—the distribution of seats that would have resulted from the 1975 election if it had been held under the boundaries used for the 1978 election (thirty Labour seats, sixty-two National seats, and a National majority of thirty-two). When the pendulum registers the mean two-party swing that actually occurred in 1978—4.3 percentage points to Labour—the arrow indicates a probable National majority of eleven seats. The shaded seats are those that actually changed hands in the 1978 election.

SOURCE: This figure was designed by Alan McRobie and Nigel S. Roberts, who performed the calculations underlying all the figures cited here and elsewhere in this chapter for electorate-level swings between 1975 and 1978. Since those two elections were conducted under different boundaries, it was necessary to calculate for each of the ninety-two districts created by the 1977 redistribution the totals of votes cast in 1975 at the polling places falling within the new district. For these calculations see Alan McRobie and Nigel S. Roberts, *Election '78: The 1977 Electoral Redistribution and the 1978 General Election in New Zealand* (Dunedin: John McIndoe, 1978), pp. 60-153.

FIGURE 11–2
The Range of the Swing, 1978 General Election

Largest Swings to Labour

West Coast	15.2
Mangere	14.9
Dunedin North	11.4
Papanui	10.4
East Coast Bays	9.9
New Lynn	9.9

Swings to National

Rangitikei (won by Social Credit)	16.5
Kaipara	4.8
Island Bay	2.2
Matamata	1.9
Birkenhead	1.7
Hauraki	1.4
Kaimai	0.9
Tauranga	0.4

Average swing: 4.3 percentage points to Labour

Status of seat before the 1978 election:

National
Labour

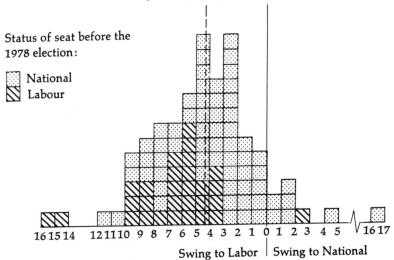

Swing to Labor | Swing to National

NOTE: In Figures 11–2 through 11–5, each of the electorates created by the 1977 redistribution is represented by a square. Each square is shaded to indicate the party that would have won the electorate in 1975 if the 1975 election had been held under the new boundaries.

SOURCE: Figures 11–2 through 11–5 are based on the official returns and on calculations by McRobie and Robert in *Election '78*, pp. 60-151.

FIGURE 11–3

CHANGE IN THE LABOUR VOTE, 1975–1978

Overall change: +0.8 percentage points

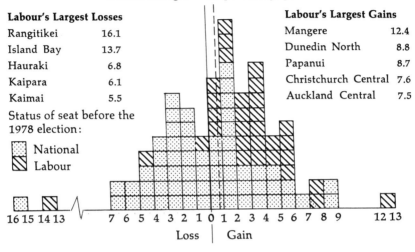

Labour's Largest Losses

Rangitikei	16.1
Island Bay	13.7
Hauraki	6.8
Kaipara	6.1
Kaimai	5.5

Status of seat before the
1978 election:

National
Labour

Labour's Largest Gains

Mangere	12.4
Dunedin North	8.8
Papanui	8.7
Christchurch Central	7.6
Auckland Central	7.5

16 15 14 13   7 6 5 4 3 2 1 0 1 2 3 4 5 6 7 8 9   12 13

Loss | Gain

FIGURE 11–4

CHANGE IN THE NATIONAL PARTY VOTE, 1975–1978

Overall change: −7.8 percentage points

National's Largest Losses

Pakuranga	22.7
East Coast Bays	22.2
West Coast	20.8
Wallace	13.8
Mangere	13.3

Status of seat before the
1978 election:

National
Labour

National's Smallest Losses

Birkenhead	1.6
Nelson	2.0
Western Maori	3.3
Onehunga	3.3
Western Hutt	3.7
Roskill	3.7

23 22 21 20   14 13 12 11 10 9 8 7 6 5 4 3 2 1 0

Decline in the National vote

FIGURE 11–5

CHANGE IN THE SOCIAL CREDIT VOTE, 1975–1978

Social Credit's Smallest Gains		Social Credit's Largest Gains	
Southern Maori	2.0	Rangitikei (won by	
Nelson	2.5	Social Credit)	26.7
Lyttelton	3.1	Hauraki	20.4
Western Hutt	3.2	Kaipara	20.3
Yaldhurst	3.7	Hastings	17.1
Pencarrow	3.7	Tauranga	15.8
		Whangarei	15.7

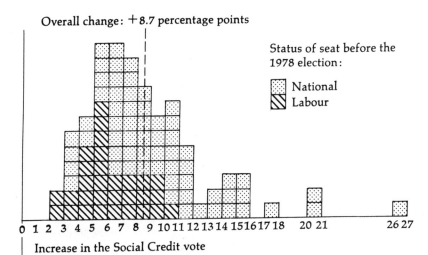

Overall change: +8.7 percentage points

Status of seat before the 1978 election:

National
Labour

Increase in the Social Credit vote

candidate won more than 2,000 votes. Alternative—or independent—National candidates were largely responsible for the major decline in National's votes in several electorates. In East Coast Bays, a twenty-eight-year-old part-time horse breeder stood against the minister of health, Frank Gill, and won 3,684 votes; in Pakuranga (the National party's equivalent of Island Bay), Gavin Downie, who had held the seat for six years for National, was not renominated but stood as an independent National candidate and took nearly 4,500 votes, more than half as many as National's winning official candidate; and in Wallace, June Slee, sister of the leader of a dissident group of Southland farmers, stood against Brian Talboys, deputy leader of the National party and New Zealand's minister of foreign affairs, and won 2,199 votes. In the West Coast electorate, Don Eadie—an independent candidate representing the West Coast party—won

3,334 votes, to come in narrowly behind the National party's 3,520 votes and marginally in front of Social Credit's 3,161. However, Labour's Kerry Burke won the seat handily with more than 9,000 votes.

On the other hand, Social Credit's share of the poll went up in every seat in New Zealand (see Figure 11–5). Its most dramatic gain was in Rangitikei (26.7 percentage points), but the Social Credit vote rose by more than 20 percentage points in Hauraki and Kaipara as well. With another strong showing in Bay of Islands (a successor to the former Hobson electorate and a traditional area of Social Credit strength), the Social Credit Political League is now within striking distance of achieving in 1981 what it had hoped to win in 1978—four seats. As Figure 11–6 shows, the National-Social Credit swings that would transfer the Bay of Islands, Hauraki, and Kaipara from National to Social Credit are 6.4, 7.2, and 1.7 percentage points, respectively.

For its part, the Labour party increased its share of the vote in fifty-seven seats but lost ground in the other thirty-five. Figure 11–3 shows that Labour's share of the vote rose predominantly in seats it had held prior to the general election. The Labour party recorded an above-average increase in its share of the vote in twenty-three of the thirty seats it would have won in 1975 had the 1977 electoral boundaries been operational then, as well as an increase in another four seats Labour had held prior to the election. Labour lost ground in only three of the seats it would have won in 1975 (Wanganui, West Coast—and inevitably—Island Bay).

Like the National party, the Values party lost ground in all ninety-two seats. Not even the leader of the Values party, Tony Kunowski, could escape the tide: the average decline in the Values vote was 2.8 percentage points, and even Kunowski's share of the poll declined by almost that much (2.5 percentage points).

Regional Results. Table 11–4 gives a regional breakdown of the results. Areas of special strength and weakness are immediately apparent. The Labour party not unexpectedly won more than three-quarters of the votes in the four Maori electorates; and—aided by swings averaging more than seven percentage points—Labour polled strongly in South Island cities, taking more than 50 percent of the votes in Christchurch and very nearly half the votes in Dunedin. The swing to Labour in the South Island was significantly higher than in the North Island. There was an average swing of 6.0 percentage points to Labour in the South Island, compared with an average swing of 3.6 percentage points in the North Island. After Labour's poor

FIGURE 11-6

NEW ZEALAND ELECTORAL PENDULUM, 1981

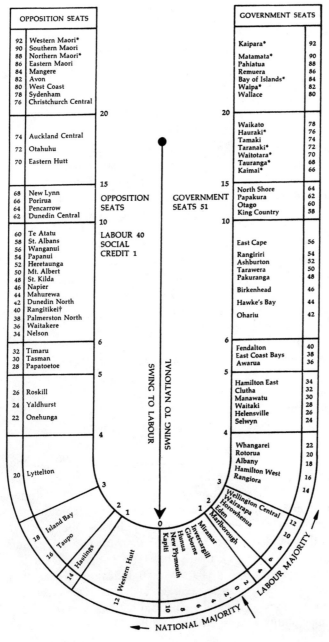

*Seat where Social Credit came second in 1978. The two-party swing required for Social Credit to capture these seats in 1981 is, in percentage points:

Kaipara	1.7
Bay of Islands	6.4
Hauraki	7.2
Tauranga	11.5
Kaimai	13.0
Waitotara	15.6
Matamata	16.9
Taranaki	17.2
Waipa	18.3
Northern Maori	18.3
Southern Maori	38.5

†Seat held by Social Credit. The two-party swing required for Labour to capture Rangitikei in 1981 is 37.7 percentage points.

NOTE: This figure summarizes the results of the 1978 general election and identifies the seats most likely to change hands with any given swing in the next general election or in any by-election before then. Like all previous pendulums, it is based on the two-party swing required for a seat to change hands from National to Labour or from Labour to National. The seats are listed in order of safeness, from Labour's safest seat at the top left, to National's safest seat at the top right. The figures around the inside of the pendulum show the percentage-point two-party swing required for the seats to fall. The figures around the outside perimeter indicate the majority that either Labour or National will be likely to have if the corresponding swing takes place.

The 1981 pendulum is different from those published for the two previous elections (see Figure 11-1) in several important ways. First, the columns are headed "Government Seats" and "Opposition Seats" instead of "National Seats" and "Labour Seats." This enables us to include Rangitikei, held by Social Credit's Bruce Beetham. Rangitikei has been listed as an opposition seat because Beetham is not a Government supporter and therefore cannot be included on the Government side of the pendulum. The alternative would have been to drop Rangitikei from the figure altogether, which would have been misleading since the Social Credit presence in the 1978–1981 Parliament cannot be ignored.

Social Credit came second in eleven electorates in 1978 (compared with only two in 1975). Like the others, these electorates are placed on the pendulum according to the National-Labour swing that would make them change hands. However, they have also been identified with an asterisk, and the two-party swing Social Credit would require to capture each from the incumbent has been listed alongside the pendulum. It will be noted that, apart from Kaipara, Bay of Islands, and Hauraki (all of which are actually much less safe for National than their placement on the pendulum indicates), the location of these seats would change only marginally if they were placed according to the swing required by Social Credit.

Miramar, which requires a two-party swing of 0.9 percentage points to change hands, is a key electorate. If there is an overall, uniform two-party swing of 0.9 percentage points to Labour in the next general election, National will lose office. With seven seats vulnerable to a two-party swing to Labour of 1 percentage point or less, the National Government is in a precarious position. Conversely, a 1 percentage point swing to National in the next election would allow the Government to capture only one extra seat from Labour; it would have to improve its position by a full 4.4 percentage points to capture as many as seven seats from Labour. Of course, swings are never absolutely uniform. Nevertheless, the winning and losing of seats is first and foremost a factor of nationwide swings and only secondarily a reflection of the unique characteristics of individual constituencies.

SOURCE: Constructed by Alan McRobie and Nigel S. Roberts from the official election returns.

TABLE 11–5

SWINGS AND SEATS IN CITY, TOWN, RURAL, AND
MAORI ELECTORATES, 1978

Type of Electorate	Average Swing to Labour (in percentage points)	Seats Won			
		Labour	National	Social Credit	Total
City	6.0	27	15	—	42
Town	3.8	6	7	—	13
Rural	2.3	3	29	1	33
Maori	5.4	4	—	—	4
New Zealand	4.3	40	51	1	92

SOURCE: Calculated from official returns. McRobie and Roberts, *Election '78,* pp. 60-151, contains the calculations of the results of the 1975 general election in the electoral boundaries used for the 1978 general election which form the basis for the swing calculations in this table and elsewhere in this chapter.

showing in the Auckland metropolitan area in 1975, the average swing of 5.9 percentage points there was particularly satisfying for the party, which won both more votes and more seats than National in Auckland.

The National party did not win more than half the votes in any of the ten regions outlined in Table 11–4. However, National's two strongholds are in the far north and the far south of the country: in both regions National won more than 45 percent of the votes cast and picked up all the seats. In the nation's thirty-three rural seats, the swing to Labour was kept to a minimum: it averaged only 2.3 percentage points. This was because Social Credit often performed well in the nation's rural seats at the expense of Labour. The Labour vote all but disappeared in seats like Kaipara and Rangitikei (Labour took fewer than 1,500 votes in each), and the Labour vote dipped drastically in seats like Hauraki, Matamata, and Waipa. In these three electorates and five others (Bay of Islands, Kaimai, Taranaki, Tauranga, and Waitotara) Labour came third to Social Credit's second. National came third to Social Credit's second in two of the Maori seats (Northern and Western Maori). Social Credit's areas of strong support are still in the northern North Island (where Vernon Cracknell, then leader of the league, held the seat of Hobson from 1966 to 1969) and the western and central areas of the North Island. It remains weakest in the city of Christchurch—ironically, the home of its first leader, Wilfred Owen.

Table 11–5 illustrates the swings in New Zealand's city, town, rural, and Maori electorates and indicates the number of seats held

TABLE 11–6
Average Swing, by the Safety of Electorates, 1975 and 1978
(in percentage points)

Classification of Electorate	Swing to National in 1975		Swing to Labour in 1978	
Safe Labour	10.0	(N=27)	8.3	(N=10)
Fairly Safe Labour	8.2	(N=12)	7.8	(N= 6)
Marginal Labour	8.3	(N=16)	4.8	(N=14)
Marginal National	7.1	(N= 9)	5.3	(N=16)
Fairly Safe National	6.9	(N=10)	3.7	(N=15)
Safe National	6.9	(N=13)	3.0	(N=31)
New Zealand	8.4	(N=87)	5.0	(N=92)

Source: Official returns, appropriate years; and McRobie and Roberts, *Election '78*, pp. 60-151.

by the political parties in these four categories of constituencies. The table tells an important tale. More than two-thirds of Labour's parliamentary seats are in the four main urban areas, while—by way of contrast—57 percent of the National party's parliamentary seats are rural. Although National has an important reservoir of suburban seats, the Labour party's eggs are very heavily drawn from just one basket. If Labour is to form another Government it must increase its share of the town seats. As Figure 11–6 (the 1981 New Zealand electoral pendulum) shows, if the Labour party cannot capture seats like Gisborne, Invercargill, and New Plymouth, it will be unlikely to win the 1981 general election. Robert Chapman noted in 1972, the "town and rural electorates . . . are the substance of National's strength."[12] This remains true today. Equally, the Labour party must make inroads into the town electorates. They are currently the key to the control of New Zealand's House of Representatives.

At the aggregate level, one final point needs to be made. Table 11–6 sets forth the swings that occurred in both 1975 and 1978 by the safety-marginality of the electorates (as classified before each general election). The fact that the swings to Labour in 1978 were greatest in safe Labour seats and that—almost without exception—they declined through marginal seats to safe National seats is indicative of a return to the Labour fold by 1975 defectors to National and by abstainers. In 1975, the swing to National was highest in safe

[12] Robert Chapman, *Marginals '72* (Auckland: Heinemann, 1972), p. 4.

Labour seats (as logic would predict)[13] but in 1978 the opposite did not occur: the swing to Labour was lowest in safe National seats.

In brief, Labour lost most support in 1975 in its own strongholds: it recouped some of that important ground in 1978. Labour lost the least ground in 1975 in safe National seats, and it made very little headway in them three years later. Had National voters been converted to Labour in large numbers, the opposite might well have occurred: there would have been more National supporters at risk in safe National seats, and thus higher swings to Labour in safe National seats.

Who Did What?

For further light on the New Zealand general election of 1978, it is necessary to turn to survey research data. Brian Murphy's chapter on polling and the election contains data from the National Research Bureau's opinion polls. New Zealand's other major public opinion polling company, the Heylen Research Centre, can also increase our understanding of the 1978 general election. Heylen's long-term results closely paralleled the National Research Bureau's. However, Heylen

---

[13] The logic is based on the following argument. Assume that two parties (let's call them Labour and National) each took 50 percent of the votes throughout an imaginary country in Election One. In blue-ribbon Constituency Q, however, the result was as follows:

	National	Labour
Votes	8,000	2,000
Percentage	80	20

Then Election Two witnesses an overall swing (throughout the country as a whole) of five percentage points to the National party—that is, the countrywide vote splits 55 percent to 45 percent in favor of the National party. However, not unreasonably, this five percentage point swing to the National party is composed of a ten percentage point swing to National by persons who voted Labour at Election One, and a five percentage point swing to Labour by persons who voted National at Election One. The result in Constituency Q would be as follows:

	National	Labour
Votes	7,800	2,200
Percentage	78	22

Therefore, despite a country-wide swing of five percentage points to National, Constituency Q—a safe National seat if ever there was one—experiences a two percentage point swing to Labour. Of course, the converse of this particular illustration is that in terms of swing, Labour would also do worst in seats that were its best, or safest, seats at Election One. For further explorations of this paradox, see for example, Denis P. Altman, "Foreign Policy and the Elections," *Politics*, vol. 2 (May 1967), pp. 60-62; and David Butler and Donald Stokes, *Political Change in Britain* (London: Macmillan, 1969), pp. 303-312.

TABLE 11–7
HEYLEN POLL FINDINGS ON VOTE SWITCHING, 1975–78
(in percentages of respondents)

Recalled Vote, November 1975	Intended Vote, November 1978				Total, 1975
	Labour	National	Social Credit	Values	
Labour	27.4	1.4	4.6	0.6	39.6
National	2.4	32.9	5.2	0.5	47.7
Social Credit	0.8	0.5	5.0	0.1	7.5
Values	1.2	0.1	1.3	1.9	5.2
New Voters	6.7	3.3	3.4	0.7	—
Total, 1978	38.5	38.2	19.5	3.8	100.0
Gain/loss[a]	−1.1	−9.5	+12.0	−1.4	

NOTE: The original sample size was N=1,000 but undecided electors and persons who did not intend to vote have been excluded from the figures used here.

[a] In percentage points.

SOURCE: "Heylen Poll 18th November 1978," p. 16.

also conducted a poll on Saturday, November 18, 1978—exactly a week before the election. The results were embargoed until the polls closed at seven o'clock in the evening on election day, an indication of both Heylen's caution and New Zealand's general timidity in the sphere of public opinion polling by comparison with other Anglo-American democracies. The opinion poll contained dramatic results and predicted the overall division of party support with uncanny precision. Table 11–7 gives the results of Heylen's November 18 survey.[14]

Additional evidence can be drawn from a survey of 600 electors in the Lyttelton constituency. The sample was representative not only of the electorate itself, but also of the nation as a whole—in 1978, 1975, and 1972 (see Table 11–8). Table 11–9 examines the 1978 stated preferences of 1975 voters. In Lyttelton, more than one in ten 1975 National voters supported Labour in 1978, while fewer than one in twenty 1975 Labour voters found National more attractive in 1978. Similarly, National lost more support to the Social Credit Political League than did Labour. Those two factors alone, however, were

---

[14] Details of the poll are contained in "Heylen Poll 18th November 1878," an unpublished sixteen-page document released by the Heylen Research Centre on November 25, 1978. I would like to thank Ken Fink-Jensen, a director of the Heylen Research Centre, for supplying me with copies of his findings.

TABLE 11–8

RESULTS OF LYTTELTON SURVEY AND OF GENERAL ELECTIONS IN LYTTELTON AND NEW ZEALAND, 1972–78
(in percentages)

Election	Party[a]	Lyttelton Survey (N=600)	Official Results, Lyttelton	Official Results, New Zealand
1972	Labour	51.5	56.9	48.4
	National	43.4	40.3	41.5
	Social Credit	4.4	2.4	6.6
	Values	0.7	—	2.0
1975	Labour	40.3	43.1	39.6
	National	51.9	47.9	47.6
	Social Credit	3.0	2.8	7.4
	Values	4.7	6.2	5.2
1978	Labour	46.1	48.6	40.4
	National	45.5	42.0	39.8
	Social Credit	5.8	6.0	16.1
	Values	2.6	2.7	2.4

[a] Votes cast for other candidates have been excluded.

SOURCE: Preelection surveys of 600 voters in the Lyttelton electorate, planned and supervised by the author, from whom further information and data are available. The other statistics are from the official returns, appropriate years.

TABLE 11–9

LYTTELTON SURVEY FINDINGS ON VOTE SWITCHING, 1975–78
(in percentages of respondents)

Recalled Vote, 1975	Intended Vote, 1978				Total, 1975
	Labour	National	Social Credit	Values	
Labour	37.3	1.5	1.3	0.2	40.3
National	5.6	42.9	2.4	1.1	52.0
Social Credit	0.6	0.7	1.7	0.0	3.0
Values	2.6	0.4	0.4	1.3	4.7
Total, 1978	46.1	45.5	5.8	2.6	100.0 (N=466)

SOURCE: Lyttelton survey, November 1978.

not enough to cause National to lose the seat, according to the survey. Labour's gains had to be consolidated by former Values party voters, who plumped for Labour rather than National by a ratio of six to one. Indeed, in Lyttelton in 1978 Labour captured twice as many 1975 Values voters as did the Values party itself!

There are no permanent benchmarks in politics, but trends at least can be discerned. In Lyttelton the data we have for three consecutive elections show large-scale defections from Labour to National in 1975: nearly 20 percent of those who voted Labour in 1972 voted National in 1975. (By contrast, fewer than 5 percent of National's 1972 voters switched to Labour three years later.) In 1978, however, 30 percent of those who voted Labour in 1972 and National in 1975 returned to the Labour fold. National retained the support of fewer than 60 percent of its 1975 Labour converts, while an additional 10 percent voted Social Credit in 1978. Six times as many people voted Labour-National-Labour in the three elections as voted National-Labour-National: evidence, indeed, that as far as the major parties are concerned, the New Zealand general election of 1978 was a reinstating election. The close division of the popular vote between the Labour and National parties throughout the 1960s was repeated in 1978. Just under a quarter of the entire sample of Lyttelton voters voted consistently National in the three general elections; the proportion voting for the Labour party in the three consecutive elections was only slightly higher.

Issues and Leadership. Explaining why voters behaved as they did is more important than describing who did what. Table 11–10 is based on data garnered by the Heylen Research Centre in its postelection public opinion poll of December 2, 1978. Voters were asked "What policy most influenced you to support the party which you supported?"[15] The noticeably different issues cited by supporters of the various political parties are a salient reminder of Austin Mitchell's assessment of the electorate in New Zealand: "two massive armies facing each other across the party lines in mutual incomprehension."[16]

While one-third of National voters said they were most influenced by the state of the economy, an almost paltry 8.2 percent of Labour voters were similarly moved. Not surprisingly, supporters of the Social Credit Political League—which has always laid great stress on

---

[15] "Post-Election Survey December 1978" (Auckland: Heylen Research Centre, December 1978).

[16] Austin Mitchell, *Politics and People in New Zealand* (Christchurch: Whitcombe and Tombs, 1969), p. 215.

TABLE 11–10

POLICY AREA MOST INFLUENCING PARTY CHOICE IN 1978, BY RESPONDENT'S PARTY

(in percentages)

Most Influential Policy Area	Respondent's Party, 1978				All Respondents[a]
	Labour	National	Social Credit	Values	
Economy	8.2	34.3	39.0	—	24.6
Environment	1.2	—	—	50.0	2.4
Superannuation	—	3.7	2.5	—	1.9
Attitude to private enterprise	—	12.0	—	—	5.1
Housing	2.4	—	7.3	—	1.9
Immigration	—	—	—	—	—
Unemployment	15.3	—	—	—	5.1
Abortion	2.3	2.8	4.9	20.0	4.3
Unions	1.2	7.4	—	—	3.5
Sporting contacts	—	—	—	—	—
Party philosophy	37.6	13.9	21.9	—	23.9
Other	22.4	17.6	12.2	20.0	17.5
Don't know	9.4	8.3	12.2	10.0	9.8
Total	100.0	100.0	100.0	100.0	100.0
	(N=85)	(N=108)	(N=41)	(N=10)	(N=256)

[a] Includes supporters of other parties and persons who refused to divulge which party they supported.

SOURCE: "Post-Election Survey December 1978" (Auckland: Heylen Research Centre, December 1978), pp. 22–23.

monetary reform—were the people most concerned about the economy. While about one-sixth of Labour supporters were influenced most by unemployment, less than 1 percent of National voters felt likewise! As might have been expected, Social Credit voters expressed a comparatively high degree of concern about housing; their party has always laid great emphasis on the availability of low-interest loans. And the handful of Values party supporters among the respondents bore out the common view that Values supporters are most concerned about the environment and abortion.

Abortion was expected to be an issue of considerable moment in the general election. Table 11–11 examines the 1978 swing in five classes of seats according to the views on this issue of the incumbent M.P. contesting the seat. (Seats like Te Atatu and West Coast, where

TABLE 11–11

SWING TO LABOUR, BY THE INCUMBENT'S STAND ON ABORTION, 1978
(in percentage points)

Classification of Electorate	Swing to Labour, 1978	Number of Electorates
Conservative National	3.4	(N=30)
Liberal National	3.9	(N=18)
Conservative Labour	5.4	(N=19)
Liberal Labour	7.7	(N=14)
No incumbent or former M.P. running	5.1	(N=11)
New Zealand	5.0	(N=92)

NOTE: Electorates are classified according to the incumbent's party and stand on abortion. Where no incumbent ran but a former M.P. was a candidate, the electorate is classified according to the former M.P.'s position.

SOURCE: Official returns, appropriate years, and McRobie and Roberts, *Election '78*, pp. 60-151. The classification of M.P.s was greatly facilitated by Erich Geiringer, *SPUC 'Em All! Abortion Politics 1978* (Martinborough, New Zealand: Alister Taylor Publishers, 1978), pp. 38-87.

no incumbent was running but where the Labour candidate was a former M.P., are classified according to the position the candidate took on the abortion issue in the House of Representatives prior to his defeat in 1975.) The lowest anti-Government swings occurred in seats where liberal Labour M.P.s were running. The conclusion to emerge from Table 11–11 is straightforward: abortion had no *overall* effect on the general election—as the campaigners on both sides of the abortion issue agree.

It is generally thought that Robert Muldoon's leadership was a clear asset for the National party in 1975. Prior to the 1978 general election, Muldoon was running well ahead of the Labour party's leader, Bill Rowling, in the Heylen Poll's question as to who would make the better prime minister. In late October, for example, 59 percent of those interviewed chose Muldoon, as against a mere 27 percent for Rowling. As Figure 11–7 reveals, this was not an aberration: Muldoon consistently outclassed Rowling during the entire three-year period 1975–1978. However, the Heylen Research Centre's preelection poll on November 18, 1978, recorded a dramatic drop in support for Robert Muldoon. He won the support of only 48 percent of those interviewed, while Bill Rowling's rating climbed to 38 percent.

FIGURE 11–7
THE BETTER PRIME MINISTER, MULDOON OR ROWLING?
RESPONSES TO THE HEYLEN POLL, 1976–1978

Survey question: "Which one of the two, Mr. Muldoon, or Mr. Rowling, would make the better prime minister?"

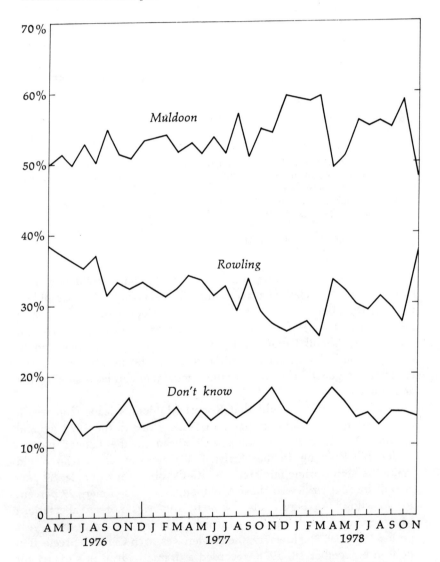

SOURCE: "Heylen Poll 18th November 1978," Heylen Research Centre, November 25, 1978, p. 7.

The 1978 survey in the Lyttelton electorate throws important light on these figures. The survey asked two similar (though slightly wider) questions. First, "Of all the politicians in New Zealand that you know of, who do you personally think would make the best Prime Minister?" And second, "Let's suppose you could cast a vote for Prime Minister separate from your vote for your local M.P. Of all the politicians in New Zealand that you know of, who would you vote for as Prime Minister?" These questions produced similar results. In answer to the first, a quarter of the sample named Muldoon while 15 percent named Rowling. In answer to the second question, 22 percent chose Muldoon and 18 percent Rowling.

But to the second, there were two follow-up questions. Any respondents who did not name one of the four main party leaders were asked who they would "vote for as Prime Minister from amongst the leaders of the four main political parties?" And any who—in answer to this question—chose neither Muldoon nor Rowling, were presented with a choice narrowed still further: "And if the choice was simply between Mr. Muldoon and Mr. Rowling, who would you vote for then as Prime Minister?" The responses to these questions are revealing:

	Muldoon	Rowling
All N.Z. politicians	21.8	18.2
Four party leaders	13.7	13.7
Muldoon and Rowling	9.7	15.3

Thus, told to pare down the alternatives to the leaders of New Zealand's four main political parties, voters accorded Rowling and Muldoon exactly the same degree of support. Instructed to go one step further and choose only between Muldoon and Rowling, the remaining voters in the sample gave the prime minister less than two-thirds the support given to the leader of the opposition.

In other words, if voters initially reluctant to commit themselves to either Muldoon or Rowling are pushed to choose one or the other, Bill Rowling's overall support increases to a point slightly *above* that of Robert Muldoon. Apparently Muldoon's support in the electorate is skin-deep. At bedrock, there is at least as much support for Rowling as there is for the prime minister.

This fact had important consequences for politics in New Zealand in 1978. More than 86 percent of both Muldoon and Rowling "first-wave" supporters in the Lyttelton electorate voted National and Labour respectively; exactly the same proportions (84.1 percent) of Muldoon and Rowling "second-wave" supporters voted National and Labour respectively; and 57 percent of Muldoon and Rowling "third-wave" supporters voted National and Labour respectively. These figures are remarkably similar. But what gave Labour the edge on National in Lyttelton in November 1978 (and, by implication at least, throughout New Zealand) was the fact that Rowling had many more "third-wave" supporters than Muldoon.[17]

A Theoretical Explanation. The 1975 general election was the first election in New Zealand since 1935 in which a major political party obtained less than 40 percent of the votes cast: Labour won only 39.6 percent. Although the Labour party inched its way back over the 40 percent mark three years later, the phenomenon recurred, and the National party won less than 40 percent of the valid votes cast in 1978.

What accounts for the violent swing away from New Zealand's third Labour Government in 1975, and almost as dramatic a swing away from the third National Government three years later? To explain the behavior of New Zealand voters in these two elections, we can turn to the theoretical basis outlined by Angus Campbell, Philip Converse, Warren Miller, and Donald Stokes in *The American Voter* and adopted by David Butler and Donald Stokes in *Political Change in Britain*. Campbell and his colleagues developed and refined the view that voters are primarily influenced by party identification, candidate orientation, and issue orientation. With respect to issues, Campbell, Converse, Miller, and Stokes

> specify at least three conditions to be fulfilled if an issue is to bear upon a person's vote decision:
> 1. The issue must be cognized in some form.
> 2. It must arouse some minimal intensity of feeling.
> 3. It must be accompanied by some perception that one party represents the person's own position better than do the other parties.[18]

David Butler and Donald Stokes define the three conditions in a similar manner and argue that "the sharpest impact on party strength will be made by issues which simultaneously meet all . . . three conditions, that is to say by issues on which attitudes are widely formed,

---

[17] More detailed examinations of the influence of leadership on voting behavior in New Zealand, utilizing the Lyttelton data, are currently being undertaken by Clive Bean, a postgraduate student in political science, and John Henderson, a lecturer in political science, at the University of Canterbury, Christchurch, New Zealand.

[18] Campbell et al., *American Voter*, pp. 169–170.

FIGURE 11–8

THE REGION OF MAXIMUM IMPACT BY ISSUES

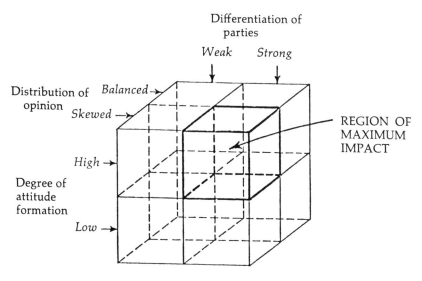

SOURCE: David Butler and Donald Stokes, *Political Change in Britain*, 2nd ed. (London: Macmillan, 1974), p. 294.

on which opinion is far from evenly divided and on which the parties are strongly differentiated in the public's mind."[19]

Butler and Stokes devised "an eight-fold geometric figure" to illustrate the region of maximum impact by political issues on voters' partisan preferences (reproduced here as Figure 11–8). The postal survey of the New Zealand electorate in 1975 conducted by Stephen Levine and Alan Robinson did not work directly within this frame, but it did identify at least eight election issues on which there were strongly unbalanced divisions of opinion within the electorate. These issues are listed in Table 11–12. On the first five issues the Labour party and the National party took widely differing stands; and in each case the view of the majority of voters was favorable to the National party. But while the final three issues (numbers six to eight in Table 11–12) produced a skewed distribution of opinion within the elector-ate, the differentiation between the parties on these issues was almost

---

[19] David Butler and Donald Stokes, *Political Change in Britain*, 2d ed. (London: Macmillan, 1974), pp. 293-294.

TABLE 11–12

POLARIZING ISSUES IN NEW ZEALAND, 1975

(in percentages; differences in percentage points)

	Response		
Survey Statement	Agree	Disagree	Difference
1. The New Zealand Government should stop the All Black rugby team from visiting South Africa next year.	17	77	(60)
2. The Government should take firm action to control wage increases.	73	14	(59)
3. Workers in any industry should not be compelled to join a union if they don't want to.	73	22	(51)
4. New Zealand has been borrowing too much overseas in the last two years.	68	20	(48)
5. Pacific Islanders coming into New Zealand to work should not be permitted to settle permanently in this country.	51	27	(24)
6. New Zealand should withdraw from the ANZUS military defense alliance with Australia and the United States.	16	69	(53)
7. New Zealand should no longer have the Queen as Head of State.	26	68	(42)
8. A woman should have the right to an abortion if she wants one in the first twelve weeks of pregnancy.	57	30	(27)

SOURCE: Stephen Levine and Alan Robinson, *The New Zealand Voter: A Survey of Public Opinion and Electoral Behaviour* (Wellington: Price Milburn for New Zealand University Press, 1976).

certainly weak. It is thus not unreasonable to surmise that the tide of *issues* favored the National party quite considerably in 1975.

What of 1978? The issues that were being talked about by the politicians and that may have aroused the passions of the populace were the state of the economy, unemployment, the power of trade unions, sporting contacts with South Africa, abortion, and leadership. In the absence of harder evidence from survey research, we can only speculate. Nevertheless, it is highly doubtful that any of these issues favored either of the parties because the chances of voters' perceiving a meaningful difference between the Labour and National parties in particular were remote. Labour had placed the country in economic jeopardy from 1972 to 1975; National had done nothing to retrieve it from the quagmire. Indeed, unemployment under the National Government had increased as much as fivefold, but Labour offered no credible schemes for reducing the number of people on the dole.

With regard to trade unions, the National party had talked tough in 1975. For example, it had promised that trade union membership would become voluntary. Not only did this *not* come to pass, but the National Government even went so far as to settle a meat workers' pay dispute by offering the freezing workers $3 million in public funds—and thus won high praise from the unionists and sharp criticism from employers.[20] In 1975 the National party had argued in its manifesto: "if the Rugby Union wishes to invite [the South African team] the Springboks to New Zealand next winter, we will make them welcome."[21] Less than two years later, the National Government disclaimed its own manifesto and endorsed the commonwealth heads of government Gleneagles Agreement and thus undertook to take "every practical step to discourage contact or competition by their nationals with sporting organizations, teams, or sportsmen from South Africa or from any other country where sports are organized on the basis of race, color or ethnic origin."[22] And, finally, the abortion and leadership questions, as we have already seen, do not appear to have decisively affected the outcome.

Faced with two failed Governments, the New Zealand voters had no policy cues to guide them. Instead they acted rationally and behaved as theories of electoral behavior suggested they would: they rejected the two major parties in record proportions, and they voted in accordance with their party identification: 83 percent of National party identifiers voted National, and 92 percent of Labour party identifiers voted Labour.

---

[20] A. J. ("Blue") Kennedy, the national secretary of the Meat Workers' Union, was reported as "happy with Mr. Muldoon's attitude." Kennedy praised the prime minister because "He demonstrated a sense of reality throughout the proceedings. He was not abrasive; he was firm and he was determined to get hold of the facts." *Press* (Christchurch), March 21, 1978. On the other hand, the executive director of the Freezing Companies Association, Peter Blomfield, expressed both "extreme concern" and "horror." *Christchurch Star*, March 20, 1978. The Government's argument to the effect that its $4 million investment had saved the country $100 million in export receipts that were *not* lost as a result of industrial dispute went almost totally unnoticed.

[21] New Zealand National Party, *1975 National Party Manifesto*, condensed version (Wellington: Dominion Headquarters, New Zealand National Party, 1975), p. 9.

[22] The text of the Gleneagles Agreement can be found as an appendix to Luke Trainor, "The Primacy of Internal Policy: National, Sport and External Relations, 1975-78," *Political Science*, vol. 30 (December 1978), pp. 63-78.

The official results for the 1978 New Zealand general election give the voter turnout as 68.41 percent. This would be an all-time low,[23] but as Alan McRobie's chapter on the electoral system makes clear, the electoral rolls for the 1978 election were drastically inflated by errors. An article in the *Christchurch Star* two days before the election estimated the number of excess voters to be 429,754.[24] McRobie has put the figure at "nearly half a million." Assuming that the actual number of imaginary voters on the rolls in November 1978 was somewhere between these two figures—say 465,000—then the turnout was about 84.6 percent. Using provisional figures, Stephen Levine reached an estimate of 83.8 percent.[25] It is important to note that both these estimates are *higher* than the turnout in 1975.

There are two possible explanations for this. The first is that the 1978 general election was a reinstating election in more ways than one. Not only did Labour voters return to the fold and the major parties return to comparative equilibrium, but 1975 nonvoters also began to return to political activity. The second explanation casts doubt upon the validity of the 1975 figure for turnout. If, as seems likely from all available evidence, poor rolls are responsible for a drop in turnout in New Zealand of about three percentage points every time a second election is held in the same set of electoral boundaries (as in 1960 and 1966, to take two other examples), then the official calculations of the turnout in 1975 are too low. It is likely, therefore, that true turnout in 1975 was of the order of 85.5 percent. If this is the case, the elections in New Zealand in the 1970s witnessed a steady decline in turnout: from 89.1 percent in 1972, turnout dropped to roughly 85.5 percent in 1975 and then fell to about 84.6 percent in 1978. This explanation is in line with the preceding argument to the effect that the voters were offered a choice between Tweedledumb and Tweedledumber in 1978—and behaved accordingly. An increase in the rate of abstention from voting would have been entirely rational in 1978 in New Zealand.

Either of these explanations concerning turnout is consistent with aspects of the theoretical explanations put forward in this chapter. The sad fact is that elections in New Zealand have been so badly mismanaged of late that the truth of the matter will probably never be known.

23 "The General Election 1978," *Appendices to the Journals of the House of Representatives* (Wellington: Government Printer, August 1979), p. 113. See also *Christchurch Star*, August 17, 1979.

24 *Christchurch Star*, November 23, 1978.

25 Stephen Levine, *The New Zealand Political System* (Sydney: Allen and Unwin, 1979), p. 195.

But then life in a democracy has never been as neat as one could wish. Even in the hopeful era of the American and French revolutions one conservative observer put it this way: "Monarchy is like a splendid ship, with all sails set; it moves majestically on, then it hits a rock and sinks for ever. Democracy is like a raft. It never sinks but, damn it, your feet are always in the water."[26]

---

[26] Attributed to the American Fisher Ames, quoted in D. W. Brogan, *The Free State: Some Considerations on its Practical Value* (London: Hamish Hamilton, 1945), p. 7.

APPENDIX A

Aftermath —The Election Petitions

Alan McRobie

At 7:30 P.M. on Thursday, May 24, 1979, the speaker of the House of Representatives, Richard Harrison, entered the Debating Chamber carrying a thick pile of papers. Before a hushed gathering he announced that, as a result of the recount of votes ordered by the Electoral Court, Winston Peters had won the Hunua seat with a majority of 192 votes. Immediately, the House ordered the clerk of the writs to attend, and at 7:51 P.M. the name of Malcolm Douglas was struck out and that of Winston Raymond Peters substituted in the official results as the duly elected member of Parliament for Hunua. As Malcolm Douglas left the chamber, escorted by the Labour party's deputy leader, Robert Tizard, chief whip, Russell Marshall, and his brother, Roger Douglas, M.P. for Manurewa, sympathetic applause rippled through the opposition benches.

At 8:42 the same evening Winston Peters, who had caught the 7 P.M. Air New Zealand flight from Auckland to Wellington, entered the chamber to prolonged applause from Government M.P.s and was sworn in as Hunua's member of Parliament—its second in eight days.[1] Thus, fully six months after the 1978 general election, the composition of New Zealand's Thirty-ninth Parliament was finally settled.

Nine days earlier, in the Wellington Supreme Court, Labour's Margaret Shields had finally conceded defeat in her attempt to have the Kapiti election result reversed. The court's ruling that the principles established during the hearing of the Hunua Election Petition would apply equally in the Kapiti hearing had undermined any chance she might have had of winning the seat on a recount. This left the way clear for Barry Brill, the incumbent M.P. who had been declared

---

[1] Douglas had been formally sworn in as Hunua's M.P. on May 16, the day Parliament reconvened after the 1978 election.

reelected with a wafer-thin majority—twenty-three votes—only after a magisterial recount, to be confirmed as Kapiti's member of Parliament for the next three years.

Hunua

The 1979 Hunua Election Petition is likely to become a landmark in New Zealand's constitutional and electoral history. The only petition to be heard in detail for more than thirty years, it was the first to be considered since the electoral rules had been extensively revised in 1956. It also subjected to judicial scrutiny the rules governing the registration of electors enacted in 1975 by the third Labour Government, which had become the focal point for a great deal of bitter interparty debate. An unusual aspect was the very large number of votes challenged—1,158 by the petitioner and 334 by the respondent. Collectively, these accounted for more than 8 percent of all votes cast in the electorate, and although many challenges were abandoned on both sides during the course of the hearing, the number of votes questioned for one reason or another was still far greater than ever before. Finally, since Parliament was in session when the recount of votes was completed, Malcolm Douglas became the first M.P. since 1873 to be expelled from Parliament after he had taken his seat.

In the official election result announced by the returning officer on December 14, 1978, the Labour party's candidate, Malcolm Douglas, received 7,935 votes to give him a majority of 301 over National's Winston Peters.[2] This result was something of a surprise, for it represented a two-party swing to Labour of nearly nine percentage points, more than double the average swing to Labour throughout the country. Recriminations followed immediately, with Labour and National accusing each other of electoral irregularities in their efforts to win the seat,[3] and the possibility of bringing an election petition to try to overturn the result was discussed openly by National party officials. On January 18, 1979 (more than two weeks before the deadline for petitions, which is forty-nine days after the declaration of the official result) Peters and two Hunua electors filed a petition in the Auckland Supreme Court in which they claimed that Peters was and should have been declared duly elected or, alternatively, that Douglas had not been properly elected and the election should therefore be voided.

---

[2] Peters received 7,634 votes. There were also two minor party candidates, Geoffrey Morell (Social Credit) who received 2,410 votes, and Peter Robinson (Values) who received 275.

[3] *Christchurch Star*, November 27, 1978—the Monday after the election.

251

The court began hearing the petition on March 19 and sat for a total of thirty-three days. Its judgment, delivered on May 11, ordered a scrutiny and recount of all votes cast in the Hunua election in accordance with the specific decisions reached. This was completed on May 24, and the result, delivered post haste to the speaker of the House of Representatives late that afternoon, was announced when the House reassembled after the tea adjournment.

The Allegations. Winston Peters initially listed twenty reasons why he should have been declared elected. A number were subsequently abandoned, and the court was ultimately required to adjudicate on eleven allegations:

1. Votes cast by persons originally enrolled in Western Maori or another Maori electoral district had been allowed, contrary to Section 43B of the 1956 Electoral Act.
2. Votes cast by persons resident in electorates other than Hunua had been allowed even though these persons were not entitled to be registered in Hunua.
3. Votes had been cast and allowed in the names of electors who were dead, were overseas, did not vote, or did not exist.
4. Some special votes had been allowed even though the voters' names were not on any Hunua roll or were not entitled to be on that roll.
5. Names had been wrongly deleted from the Hunua roll, and as a consequence some valid votes had not been included in the count.
6. Some special votes had not been counted even though the electors were entitled to be enrolled and had taken steps to become enrolled.
7. More ballot papers had been issued on election day than there were electors recorded as having voted.
8. Douglas and/or his agents had endeavored to influence voters in a manner contrary to Section 127 of the 1956 Electoral Act.
9. Officials conducting the election had refused to put certain questions to electors when asked to do so by Peters's scrutineers.
10. The votes of electors who voted more than once had been allowed.
11. Ballot papers marked in a manner other than that authorized by Section 106 of the 1956 Electoral Act had been wrongly allowed and counted.[4]

---

[4] No. M38/79 Supreme Court of New Zealand, Auckland Registry, *Hunua Election Petition: Judgement*, May 11, 1979, pp. 2-3 (précis).

Douglas's response was to submit ten objections of his own:

1. Winston Peters was not a valid candidate and therefore had not been entitled to be elected.

2. Peters's own vote had been wrongly allowed.

3. Some of the persons listed as being on both the Hunua and the Western Maori rolls, and those alleged to be wrongly on the Hunua roll, were validly registered as electors in Hunua.

4. Some ordinary and special votes were disallowed when, in fact, they had been cast by electors entitled to be enrolled in Hunua and who had taken steps to become enrolled.

5. Some votes had been allowed which were cast by electors who did not have the necessary residential qualification to be enrolled in Hunua.

6. Peters had breached Section 103 of the 1956 Electoral Act by speaking to electors inside polling booths.

7. Scrutineers appointed by Peters had also breached the provisions of Section 103 of the act by speaking to voters in polling booths.

8. Peters had endeavored to influence voters in a manner contrary to Section 127 of the 1956 Electoral Act.

9. In response to the complaint by Peters that officials conducting the election had failed to put certain questions to electors when asked to do so by scrutineers, Douglas argued that Peters and his agents had acted outside the scope of, and in contravention of, certain sections of the 1956 Electoral Act.

10. Some ballot papers had been rejected as informal even though the voters' intentions had been clearly indicated.[5]

These allegations illustrate clearly the animosity existing between the two candidates and their respective party organizations as both sides sought to use every argument possible, both legal and moral, in support of their claim to the seat.[6] A number of these allegations

---

[5] Ibid., pp. 3-4.

[6] A close study of document M38/79 *Hunua Election Petition: Notes of Evidence* reveals clearly how far *both* major parties were prepared to go to win the parliamentary seat. For example, a Labour party organizer admitted that she had signed special vote declaration forms as a witness to the applicant's signature although they had not been completed in her presence. The party organization was also very active in the months before election day in persuading potential voters to register in Hunua without first checking to make sure that they were not already enrolled elsewhere. For their part, National party workers clearly had a very thorough knowledge of the contents of the Electoral Act and were determined to use it to the full to secure their objectives. During polling National party scrutineers challenged the right of a sizable number of electors to vote in Hunua. The effect of this was to delay considerably the voting procedures and thus create long queues of voters because each voter challenged was required to sign a declaration to the effect that he was entitled to vote in

were rejected by the court, and the judgment ultimately centered on six main questions.

(1) Was Winston Peters a valid candidate? Peters is a Maori who, at the time of the 1976 census, had exercised his option to be enrolled as a Maori elector. His name had therefore been duly entered on the Northern Maori electoral roll. Subsequently, Peters had moved his residence to the Auckland suburb of Howick, which is within the Hunua General Electoral District and the Western Maori Electoral District. In May 1978, after winning the National party's nomination for Hunua, he had applied for registration as an elector at his new address and had been placed on the Hunua roll. Counsel for Douglas argued that Peters could not transfer his enrollment from a Maori to a general roll because, having chosen to be registered as a Maori elector at the time of the census, he was prevented by Section 43B of the Electoral Act from changing his option before the next census, in 1981. It was claimed that by moving to Howick, Peters had lost his qualification to be included on the Northern Maori roll, that he could not legally register on the Hunua roll, and that he had failed to register on the Western Maori roll. Thus, Douglas's counsel reasoned, since Peters was not legally registered on any roll he was not entitled to be a candidate.[7]

Had the court accepted this view the petitioner's case would have collapsed. But the argument put forward by the respondent was not upheld. The court's decision was based on two main grounds: that an elector is a person who is registered *or who is qualified to be registered* as an elector (which Peters undoubtedly was), and a rather obscure section of the Electoral Act which stated that the nomination or election of any person was not to be questioned on the ground that he or she was registered on a wrong roll.[8] It was held that Peters was

---

the electorate and that he had not previously voted that day. It was averred that many voters became tired of waiting and left the polling place although there was no evidence to suggest that they had not gone to another. The petitioner was also successful in overturning some special votes cast at a booth in the adjoining Papatoetoe electorate where it could be shown that the voter had been within two miles of a booth in his own electorate at some stage during the day. The court was thus required to impose a narrow legal decision which effectively removed the votes of some persons who were otherwise properly entitled to have their votes counted.

[7] According to Section 25 of the Act, ". . . every person registered as an elector of any electoral district, but no other person, is qualified to be a candidate and to be elected . . ."

[8] This section had been inserted into the electoral law in the dying hours of the 1925 parliamentary session to clarify the position of some sitting members because doubts had been raised as to the validity of their enrollment and, therefore, their eligibility to vote.

entitled to be registered on the Western Maori roll, that he *was* registered on the Northern Maori roll, and that he was therefore entitled to be a candidate.

This decision led to a very curious situation. Although his candidacy was valid, Peters's own vote, cast in Hunua, was disallowed because he was not entitled to be registered there. Nor could he have cast a valid vote in Northern Maori since he had lost his residential qualification by moving to Howick. The court has, in effect, ruled that it is possible for a person to be a candidate and win election to Parliament even though he or she cannot cast a valid vote in any electorate.

(2) Were the electoral rolls properly compiled? From the time the first computer printout became available at the end of April 1978 the state of the new electoral rolls was severely criticized. People who claimed to have completed reenrollment cards were unable to find their names listed—yet the names of many who had long since moved away from a given address were still included, and many found that their names were entered more than once. Public panic, stimulated at least in part by the Labour party's persistent attacks on both the Government and the Electoral Office and also by its extensive campaign to persuade all people whose names did not appear on the printed rolls to complete registration cards regardless of whether they had already enrolled, resulted in a rush of additional registration in the three months before the general election. By the time enrollments finally closed[9] there were nearly half a million more names listed than there were eligible voters.

Douglas's counsel alleged that the compilation of the roll was so defective that it did not meet the requirements laid down in the Electoral Act. Given this, it was argued, the election should be voided and a by-election held.

The court regarded this allegation as a "serious constitutional issue" warranting a thorough examination. The real electoral roll, the judges pointed out, is a "compilation of cards," and to enter an elector's name on the roll is to add his registration card to this file. Although the Electoral Act requires that each electorate officer maintain the roll for his electoral district, it was decided in August 1976 to centralize all enrollment cards at the Chief Electoral Office in Lower Hutt.[10] While the court agreed that this procedure was irregular, it

[9] Enrollments close at 6 P.M. on the day the writs are issued.

[10] The purpose of this decision was to simplify the checking of enrollments for duplications and transfers. See *Report of the Committee of Inquiry into the Administration of the Electoral Act, Wellington,* August 1979 (typescript), Section 6.

nevertheless held that the conduct of the election was not materially affected thereby. It therefore rejected the claim that the election should be voided on this ground.

Even more significant was the court's ruling that the "carrying forward" of names from the pre-1976 rolls was valid for general rolls. Until 1975 all electors were required to reenroll within three months of any change in electoral boundaries. When the Labour Government provided for reenrollment to take place in conjunction with the quin-quennial census, the requirement to reenroll after each redistribution of electoral boundaries was dropped, and the court held that the phrase "who have applied for registration as electors"[11] related to *any* past application for enrollment. This view appears to imply that, provided an elector remains at the same residence, an application for enrollment made many years ago still holds good. This, clearly, was not Parliament's intention, for it undermines the whole rationale for conducting a general reenrollment along with the census—the prep-aration of accurate and up-to-date electoral rolls.

The court, however, took a quite different view of the "carrying forward" procedure for Maori rolls. Under the 1975 legislation all Maoris (that is, persons of New Zealand Maori ancestry who wished to be regarded as Maoris for electoral purposes) were required to choose which roll—Maori or general—they wished to be registered on. Any Maori who failed to exercise either option, even if previously registered on a Maori roll, was not thereafter legally registered on *any* roll. The judgment noted that "the Maori rolls compiled and used for the 1978 General Election doubtless contained a large number of persons who were not qualified as Maori electors because they were carried forward without having exercised the entitling option." The effect of this decision, the court observed, was that had the petition related to a Maori electorate the likely outcome would have been a voiding of *all* elections in Maori electorates because the rolls included an unknown number of unqualified persons. But, as the petition be-fore the court related to a general electorate, no such problem existed and the hearing could proceed. This disposed of the second of the respondent's grounds, that the irregular compilation of the roll was a good and proper reason for the election in Hunua to be voided.[12]

(3) *Could non-Maori electors who had chosen to be registered on a Maori roll later change to a general roll?* Winston Peters challenged the validity of over 400 votes cast by people who were alleged to have opted to be placed on a Maori roll at the time of the 1976 census but

---

[11] 1956 Electoral Act, Section 60(3).
[12] *Hunua Judgement*, pp. 30-31.

who later registered on the Hunua general roll. Evidence submitted by Douglas's counsel showed that many were in fact Pacific Islanders and some were even Europeans who had been included on a Maori roll because they had ticked the box on the enrollment card alongside the statement "I am a Maori and wish to be registered as an elector of a Maori electoral district."[13] The court held that the information supplied by electors when completing the enrollment cards must be presumed to be correct and that "the enrollment on Maori Electoral Rolls of persons who were not entitled to be so enrolled because they were not New Zealand Maoris was brought about as a result of the elector's own choice ... and he must accept the consequences of his own error."[14]

The key question was whether an elector who had initially placed him or herself on a Maori roll (although not qualified to be there) and who later completed an enrollment card with the intention of enrolling in a general electorate was entitled to cast a valid vote in the latter. The court's view was that entitlement to enroll, not qualification for enrollment, was the substantive issue and that, in terms of Section 40 of the Electoral Act, no one was entitled to be registered on more than one electoral roll. Thus, those who had registered on a Maori roll at the time of the census and who later registered as electors on the Hunua general roll were not entitled to cast a valid vote in Hunua *unless they had first notified the Electorate Officer of the Maori electorate, in writing, that they wished to have their name removed so that it could be placed on the proper roll.*[15] This can only be interpreted to mean that the completion of a new enrollment card was not deemed to be sufficient notice in writing—yet electors moving from one general electorate to another are able to transfer to a new roll simply by completing another enrollment card once they have lived in their new electorate for at least three months.[16]

---

[13] As defined in the Electoral Act, the word "Maori" is restricted to members of New Zealand's aboriginal race and their descendents. But Cook Islanders, of whom there were 18,610 living in New Zealand at the time of the 1976 census, are officially known as "Cook Island Maoris" and were asked to identify themselves as such on the 1976 census schedule. It is not, therefore, surprising that a number responded positively to the question included on the enrollment card despite the fact that the "Information for Electors" printed on the *front* of the card explains the nature of the "Special Provisions for Maoris." (To be able to read *and understand* these instructions an elector needs to be able to read at a level which would enable him to cope with the work undertaken by a senior secondary school student, sixteen or seventeen years old.)

[14] *Hunua Judgement*, p. 44.

[15] Ibid., pp. 49-50.

[16] During the hearing of the evidence the deputy chief electoral officer, Peter Horne, stated that Winston Peters's enrollment cards for Northern Maori and

The ruling meant that 212 votes that had previously been accepted as valid were disallowed. Some had been cast by Maoris who had breached Section 43B of the Electoral Act by enrolling in Hunua after they had exercised their option to be registered as electors on a Maori roll: the decision to disallow these votes cannot be questioned. But a significant number of votes disallowed in this category were cast by Pacific Islanders who were not qualified to be included on a Maori roll in the first place.[17] The legal requirement that an elector make a written request to have his name removed from a wrong roll *before* he can register legally on the correct one is a little-known provision, even among educated Europeans. Undoubtedly, the court's ruling effectively prevented some people from casting a valid vote, and the available evidence suggests strongly that those most disadvantaged belonged to a minority ethnic group. This was clearly contrary to Parliament's intention as expressed by M.P.s during the 1956 debate on the Electoral Act. For example, the then minister of justice, Jack Marshall, repeatedly emphasized that "no qualified person should be deprived of the opportunity to register or to vote. In other words, everybody who is entitled to vote should be able to vote."[18] Marshall also noted another principle accorded bipartisan support by the select committee that had studied the bill: "that where an election is contested the court should look to the substance and not to the technicality in deciding whether or not votes should be allowed or whether incorrect practices have occurred."[19] It is very difficult indeed to reconcile the court's ruling with these sentiments.

(4) *Did some people vote when they were not legally entitled to?* In order to qualify as an elector of a particular electoral district a person is required to have lived in the electorate "for not less than three months immediately preceding the date of his application for registration."[20] Where an elector moves permanently to a new address,

---

Hunua "came together in a national alphabetical sorting of all rolls" after the election, and since the second card did not match the Maori option stated on the first card his name was deleted from the Hunua record and he was enrolled in Western Maori. See *New Zealand Herald*, March 20, 1979.

[17] *Hunua Notes of Evidence*, pp. 7-97 passim; *Hunua Judgement*, pp. 56-63. All voters challenged were numbered consecutively for reference purposes. From the *Notes of Evidence* it is possible to determine the ethnicity of individual voters, and the *Judgement* itself makes it possible to determine which of the challenged votes were disallowed. It should be stressed that the numbering of voters (not votes) was instituted to protect the secrecy of the ballot; the court was not concerned to know how each individual voter voted.

[18] *Parliamentary Debates*, 1956, vol. 310, p. 2840.

[19] Ibid., pp. 2840-2841.

[20] 1956 Electoral Act, Section 39(1) (d).

and once he has resided there for three months, his residential qualification arising from the first address lapses and he is obliged to complete a new enrollment card. Failure to notify the Electorate Officer of the new address is an offense punishable by a fine not exceeding $2, although where a person changes residence within an electorate, failure to do so does not disqualify him from voting in the next election.[21] Since New Zealanders are a very mobile people (about 9 percent change residence each year) it follows that all electorates are likely to have rolls which include the names of some persons no longer qualified by residence to vote there.

The court disallowed ninety votes cast by people whose names were included on the printed rolls for Hunua but who had either gained a residential qualification in another electorate or moved elsewhere and thus lost their entitlement to be registered from the address recorded on the roll. In addition, another twenty-two votes were disallowed because the electors concerned did not have the requisite residential qualification to be enrolled in Hunua. Eleven of these, although included in the Hunua roll, lived at addresses located outside the boundaries of that electorate; another four were shown to have not completed the three month residential requirement at the date enrollments closed; and seven had their principal residence in another electorate.

While there can be no doubt that most, if not all, of these votes were properly disallowed, two questions arise. First, included among those who had lost their entitlement to vote in Hunua were seventy-eight voters who had moved away from the address given on the roll and whose current address was unknown. Counsel for the respondent argued that this did not necessarily mean that they had shifted to another electorate and that the onus was on the petitioner to show that the voter in question had acquired the right to register in another electorate before he lost his right to vote in Hunua. The court's view was the opposite: that for these votes to remain valid it was up to the respondent to show that the electors were still qualified to vote in Hunua. In disallowing these seventy-eight votes the court commented that it was satisfied that "the majority" had been cast by electors who had "lost their residential qualification having permanently left the address at which they are registered."[22] Yet a niggling doubt remains: it is just possible that a few electors who were properly qualified had their votes disallowed because they had failed to notify the electorate officer of their change of address within the

[21] Ibid., Sections 44-45.
[22] *Hunua Judgement*, pp. 66-67.

electorate—an omission that should not, of itself, result in a vote's being disallowed.

The second question relates to the eleven electors whose names were included on the Hunua roll but at addresses which, the court found, lay clearly beyond the electorate's boundaries. How, then, did they come to be included on the Hunua roll at all? If, as seems certain, these electors supplied the Electoral Office with correct information, the error which resulted in their inclusion in Hunua must have been an administrative one. If this is indeed the case, eleven voters at least appear to have been disfranchised through no fault of their own.

(5) *Were there any corrupt or illegal practices which may have· affected the outcome of the election?* The Electoral Act defines corrupt practices as personation (plural voting, voting in the name of another person, or attempting to do these), bribery, treating, and undue influence. Illegal practices are limited to paying to have election notices displayed, using loudspeakers in a public place for campaigning without authority, providing money for illegal purposes, or inducing disqualified persons to vote.[23] The essential difference between the two types of offense is that corrupt practices, if proved, may result in an election's being voided, but this does not apply to illegal practices. In addition, there are a number of offenses, for example interfering with or influencing voters on polling day while the poll is being held, punishable on conviction by a fine or even imprisonment.

The petitioner and the respondent had each alleged that election-day illegalities had been committed by the other party, but these were not proved to the court's satisfaction. Personation, however, was proved in thirteen instances, and twenty-two votes were disallowed as a result. In one or two instances the plural voting appears to have stemmed from stupidity rather than deliberate malpractice, but most of the evidence pointed to outright dishonesty by a handful of voters. In its Special Report to Parliament the court noted its concern at the ease with which personation could occur. To eliminate this abuse it recommended that

> an acceptable system of identification, if only for electoral purposes, would be of immense value in the running of an election, especially in areas where there are a number of non-European voters, and that some form of identification could give greater confidence in the validity of the ballot

---

[23] 1956 Electoral Act, Sections 140-148.

and could avoid to a large measure those abuses which have been revealed in our consideration of this case.[24]

Although somewhat larger than normal, the number of proven plural votes was still very small compared with the total number of votes cast. The suggestion that voters be required to produce identity cards in order to obtain voting papers is anathema to the overwhelming bulk of New Zealanders. Even if it were effective (despite the inevitable problems arising from lost and misplaced cards), it would be rather like using a sledgehammer to crack a nut. Printed electoral rolls that were both accurate and up-to-date would achieve the same goal without antagonizing the electorate.

(6) How should a voter be required to show his preference for a particular candidate? Both Section 106 of the Electoral Act and the ballot paper require a voter to indicate his choice "by striking out the name of every candidate except the one for whom he wishes to vote."[25] While this seems clear and unequivocal, it has, in the past, been regarded as being qualified by Section 115 which deals with informal votes. This clause requires returning officers to reject

> any ballot paper that does not clearly indicate the candidate for whom the voter decided to vote:
> Provided that no ballot paper shall be rejected as informal by reason only of some informality in the manner in which it has been dealt with by the voter if it is otherwise regular, and if in the opinion of the Returning Officer the intention of the voter is clearly indicated.

Traditionally, the New Zealand practice has been to encourage as many electors as possible to record their votes. Parliament's view, as expressed by Jack Marshall in 1956, was that "the principle that should be followed is that if the intention of the voter is clear, then his vote ought to count."[26] This sentiment has been applied by returning officers throughout the country for the past twenty years, and it was reiterated in a circular memorandum prepared by the chief electoral officer and sent to all returning officers just before the election. This set out guidelines for dealing with a "party" (as distinct from a "candidate") vote and with votes indicated by ticks or

---

[24] *Hunua Election Petition: Special Report*, p. 10.

[25] The first instruction printed on the ballot paper reads: "Strike out the name of every candidate *except the one for whom you wish to vote.*" To many Maoris and Pacific Islanders, particularly those working in unskilled occupations, the usual meaning of the word "strike" is to "down tools and walk off the job." But if such an elector were to seek some other explanation of the word "strike" as it appears on a ballot paper he would probably be told that it meant to "cross out." Clearly, colloquial expressions can be very confusing.

[26] *Parliamentary Debates*, 1956, vol. 310, p. 2842.

crosses. In part the memorandum stated: "It is fundamental to our electoral system that everyone qualified as an elector should cast a vote and it follows that an 'informal' vote is only where the intention of the elector is *NOT CLEAR.*" The document concluded:

> REMEMBER—IS THE INTENTION OF THE ELECTOR
> CLEAR?
> IF SO, ALLOW IT,
> IF NOT—INFORMAL and thus
> DISALLOWED.[27]

The court took the opposite view. Section 106 was held to be mandatory: voters were required to exercise their franchise exactly as instructed for the vote to be allowed. By requiring both that a vote be regular and the intention clear, the court held that Section 115 left returning officers little room for discretion. On the basis of this ruling, all ballot papers which had been marked with ticks and/or crosses were informal.[28] In giving its decision the court noted that most of New Zealand's previous electoral courts had ruled against accepting ticks and crosses and that it "did not approve of" the two 1926 decisions (Westland and Lyttelton) where they had been accepted as valid.

The same reasoning led the court to reject all votes where electors had expressed a preference for a political party but not its candidate. One of the changes introduced by Labour in 1975 was a law providing that party designations be included on ballot papers, in brackets, immediately after each candidate's name. The intention

---

[27] Department of Justice, Circular R/O 23/1978, *To All Returning Officers,* November 24, 1978. There is a fine distinction between an "informal" and a "disallowed" vote. An "informal" vote is one where the voter has met all the preconditions for casting a vote—that is, the residential requirements have been fulfilled and the elector has completed an application for registration as a voter— but fails to indicate his choice of candidate clearly and unequivocally on the ballot paper. By contrast, a vote which is "disallowed" is rejected because the person casting it is not qualified to be registered or, if qualified, has not taken the trouble to register as an elector, or because some error has been made in completing a special vote declaration form. Disallowed votes are, therefore, invalid.

[28] *Hunua Judgement,* pp. 90-107. The court accepted, for example, that if a voter had inadvertently struck out the names of all the candidates listed and had then written the name of one of them on the ballot paper, this would be acceptable as an indication of clear intent. (In my view the court may have erred in judging the phrase "if it is otherwise regular" to mean that a vote had to be "dealt with in accordance with the provision of Section 106" if it was to be adjudged formal. I think it can be argued that this phrase refers to the regularity of the ballot paper in all respects *other* than in the way it has been dealt with by the voter. If this interpretation is valid, Section 115(2) (a) (ii) cannot be held to apply to Section 106 because that section does no more than specify the action to be taken by a voter in dealing with his ballot paper.)

was to assist voters to identify the candidate of their choice; nevertheless the Electoral Act still required electors to choose between *candidates,* and the court thus held that "party votes" were inadmissible. In fact, the court went even further to observe:

> The purported party vote in our view is a particularly objectionable method to allow because all it may indicate is that a voter has a preference for one particular party but that the candidate who is representing that party is not one for whom the voter wishes to cast a vote. This could be for many reasons: dislike of the candidate's views on a particular subject, or a feeling that at that time the particular candidate would not be a proper person to be a Parliamentary representative.[29]

Although research into voting behavior both in New Zealand and elsewhere shows that present-day electors vote overwhelmingly for a party and not a person, the court chose to adopt a literal interpretation of a law first written in its present form in 1881—long before mass-based parties appeared in the political arena. To some degree, then, the third Labour Government had been hoist with its own petard.

As a consequence 378 votes which had been accepted by the returning officer as valid during the official count were declared informal. On 354 of them voters had struck out three of the party labels while leaving the fourth unmarked. But while the intention of these voters may appear to be beyond doubt, the court's ruling that the law required them to choose between candidates, not parties, meant that these votes were rejected during the court-ordered recount.

The Recount. The overall effect of these decisions was that nearly 900 votes treated as valid during the official count in December 1978 were disallowed on the ground that the person casting the vote was not qualified to do so (503) or rejected as informal (378). In addition, 12 special votes which had previously been disallowed by the returning officer were restored,[30] and 31 votes originally declared informal were allowed. As a result the total number of votes counted dropped by 815.[31]

---

[29] *Hunua Judgement*, p. 106.

[30] The reasons given were: voter's identity established (2), address within Hunua (1), voter qualified (3), name wrongly deleted from roll (3), voter had made correct application for enrollment (2), and vote disallowed by mistake (1).

[31] There is some dispute about the accuracy of these figures. On June 7, Richard Prebble (M.P. for Auckland Central) pointed out in a parliamentary question that, although the court had disallowed 491 votes, the difference between the number of votes counted during the official count in December 1978 was only 468 greater than the number counted in the court-ordered recount. The minister of justice, Jim McLay, could not throw any light on this discrepancy.

Of the 503 votes disallowed by the court, 158 were special votes. A number were rejected for reasons which apply to many special votes—that the elector was not qualified to vote (that is, he had not taken the necessary steps to become enrolled within the time limits prescribed by the Electoral Act, or he did not live in Hunua and was therefore not qualified to vote in that electorate), or that the special vote declaration form had not been signed by the voter or properly witnessed. Even so, over one-third were cast by electors who lived outside the Hunua electorate even though the addresses at which they lived appeared, in many instances, on the Hunua roll. How these votes came to be allowed in the first place is still not clear, but it does seem certain that the checking of special vote declarations was less than exhaustive. The available evidence suggests that, in part at least, this situation may have arisen as a result of the earlier decision to centralize all enrollment cards at the Chief Electoral Office. In the week following the election that office was inundated with some 56,000 special vote declarations (about one-quarter of the total) sent in by returning officers because they did not have the requisite information to determine their validity. According to counsel for Douglas,

> because of the pressure, the staff involved were instructed when checking whether someone was entitled to vote to check whether there was a card in that voter's name and address. No attention was paid to the electorate. As a result, there was no check that the voter resided in the electoral district.[32]

The Certificate of Result sent to the speaker of the House gave Winston Peters 7,507 votes to Malcolm Douglas's 7,315. It is clear from these figures that Douglas was most affected by the court's rulings; 76.1 percent of the votes disallowed or declared informal had been cast in his favor compared with only 15.6 percent for Peters. In view of the very large number of Pacific Islanders whose names appear in the lists of disallowed votes it seems highly probable that the literacy level among this group of voters played an important part in the final result.[33]

Kapiti

The Hunua judgment and the court's ruling that its findings had established clear-cut precedents meant that the Kapiti election petition

---

[32] "First Respondent—Preliminary Comments on Evidence," p. 13.
[33] *Hunua Petition: Special Report*, pp. 8-11.

brought by the Labour candidate, Margaret Shields, collapsed. Although significantly fewer votes had been challenged by both petitioner and respondent (National's Barry Brill), the allegations listed by both parties were substantially those traversed by the court in the Hunua hearing.

On election night Margaret Shields had led the incumbent, Barry Brill, by nine votes, and against all expectations her majority had increased to fifteen when the official result was declared. Brill refused to accept the declaration and immediately applied for a magisterial recount. A magistrate supervising a recount is vested with all the powers of a returning officer and may reverse decisions taken by that officer during the official count. Walter Willis, the magistrate appointed to supervise the recount, outlined four principles to help determine the validity of votes which were questioned by scrutineers for the two principal candidates: (1) that the "party vote" would be accepted where the voter had struck out the names of three of the parties and had left the fourth untouched, (2) that ticks and crosses on ballot papers, in any number or combination were to be treated as informal, as were (3) ballot papers marked with something other than a tick or cross, and (4) ballot papers in which all names had been crossed out and a tick was placed beside the name of one of the candidates.[34] The recount conducted under these rules eliminated eighty-three votes previously counted as formal and, in doing so, reversed the result. Barry Brill was declared elected by twenty-three votes.

After investigation, Margaret Shields decided to petition the Supreme Court to overturn the result or to have the election voided. Her claim to the seat was based on two main grounds: that a number of votes had been improperly allowed or disallowed (including, in the latter instance, votes not marked in strict accordance with the

---

[34] *Kapiti Petition: Ruling of Walter Willis* (no date). The last ruling was challenged by the scrutineer for Shields on the grounds that since the word "stet" written alongside the name of one candidate (all names being crossed out) had been allowed as valid, ticks alongside the name of a candidate must also be accepted in the interest of uniformity. To do otherwise, argued the memorandum, "unfairly discriminates against electors who have no knowledge of latin either through lack of education or lack of knowledge of the printing trade." (Memorandum of Jeff Forman, scrutineer for Margaret Shields, December 19, 1978.) Willis's response, as recorded in a further ruling, was, "it is unclear to me whether the elector had a change of heart by first ticking one candidate's name and then striking out the lot or alternatively by crossing out all the names and then having a change of heart and adding a tick." It should also be noted that Willis's decision on the question of the acceptability of ticks and crosses differed from that given by the magistrates supervising the recounts in Hastings and Western Hutt a few days earlier.

provision of Section 106 of the Electoral Act but where the voter's intention was believed to be clear) and that errors and omissions by the electorate officer and the chief electoral officer had prevented the accurate compilation of an electoral roll for the electoral district. ⸰ Brill counter-claimed on each of these grounds and added a few allegations of his own—plural voting, the votes of people enrolled on a Maori roll at the time of the census and who had subsequently enrolled in Kapiti, two votes marked "Labour," and seventeen votes "cast on pieces of paper not being ballot papers prescribed by Regulation 12(2). . . ."[35]

Following the decision that the Hunua judgment would be applied to her own petition, Shields reassessed her position and concluded that its net effect would be to increase Barry Brill's 23 vote majority by at least 180. Without doubt she also took into account the court's decision to allow the respondent to amend his list of objections to include some 500 "party votes," previously accepted as formal, which would clearly increase his majority even further.[36] When the court reconvened after a twenty-four-hour adjournment Margaret Shields offered no evidence in support of her claim to the seat and Barry Brill was declared to have been duly elected M.P. for Kapiti.[37]

Issues and Implications

The Hunua judgment has undoubtedly clarified many aspects of the electoral law as it is currently written. It has provided a body of case law in an area where little or none previously existed. Clear-cut rules as to what constitutes an electoral roll, the strict procedures to be followed by electors when changing their electoral registration from one district to another, the constraints surrounding the issuing and acceptance of special votes, and the validity of ballot papers not marked exactly as instructed, have all been established for the first time. Undoubtedly, with such precise directives as guides, the task of returning officers will be made very much more straightforward.

In some respects a more equitable decision might have been for the Hunua election to have been voided. There was undoubtedly confusion over the correct enrollment procedures, and this com-

---

[35] No. 41/79 Supreme Court of New Zealand, Wellington Registry. *Kapiti Election Petition: First Respondent's List of Objections*, April 6, 1979, pp. 4-5. (The booths where these votes were cast had apparently run out of ballot papers and some emergency ballot papers had therefore been drawn up on plain paper.)
[36] *Kapiti Election Petition: Motion to Amend List of Objections*, May 14, 1979.
[37] *Kapiti Election Petition: Judgement*, May 15, 1979, p. 2.

pounded the difficulties arising from the failure of many potential electors to complete enrollment cards at census time and the subsequent administrative decision to "carry forward" entries from the existing rolls. But to have taken this action on the ground that the roll for that electorate had been inadequately, improperly, incorrectly, or even illegally compiled would have been contrary to the greater general good. To have come to this decision would have been to bring the entire 1978 general election into question because similar imperfections in the electoral rolls were likely to be found right across the country.

Even so, the court seems to have reinforced the double standard for Maori and non-Maori representation. By ruling that it was right and proper to carry forward the names of electors registered on the 1975 general rolls but that this was not the case with the equivalent Maori rolls, it has placed yet another barrier between Maori and non-Maori in the political arena. Non-Maoris who fail to fulfill their legal obligations in the matter of enrollment are excused; Maoris in exactly the same position may be penalized. Furthermore, the court commented that had the Hunua petition related to a Maori electorate, all elections in Maori electorates probably would have been voided because their rolls included an unknown number of unqualified persons; but this comment appears to have been beyond the court's competence to make. Its effect is likely to be threefold: to accentuate the present differences between Maori and non-Maori parliamentary representation, to seriously undermine the electoral position (and, therefore, the effectiveness) of the four M.P.s elected in the Maori electorates, and, perhaps most important of all, to increase doubts already present in the minds of a number of Maoris that their views and interests can be represented adequately through the parliamentary system.

The court was very properly concerned about the corrupt practices and other serious irregularities uncovered during the Hunua hearing, and its Special Report to Parliament contains recommendations designed to eliminate these in future elections. Nevertheless, experience has shown that rolls which are complete and up-to-date are as good an insurance as any against possible malpractice. Certainly these will not totally prevent personation, but by making detection very much easier they will reduce it to an absolute minimum. Accurate and up-to-date rolls have the further effect of reducing the incidence of special votes, and those who are forced by circumstance to apply for one have a greater guarantee that it will be accepted as formal.

New Zealand's electoral laws reflect the values held by the country's dominant socioeconomic group, the educated middle-class Europeans. To a large extent they are the product of mid-nineteenth-century society, and the amendments and revisions which have taken place from time to time have done little more than refine the original premises. It is often assumed that the electoral system is simple and easily understood, yet the evidence of the two recent election petitions suggests otherwise. Difficulties arising from minimal literacy levels were very real in Hunua, but while the court recognized the problems thus created it did not seem to appreciate their full significance.[38] Plainly, it cannot be assumed that all electors are able to read, nor can it be assumed that illiterate or semiliterate voters know they can seek assistance from the returning officer. Nevertheless the court, following a precedent established in the 1915 Hawke's Bay Election Petition, held that this assumption should be made. The instructions included on the ballot paper would present serious difficulties to voters with little formal education or whose cultural background differed from the norm, and this is likely to be compounded by the requirement that voters strike out the names of those candidates they do *not* wish to vote for rather than indicating directly the candidate of their choice. While help is available for an elector who needs it, few would be ready to admit this even if they were aware that it could be had.

One thing has been made abundantly clear. The laws that are studied and debated at length in Parliament do not always incorporate the values and provisions the members think they are putting in place. There is no doubt that the M.P.s who passed the 1956 Electoral Act thought they were enacting legislation that was fair, just, and liberal. The entire thrust of New Zealand's electoral provisions has been to place as few impediments as possible in the way of an individual seeking to cast a valid vote and to encourage everyone

---

[38] See *Hunua Petition: Special Report*, pp. 4 and 13. On page 13 the judges expressed surprise "that in view of the specific instructions written on ballot papers so many of the voters cast informal votes." Yet during the hearing it was reported that two subpoenaed witnesses failed to appear before the court until visited by a court bailiff who carried a bench warrant for their arrest if they failed to attend. It transpired that both were Pacific Islanders, neither of whom could read English. (See the *Press*, April 30, 1979). A few days later the court refused permission for Douglas's counsel to call a professor of English at the University of Auckland to give evidence about the wording of the instructions on the ballot paper and about the average level of literacy of the voting population. According to a newspaper report, "The Court ruled that it was not prepared to hear the evidence. It was not the response of an individual which was relevant in deciding the validity of his vote, but a question of what the statute meant" (*Christchurch Star*, May 8, 1979).

qualified to exercise this democratic right. In 1956 Parliament even sought to widen the Supreme Court's jurisdiction in electoral matters by inserting a new section into the Electoral Act. Section 166, which was adapted from Australia's Commonwealth Electoral Act of 1918 and which carries the side-note "Real justice to be observed," provides:

On the trial of any election petition—
(a) The Court shall be guided by the substantial merits and justice of the case without regard to legal forms or technicalities:
(b) The Court may admit such evidence as in its opinion may assist it to deal effectively with the case, notwithstanding that the evidence may not otherwise be admissible in the Supreme Court.

Initially it was assumed that this meant that substantive issues would not be discarded on mere technicalities.[39] The Electoral Court, however, ruled instead that the provision applied only to the conduct of the trial of a petition, not to the manner or method of voting. There is little doubt that the court's judgment was grounded on a narrow, strictly legal interpretation of the Electoral Act, and while this may certainly be correct in point of law, it did not reflect the intention of the lawmakers. The number of "party votes" rejected as informal in Hunua and Kapiti suggests that, had the ruling been applied in every electorate, around 40,000 additional votes would have had to be eliminated from the count. No one can seriously suggest that this is what Parliament had intended should happen.

The reverberations from the Hunua decision are still being felt. Tensions between the two major parties have risen perceptibly since the decision was announced as each has endeavored to use the outcome to further its political advantage. The unseated M.P., Malcolm Douglas, charged the Electoral Office with gross incompetence; his opponent, Winston Peters, responded by claiming to have further evidence of serious irregularities which he intended to make public at an appropriate time—whereupon Roger Douglas (M.P. for Manurewa, the expelled member's brother) accused him of withholding evidence during the trial. On a broader front, Prime Minister Rob Muldoon took the offensive at several of the National party's Divisional Conferences and several times referred to "slick dodges" by very "clever people" in the Labour party who were "not terribly scrupulous" in their interpretation of the electoral law. For their

---

[39] The provision was incorporated in the act following the dismissal on technical grounds of the Lyttelton Election Petition which had been lodged in 1955. See Chapter 3, footnote 54.

part, Labour party officials have alluded to the National party's "unsavory" smear campaign, and Labour M.P.s have more than once referred to the M.P.s from Hunua and Kapiti as "Court appointed members." A Labour party inspired petition calling for a by-election in Hunua circulated around Auckland for a period, and the party also announced its intention of seeking a declaratory judgment in the court of appeal on the question of the ticks and crosses argument.[40] Neither party, it seems, is willing to acknowledge that the 1978 general election is really over.

What chances are there for reform? With the climate of opinion among politicians as tense as it is they do not appear to be very great. In February 1979 the Government appointed an ad hoc, nonpolitical committee to examine the administration of the electoral law in the light of the experience of 1978 and to make recommendations for improvements. This committee reported to the Government at the end of August 1979. It also received an evaluative report from the chief electoral officer and a Special Report prepared by the Supreme Court after the announcement of the Hunua result. And on August 24, the Government formally moved that a parliamentary select committee to review the electoral law (promised back in December, shortly after the election) be set up to examine the present Electoral Act and to recommend any changes deemed desirable or necessary. Undoubtedly the law will be amended, but the changes almost certainly will be refinements in the administrative aspects of the present law—electoral enrollments and special votes—rather than wide-ranging reforms. As the Hunua and Kapiti hearings amply demonstrated, the present electoral laws are advantageous to National, which, as long as it is in power, is unlikely to acquiesce in changes that would reduce its advantage to any significant extent. Its strategy, therefore, is likely to be directed towards improving the machinery and administration of the present law while avoiding any real change to its fundamental structure. For their part, both Labour and Social Credit, along with one or two nonpartisan groups and concerned individuals, will seek more sweeping changes. The most likely outcome of these efforts is that they will founder on the rocks of interparty distrust.

---

[40] See the *Press* May 24, 26, 28, 29, 31, June 2, 4, 6, 1979; *Christchurch Star*, May 25, 26, 28, 31, June 6, 1979; *New Zealand Herald*, May 28, 30, June 6, 1979.

APPENDIX B

New Zealand Ballot, 1978

This is a sample of the ballot used in New Zealand general elections in both European and Maori districts. Actual ballots measure roughly five and a half by thirteen inches and are numbered consecutively. At the polling place, the clerk records the voter's electoral roll reference —the number of the page and line of the electoral roll on which his name appears—on the stub at left. The clerk then tears the ballot along both perforations, leaving the stub in the book, and hands the voter the ballot he will use to vote for a member of Parliament and the one he will use to vote in the triennial referendum on the sale of liquor.

No. 00000

No. 00000   BALLOT PAPER

Kaiapoi Electoral District

Election of Member of Parliament

DIRECTIONS—Strike out the name of every candidate except the one for whom you wish to vote.

After voting, fold this paper and place it in the ballot box. You must not take it out of the polling booth. If you spoil this paper, return it to the Issuing Officer and obtain another.

(Official Mark)

BROWN   (Labour)

JONES   (National)

ROBINSON   (Social Credit)

WILLIAMS, James   (Values)

WILLIAMS, John   (Independent)

Electoral—7

No. 00000

No. on Roll:
(To be entered here only)

Page	Line

Initials of
Issuing Officer:

VOTING PAPER

GENERAL LICENSING POLL   No. 00000

(Official Mark)

DIRECTIONS—Strike out the two proposals for which you do not wish to vote.

After voting, fold this paper and place it in the ballot box. You must not take it out of the polling booth. If you spoil this paper, return it to the Issuing Officer and obtain another.

I VOTE FOR NATIONAL CONTINUANCE

I VOTE FOR STATE PURCHASE AND CONTROL

I VOTE FOR NATIONAL PROHIBITION

APPENDIX C

Results of New Zealand General Elections, 1975 and 1978

Compiled by Richard M. Scammon

EDITOR'S NOTE: Between the general elections of 1975 and 1978, New Zealand's electoral districts were redrawn. The redistribution of 1977 increased the total number of districts from eighty-seven to ninety-two, leaving only five general electorates intact and creating five entirely new ones, all of them in the North Island. All of the other districts apart from the four Maori electorates were altered, many so drastically that they had to be renamed. The rules under which redistributions are conducted and the political consequences of the 1977 redistribution are discussed in Chapter 3.

1975 ELECTION RESULTS, NEW ZEALAND HOUSE OF REPRESENTATIVES
(popular vote totals and percentages, by district)

Electoral District	Total Vote	Labour	National	Social Credit	Values	Other[a]
General Electorates						
Auckland Central	15,362	6,506	6,217	410	1,939	290
		42.4	40.5	2.7	12.6	1.9
Avon	17,494	10,395	4,892	1,067	1,140	—
		59.4	28.0	6.1	6.5	—
Awarua	17,372	6,652	8,802	1,542	371	5
		38.3	50.7	8.9	2.1	—
Bay of Plenty	19,181	6,243	10,203	1,817	918	—
		32.5	53.2	9.5	4.8	—
Birkenhead	21,100	8,055	10,871	907	1,253	14
		38.2	51.5	4.3	5.9	.1
Christchurch Central	16,294	8,630	5,657	555	1,415	37
		53.0	34.7	3.4	8.7	.2
Clutha	16,754	5,286	10,021	948	416	83
		31.6	59.8	5.7	2.5	.5
Coromandel	20,101	5,897	10,621	2,620	963	—
		29.3	52.8	13.0	4.8	—
Dunedin Central	18,001	8,352	6,924	1,327	1,353	45
		46.4	38.5	7.4	7.5	.3
Dunedin North	19,777	7,782	8,740	1,180	2,075	—
		39.3	44.2	6.0	10.5	—
East Coast Bays	22,976	7,145	12,739	1,253	1,839	—
		31.1	55.4	5.5	8.0	—
Eden	19,653	8,394	9,725	497	991	46
		42.7	49.5	2.5	5.0	.2
Egmont	16,519	4,670	8,790	2,657	402	—
		28.3	53.2	16.1	2.4	—
Franklin	16,711	3,239	10,844	1,657	950	21
		19.4	64.9	9.9	5.7	.1
Gisborne	19,361	8,134	9,455	1,003	769	—
		42.0	48.8	5.2	4.0	—
Grey Lynn	16,207	8,268	5,429	977	1,472	61
		51.0	33.5	6.0	9.1	.4
Hamilton East	20,330	7,765	10,011	1,754	783	17
		38.2	49.2	8.6	3.9	.1
Hamilton West	21,581	8,403	10,472	2,069	637	—
		38.9	48.5	9.6	3.0	—
Hastings	20,026	8,580	9,071	1,788	587	—
		42.8	45.3	8.9	2.9	—

New Zealand: 1975 House of Representatives

Electoral District	Total Vote	Labour	National	Social Credit	Values	Other[a]
Hawke's Bay	19,600	6,753	10,558	1,603	686	—
		34.5	53.9	8.2	3.5	—
Henderson	17,758	7,665	7,264	1,572	1,222	35
		43.2	40.9	8.9	6.9	.2
Heretaunga	18,366	8,330	7,994	1,129	913	—
		45.4	43.5	6.1	5.0	—
Hobson	18,494	2,703	9,559	5,458	774	—
		14.6	51.7	29.5	4.2	—
Hutt	19,831	9,540	8,521	985	785	—
		48.1	43.0	5.0	4.0	—
Invercargill	18,471	7,180	9,713	1,045	533	—
		38.9	52.6	5.7	2.9	—
Island Bay	16,493	7,964	6,690	675	1,065	99
		48.3	40.6	4.1	6.5	.6
Kapiti	22,080	8,846	11,068	1,285	881	—
		40.1	50.1	5.8	4.0	—
Karori	19,877	6,405	11,235	829	1,379	29
		32.2	56.5	4.2	6.9	.1
King Country	16,349	4,864	9,180	1,759	546	—
		29.8	56.2	10.8	3.3	—
Lyttelton	21,107	9,108	10,107	592	1,300	—
		43.2	47.9	2.8	6.2	—
Manawatu	19,596	7,201	10,119	1,492	784	—
		36.7	51.6	7.6	4.0	—
Mangere	17,128	8,332	6,728	1,057	983	28
		48.6	39.3	6.2	5.7	.2
Manukau	15,726	7,495	6,817	760	626	28
		47.7	43.3	4.8	4.0	.2
Manurewa	20,019	8,200	9,558	1,296	925	40
		41.0	47.7	6.5	4.6	.2
Marlborough	18,619	7,037	10,047	928	607	—
		37.8	54.0	5.0	3.3	—
Miramar	18,851	7,664	9,413	773	956	45
		40.7	49.9	4.1	5.1	.2
Mt. Albert	18,217	8,231	7,984	914	1,060	28
		45.2	43.8	5.0	5.8	.2
Napier	20,800	9,395	8,464	1,841	1,084	16
		45.2	40.7	8.9	5.2	.1
Nelson	18,540	8,705	7,612	992	1,231	—
		47.0	41.1	5.4	6.6	—

New Zealand: 1975 House of Representatives

Electoral District	Total Vote	Labour	National	Social Credit	Values	Other[a]
New Lynn	18,116	8,033	7,143	1,524	1,373	43
		44.3	39.4	8.4	7.6	.2
New Plymouth	20,904	8,395	10,330	1,381	798	—
		40.2	49.4	6.6	3.8	—
North Shore	19,913	5,955	11,202	1,153	1,581	22
		29.9	56.3	5.8	7.9	.1
Oamaru	19,105	7,367	9,563	1,713	462	—
		38.6	50.1	9.0	2.4	—
Onehunga	17,912	8,264	7,220	1,264	1,129	35
		46.1	40.3	7.1	6.3	.2
Otago Central	19,789	7,983	10,354	910	542	—
		40.3	52.3	4.6	2.7	—
Otahuhu	15,838	8,838	5,053	1,020	879	48
		55.8	31.9	6.4	5.5	.3
Pahiatua	16,236	3,654	10,423	1,585	574	—
		22.5	64.2	9.8	3.5	—
Pakuranga	24,369	7,176	14,192	1,265	1,349	387
		29.4	58.2	5.2	5.5	1.6
Palmerston North	20,291	8,659	8,801	1,453	1,378	—
		42.7	43.4	7.2	6.8	—
Papanui	19,490	7,253	10,238	509	1,490	—
		37.2	52.5	2.6	7.6	—
Petone	16,248	8,333	5,499	1,155	1,168	93
		51.3	33.8	7.1	7.2	.6
Piako	17,104	4,074	10,248	2,322	460	—
		23.8	59.9	13.6	2.7	—
Porirua	16,175	7,692	5,427	834	2,176	46
		47.6	33.6	5.2	13.5	.3
Raglan	18,187	6,139	9,895	1,719	434	—
		33.8	54.4	9.5	2.4	—
Rakaia	17,558	5,295	10,532	988	743	—
		30.2	60.0	5.6	4.2	—
Rangiora	21,065	9,113	10,499	633	820	—
		43.3	49.8	3.0	3.9	—
Rangitikei	16,144	2,263	7,631	5,875	253	119
		14.0	47.3	36.4	1.6	.7
Remuera	18,020	2,827	11,483	809	2,363	538
		15.7	63.7	4.5	13.1	3.0
Riccarton	19,106	6,171	10,937	503	1,440	55
		32.3	57.2	2.6	7.5	.3

New Zealand: 1975 House of Representatives

Electoral District	Total Vote	Labour	National	Social Credit	Values	Other[a]
Rodney	21,132	4,354	12,171	3,528	1,060	19
		20.6	57.6	16.7	5.0	.1
Roskill	18,031	8,276	7,746	955	1,037	17
		45.9	43.0	5.3	5.8	.1
Rotorua	22,059	7,956	11,561	1,617	925	—
		36.1	52.4	7.3	4.2	—
Ruahine	19,876	7,102	9,865	1,952	957	—
		35.7	49.6	9.8	4.8	—
St. Albans	18,547	9,013	7,443	647	1,304	140
		48.6	40.1	3.5	7.0	.8
St. Kilda	20,077	9,663	7,773	1,414	1,227	—
		48.1	38.7	7.0	6.1	—
South Canterbury	19,904	6,916	11,217	1,142	629	—
		34.7	56.4	5.7	3.2	—
Stratford	16,929	4,158	9,825	2,137	788	21
		24.6	58.0	12.6	4.7	.1
Sydenham	18,613	10,086	6,269	898	1,306	54
		54.2	33.7	4.8	7.0	.3
Tamaki	18,971	5,101	11,836	725	1,258	51
		26.9	62.4	3.8	6.6	.3
Tasman	18,110	8,344	7,815	1,020	693	238
		46.1	43.2	5.6	3.8	1.3
Taupo	18,067	7,207	8,821	1,177	862	—
		39.9	48.8	6.5	4.8	—
Tauranga	21,798	6,674	11,517	2,571	1,036	—
		30.6	52.8	11.8	4.8	—
Timaru	18,562	8,815	7,804	1,140	803	—
		47.5	42.0	6.1	4.3	—
Waikato	16,118	3,200	10,273	2,003	642	—
		19.9	63.7	12.4	4.0	—
Wairarapa	18,703	7,777	9,245	1,167	514	—
		41.6	49.4	6.2	2.7	—
Waitemata	19,095	7,580	8,965	1,460	1,046	44
		39.7	46.9	7.6	5.5	.2
Wallace	16,164	3,455	10,433	1,792	484	—
		21.4	64.5	11.1	3.0	—
Wanganui	19,976	9,313	8,069	1,937	541	116
		46.6	40.4	9.7	2.7	.6
Wellington Central	19,836	8,477	9,553	467	1,326	13
		42.7	48.2	2.4	6.7	.1

NEW ZEALAND: 1975 HOUSE OF REPRESENTATIVES

Electoral District	Total Vote	Labour	National	Social Credit	Values	Other[a]
West Coast	18,526	9,522	7,121	1,019	698	166
		51.4	38.4	5.5	3.8	.9
Western Hutt	18,969	8,225	8,334	1,194	1,216	—
		43.4	43.9	6.3	6.4	—
Whangarei	21,232	7,792	10,502	2,133	805	—
		36.7	49.5	10.0	3.8	—
Wigram	19,348	9,617	7,650	957	1,124	—
		49.7	39.5	4.9	5.8	—
Total, General Electorates	1,560,932	602,121	756,593	116,680	82,306	3,232
		38.6	48.5	7.5	5.3	.2
Maori Electorates						
Eastern Maori	11,477	8,491	2,230	548	208	—
		74.0	19.4	4.8	1.8	—
Northern Maori	8,556	5,988	1,837	500	231	—
		70.0	21.5	5.9	2.7	—
Southern Maori	10,332	7,708	1,256	598	246	524
		74.6	12.2	5.8	2.4	5.1
Western Maori	12,436	10,145	1,220	821	250	—
		81.6	9.8	6.6	2.0	—
Total, Maori Electorates	42,801	32,332	6,543	2,467	935	524
		75.5	15.3	5.8	2.2	1.2
Total, New Zealand	1,603,733	634,453	763,136	119,147	83,241	3,756
%		39.6	47.6	7.4	5.2	.2
Seats		32	55	—	—	—

[a] Includes twenty-five minor parties. The largest went to the Independents, whose 809 votes were divided among eight candidates.

SOURCE: *The General Election, 1975* (Wellington: The Government Printer, 1976).

1978 ELECTION RESULTS, NEW ZEALAND HOUSE OF REPRESENTATIVES
(popular vote totals and percentages, by district)

Electoral District	Total Vote	Labour	National	Social Credit	Values	Other[a]
General Electorates						
Albany	20,976	7,438	8,597	4,091	543	307
		35.5	41.0	19.5	2.6	1.5
Ashburton	20,987	7,473	10,478	2,765	271	—
		35.6	49.9	13.2	1.3	—
Auckland Central	16,436	9,603	4,319	1,683	704	127
		58.4	26.3	10.2	4.3	.8
Avon	18,483	11,972	3,757	2,335	399	20
		64.8	20.3	12.6	2.2	.1
Awarua	19,448	6,633	8,083	4,604	128	—
		34.1	41.6	23.7	.7	—
Bay of Islands	16,721	2,935	7,430	5,748	608	—
		17.6	44.4	34.4	3.6	—
Birkenhead	19,229	6,816	9,350	2,583	480	—
		35.4	48.6	13.4	2.5	—
Christchurch Central	16,721	10,229	4,282	1,564	616	30
		61.2	25.6	9.4	3.7	.2
Clutha	19,218	7,381	8,808	2,757	272	—
		38.4	45.8	14.3	1.4	—
Dunedin Central	18,307	9,193	5,780	2,649	685	—
		50.2	31.6	14.5	3.7	—
Dunedin North	20,428	9,846	6,996	2,228	799	559
		48.2	34.2	10.9	3.9	2.7
East Cape	16,538	5,335	7,868	2,898	437	—
		32.3	47.6	17.5	2.6	—
East Coast Bays	22,255	6,109	7,675	4,448	339	3,684
		27.5	34.5	20.0	1.5	16.6
Eastern Hutt	18,869	10,640	5,267	2,394	400	168
		56.4	27.9	12.7	2.1	.9
Eden	19,998	8,005	8,653	1,836	877	627
		40.0	43.3	9.2	4.4	3.1
Fendalton	19,624	7,524	9,480	1,603	1,017	—
		38.3	48.3	8.2	5.2	—
Gisborne	17,785	7,418	7,631	2,366	370	—
		41.7	42.9	13.3	2.1	—
Hamilton East	19,439	6,991	8,352	3,659	399	38
		36.0	43.0	18.8	2.1	.2
Hamilton West	18,780	7,095	8,101	3,222	296	66
		37.8	43.1	17.2	1.6	.4

New Zealand: 1978 House of Representatives

Electoral District	Total Vote	Labour	National	Social Credit	Values	Other[a]
Hastings	20,703	7,748	7,414	5,373	148	20
		37.4	35.8	26.0	.7	.1
Hauraki	18,083	3,668	8,022	6,003	390	—
		20.3	44.4	33.2	2.2	—
Hawke's Bay	17,198	6,240	8,148	2,501	309	—
		36.3	47.4	14.5	1.8	—
Helensville	19,247	6,584	7,783	4,510	370	—
		34.2	40.4	23.4	1.9	—
Heretaunga	18,237	9,086	6,342	2,110	699	—
		49.8	34.8	11.6	3.8	—
Horowhenua	20,895	8,212	8,956	3,231	346	150
		39.3	42.9	15.5	1.7	.7
Hunua	17,436	7,315	7,507	2,346	268	—
		42.0	43.1	13.5	1.5	—
Invercargill	20,011	8,410	8,666	2,760	175	—
		42.0	43.3	13.8	.9	—
Island Bay	18,425	6,524	5,874	1,502	751	3,774
		35.4	31.9	8.2	4.1	20.5
Kaimai	18,499	4,521	8,457	4,981	540	—
		24.4	45.7	26.9	2.9	—
Kaipara	17,723	1,422	8,234	7,714	336	17
		8.0	46.5	43.5	1.9	.1
Kapiti	19,049	8,188	8,211	2,345	305	—
		43.0	43.1	12.3	1.6	—
King Country	15,244	4,034	6,804	3,997	409	—
		26.5	44.6	26.2	2.7	—
Lyttelton	21,604	10,493	9,070	1,294	577	170
		48.6	42.0	6.0	2.7	.8
Manawatu	18,260	6,750	8,053	3,064	393	—
		37.0	44.1	16.8	2.2	—
Mangere	13,744	9,104	2,841	1,655	144	—
		66.2	20.7	12.0	1.0	—
Manurewa	17,814	8,449	5,982	3,079	224	80
		47.4	33.6	17.3	1.3	.4
Marlborough	19,717	8,291	8,614	2,365	381	66
		42.1	43.7	12.0	1.9	.3
Matamata	16,279	3,010	8,731	4,324	214	—
		18.5	53.6	26.6	1.3	—
Miramar	20,833	8,921	9,236	2,065	611	—
		42.8	44.3	9.9	2.9	—

New Zealand: 1978 House of Representatives

Electoral District	Total Vote	Labour	National	Social Credit	Values	Other[a]
Mt. Albert	19,299	9,718	6,857	2,353	371	—
		50.4	35.5	12.2	1.9	—
Napier	20,099	9,987	7,060	2,664	388	—
		49.7	35.1	13.3	1.9	—
Nelson	19,033	9,605	7,366	1,506	556	—
		50.5	38.7	7.9	2.9	—
New Lynn	17,967	9,565	5,175	2,949	278	—
		53.2	28.8	16.4	1.5	—
New Plymouth	20,298	8,538	8,650	2,634	476	—
		42.1	42.6	13.0	2.3	—
North Shore	20,340	5,701	10,351	3,485	803	—
		28.0	50.9	17.1	3.9	—
Ohariu	18,881	6,851	8,809	2,015	735	471
		36.3	46.7	10.7	3.9	2.5
Onehunga	18,804	8,837	7,420	2,135	390	22
		47.0	39.5	11.4	2.1	.1
Otago	18,162	5,387	9,109	3,236	430	—
		29.7	50.2	17.8	2.4	—
Otahuhu	15,577	8,896	4,134	2,288	236	23
		57.1	26.5	14.7	1.5	.1
Pahiatua	18,559	4,296	10,971	2,898	394	—
		23.1	59.1	15.6	2.1	—
Pakuranga	20,761	5,504	7,615	2,918	269	4,455
		26.5	36.7	14.1	1.3	21.5
Palmerston North	21,679	10,629	7,893	2,558	551	48
		49.0	36.4	11.8	2.5	.2
Papakura	17,128	4,959	8,581	3,401	187	—
		29.0	50.1	19.9	1.1	—
Papanui	20,287	10,737	7,448	1,359	735	8
		52.9	36.7	6.7	3.6	—
Papatoetoe	18,391	8,412	6,901	2,861	217	—
		45.7	37.5	15.6	1.2	—
Pencarrow	18,206	9,679	6,030	1,901	596	—
		53.2	33.1	10.4	3.3	—
Porirua	16,917	8,142	4,485	2,177	2,043	70
		48.1	26.5	12.9	12.1	.4
Rangiora	20,941	8,584	9,729	2,195	433	—
		41.0	46.5	10.5	2.1	—
Rangiriri	16,654	5,658	7,934	2,824	238	—
		34.0	47.6	17.0	1.4	—

NEW ZEALAND: 1978 HOUSE OF REPRESENTATIVES

Electoral District	Total Vote	Labour	National	Social Credit	Values	Other[a]
Rangitikei	20,066	1,490	7,716	10,569	291	—
		7.4	38.5	52.7	1.5	—
Remuera	17,184	3,740	9,511	2,062	1,288	583
		21.8	55.3	12.0	7.5	3.4
Roskill	19,887	9,584	7,913	2,157	233	—
		48.2	39.8	10.8	1.2	—
Rotorua	16,118	6,106	7,126	2,565	321	—
		37.9	44.2	15.9	2.0	—
St. Albans	21,393	11,279	7,600	1,909	577	28
		52.7	35.5	8.9	2.7	.1
St. Kilda	20,529	10,064	7,105	2,638	698	24
		49.0	34.6	12.9	3.4	.1
Selwyn	18,386	7,103	8,335	2,537	411	—
		38.6	45.3	13.8	2.2	—
Sydenham	19,765	11,847	4,807	2,463	610	38
		59.9	24.3	12.5	3.1	.2
Tamaki	20,837	5,504	11,814	2,360	791	368
		26.4	56.7	11.3	3.8	1.8
Taranaki	18,198	4,351	8,968	4,395	484	—
		23.9	49.3	24.2	2.7	—
Tarawera	16,064	5,051	7,073	3,636	304	—
		31.4	44.0	22.6	1.9	—
Tasman	18,280	8,973	7,179	1,726	362	40
		49.1	39.3	9.4	2.0	.2
Taupo	16,904	7,119	6,510	2,798	477	—
		42.1	38.5	16.6	2.8	—
Tauranga	19,628	4,665	8,924	5,606	433	—
		23.8	45.5	28.6	2.2	—
Te Atatu	17,634	8,640	5,821	2,923	250	—
		49.0	33.0	16.6	1.4	—
Timaru	20,463	9,977	7,794	2,180	512	—
		48.8	38.1	10.7	2.5	—
Waikato	17,702	4,186	9,249	3,898	369	—
		23.6	52.3	22.0	2.1	—
Waipa	17,846	3,809	9,360	4,454	223	—
		21.3	52.4	25.0	1.2	—
Wairarapa	19,783	8,131	8,968	2,426	258	—
		41.1	45.3	12.3	1.3	—
Waitakere	19,565	8,612	6,596	3,731	452	174
		44.0	33.7	19.1	2.3	.9

NEW ZEALAND: 1978 HOUSE OF REPRESENTATIVES

Electoral District	Total Vote	Labour	National	Social Credit	Values	Other[a]
Waitaki	19,513	7,060	8,375	3,841	237	—
		36.2	42.9	19.7	1.2	—
Waitotara	19,174	4,726	9,133	5,024	291	—
		24.6	47.6	26.2	1.5	—
Wallace	18,704	3,929	9,253	3,147	176	2,199
		21.0	49.5	16.8	.9	11.8
Wanganui	20,743	9,703	6,601	3,956	449	34
		46.8	31.8	19.1	2.2	.2
Wellington Central	21,756	8,825	9,741	1,893	1,217	80
		40.6	44.8	8.7	5.6	.4
West Coast	19,391	9,167	3,520	3,161	209	3,334
		47.3	18.2	16.3	1.1	17.2
Western Hutt	18,732	8,368	8,200	1,645	348	171
		44.7	43.8	8.8	1.9	.9
Whangarei	21,069	7,008	8,184	5,485	335	57
		33.3	38.8	26.0	1.6	.3
Yaldhurst	20,891	10,186	8,548	1,670	487	—
		48.8	40.9	8.0	2.3	—
Total, General Electorates	1,663,431	654,494	676,294	269,864	40,649	22,130
		39.3	40.7	16.2	2.4	1.3
Eastern Maori	12,147	9,085	1,685	1,195	182	—
		74.8	13.9	9.8	1.5	—
Northern Maori	8,495	6,071	1,049	1,227	148	—
		71.5	12.3	14.4	1.7	—
Southern Maori	12,450	10,250	1,070	1,013	117	—
		82.3	8.6	8.1	.9	—
Western Maori	13,650	11,176	893	1,457	124	—
		81.9	6.5	10.7	.9	—
Total, Maori Electorates	46,742	36,582	4,697	4,892	571	—
		77.6	10.3	10.8	1.3	—
Total, New Zealand	1,710,173	691,076	680,991	274,756	41,220	22,130
%		40.4	39.8	16.1	2.4	1.3
Seats		40	51	1	—	—

a Includes twenty-eight minor parties, of which thirteen won fewer than 100 votes and six won more than 1,000. The latter were: Independent National, 4,774; National Alternative, 4,209; Independent Labour (Island Bay), 3,632; West Coast, 3,334; Alternative National Independent, 2,199; and Right to Life, 1,100.

SOURCE: *The General Election, 1978* (Wellington: The Government Printer, 1979).

CONTRIBUTORS

JUDITH E. AITKEN is a junior lecturer in the School of Political Science and Public Administration at the Victoria University of Wellington. She is the author of *A Woman's Place*, a study of the changing role of women in New Zealand, and is currently engaged in research on education planning.

RODERIC ALLEY is a senior lecturer in political science at the Victoria University of Wellington. He writes and broadcasts regularly on New Zealand politics and in 1978 covered the Labour and National party annual conferences for Radio New Zealand.

LES CLEVELAND is a senior lecturer at the School of Political Science and Public Administration at the Victoria University of Wellington. Formerly a journalist, he is the author of *The Anatomy of Influence*, a study of pressure groups in New Zealand politics, and of *The Politics of Utopia*, an analysis of New Zealand's welfare state.

WILLIAM KEITH JACKSON is professor of political science and chairman of the department at the University of Canterbury. His books include *Fight for Life: New Zealand, Britain and the EEC* and *New Zealand Politics of Change*.

COLIN C. JAMES is political editor of the *National Business Review*, New Zealand's widest circulating journal of financial and political affairs. He is a former political correspondent for the *Dominion* and the *New Zealand Herald* and coauthor (with James Eagles) of *The Making of a New Zealand Prime Minister* in 1973.

STEPHEN LEVINE is a senior lecturer in political science at the Victoria University of Wellington. He is the editor of several volumes on New Zealand political behavior, author of *The New Zealand Political System*, and coauthor of *The New Zealand Voter*.

ALAN McROBIE is a lecturer in social sciences at the Christchurch Teachers College. He is a coauthor (with Nigel S. Roberts) of *Election '78: The 1977 Electoral Redistribution and the 1978 General Election in New Zealand* and has written a number of articles on New Zealand's electoral system.

BRIAN D. MURPHY is a senior lecturer in economics at Auckland University as well as cofounder and director of the National Research Bureau. His specialty is attitudinal survey research.

KEITH OVENDEN is a senior lecturer in political science at the University of Canterbury. Author of *The Politics of Steel,* he is interested in the political sociology of advanced industrialized democracies.

NIGEL S. ROBERTS is a senior lecturer in political science at the University of Canterbury. He is the author of *New Zealand and Nuclear Testing in the Pacific* and coauthor (with Alan McRobie) of *Election '78: The 1977 Electoral Redistribution and the 1978 General Election in New Zealand*, in addition to numerous articles on Australian, New Zealand, and Scandinavian politics.

RICHARD SCAMMON, coauthor of *This U.S.A.* and *The Real Majority,* is director of the Elections Research Center in Washington, D.C. He has edited the biennial series *America Votes* since 1956.

GILBERT ANTONY WOOD is associate professor in the political studies department at the University of Otago. He is the author of a *Guide for Students of New Zealand History, The Governor and His Northern House,* and various essays on New Zealand politics and political history.

INDEX

286

abortion: 100–101, 138, 139, 164, 207–208, 240–241
economic problems: 49, 51, 174, 176–178, 239–240
elector registration controversy: 89
electoral system: 96–98
immigration: 44
opinion polls on: 239–241
redistribution of electorates: 75, 79–80, 84, 100
social problems: 173–174, 176–178
unemployment: 51, 239–241
Campaign strategies:
media, use of: 188–189
see also Beetham, Bruce C.; Muldoon, Robert D.; Rowling, Wallace E.; specific political parties
Canada:
electoral system, proportional representation problem: iii–iv, 29n
New Zealand political system, comparison: 9–10
Social Credit party in: 149n
Candidate selection:
age requirements: 103, 110n
alternative and independent candidates: 109–110
central and local control of, patterns and conflicts: 101–103, 117–118
in Maori electorates: 105n
nomination requirements: 89–90
parties' control over: 15–16, 99–100
problems and changes in: 103–106
trade unions' role in: 105
see also Incumbents, challenging of
Candidates:
advanced education as desirable qualification: 116
age of, average: 112–113, 116
alternative and independent candidates, major parties: 112, 230–231
electoral experience of new members, table: 115
independent candidates, fringe parties: 89, 101n, 112
local connections, importance of: 116
Maori candidates in general elections: 113–114
nonincumbent winners: 114–116
number of, 1972, 1975, 1978: 89, 101n, 112
sex of: 112–113, 115–116

women candidates for local office: 204–206
women candidates for Parliament: 198–204
Carroll, Sir James: 113
Carter, Sir Douglas: 223
Caucus: see Parliamentary democracy
Chapman, George: 79, 80, 125
Citizens party: 205
Clark, Helen: 139
COACTION (organization): 214
Colenso Communications: 125, 126
Compton Associates: 155
Compulsory voting: see Elector registration and voting
Confidence Index, NRB: 177
Connolly, Michael: 84, 138, 220
Conservative party: 8
Constituencies: see Electorates
Constitution: see Parliamentary democracy
Controversies:
elector registration: 85–89
Moyle affair: 136
Muldoon Government, controversial activities: 25–26
Corrupt practices, definition: 260
Couch, Ben: 114
Country party: 148, 150
Country Women's Institute: 203
Cracknell, Vernon: 151–152, 154, 158, 234
Crozier, Margaret: 166, 212

Daily press: see Newspapers
Davies, Sonja: 211
Democracy, parliamentary: see Parliamentary democracy
Democratic party: 119
Dewe, Colleen: 199n, 202n, 220
Disputed elections:
election petitions, grounds for: 94
implications of: 96
overview: 94–96
recount procedures: 94
see also Hunua disputed election; Kapiti disputed election
Districts: see Electorates
Domestic policies: 19, 25
see also Economic issues
Douglas, Clifford Hugh (Douglas credit): 148–151
Douglas, Malcolm: 144, 269
unseating in Hunua disputed election: 250–264 passim
Douglas, Roger: 140, 220, 250, 269

as source of conflict between political parties: 64–65, 96–98

votes versus seats discrepancy: iii–iv, 29, 68–69

Electorate:
age distribution, table: 35
education levels: 52–53
ethnic composition: 35–36
immigration, attitude toward: 44–45
industrialization, effect on cultural self-image: 38–44
political attitudes: 9–12, 64
population distribution, tables: 40–43
religious affiliations, table: 45
religious attitudes: 44–45
social structure: 58–63
standard of living, overview: 46
urban growth, table: 39
voting behavior: 206–208

Electorates:
"European," explanation of: 66n
Maori: iv, 3, 69–74, 105n
number of, 1978: 66
size: 4
see also Redistribution of electorates

Electronic media:
government regulation of: 182–184
operational characteristics: 185–186
radio, campaign coverage by: 190
see also Mass media; Newspapers; Television broadcasting

Employment issues: see Economic issues

Enrollment of electors: see Elector registration and voting

Equal Pay Act: 198n

Ethnic groups: 35–36

European electorates: see Electorates

Evening Post: 191–192

Faulkner, Arthur: 80, 137, 144

Feminist issues: see Women

Feminists for Life (organization): 213

Fenton, Robert: 220

Finlay, Martin: 195, 221

Fiscal policies: see Economic issues

Foreign policies:
Kirk Government: 18–19
Muldoon Government: 24
overview: 12–15

Formal ballot: 95, 261–263

France:
publication of polls, policy regarding: iii

Fraser, Peter: 134

Freer, Warren: 137

Fringe parties:
number of candidates: 89, 101n, 112

Gallup poll: see Opinion polls

Gandar, Leslie: 82n, 158, 221, 223

Garden party: 112

Geiringer, Eric: 208

General elections: see Election results

General electorates: see Electorates

Germany:
publication of polls, policy regarding: ii–iii

Gill, Frank: 230

GNP (Gross National Product): see Economic issues

Gordon, J. B. (Peter): 88

Government: see Parliamentary democracy

Governor general, role of: 5–6

Great Britain: see Britain

Grey, George: 10

Grigg, Mary: 202n

Hamilton, Adam: 124

Hunua disputed election:
allegations cited: 251–253
compilation of electoral rolls, problems in: 255–256
corrupt practices identified: 260–261
eligibility of electors in: 258–260
enrollment of non-Maori electors on Maori rolls, issue of: 256–258
informal ballots, rejection of: 261–263
petitioner's candidacy, validity of: 254–255
recount, results of: 250, 263–264
significance of: 251, 266–270

Harrison, Richard: 250

Hercus, Ann: 139, 201, 202n

Heylen Research Centre:
publication of polls, policy regarding: ii, 179, 237
see also Opinion polls

Hicks, Colleen: 144

Holland, Sidney: 122n, 124

Holyoake, Sir Keith: 14n, 16, 17, 124, 128, 170
House elections: see Election results
House of Representatives: see Parliamentary democracy
Howard, Mabel: 199n, 202n
Human Rights Act: 198n
Hunter, Les: 159

Illegal practices, definition: 260
Immigration:
    attitudes toward: 44–45
    as campaign issue: 44
    by country of origin, table: 37
    migration losses: 44n
    overstayer, definition of: 44n
Incumbents, challenging of:
    alternative and independent candidates: 109–110
    illustrative cases: 107–109
    party policy: 106
    reasons: 111–112
    redistribution as cause for: 111
Independent candidates:
    Labour party: 110
    National party: 109–110, 112, 230–231
    non-major-party candidates: 89, 101n, 112
Industrialization:
    cultural self-image, effect on: 38–39
    development of: 38
    factories, work force of: 38n
    social structure, impact on: 59–61
    urban growth, encouragement of: 39–44
Inflation: see Economic issues
Informal ballot: 261–263
International affairs: see Foreign policy
Isbey, Eddie: 111, 220

Jack, Sir Roy: 83n, 156, 221
Jeffries, Bill: 138
Jelicich, Dorothy: 202n
Judiciary, role of: 5
Juries Amendment Act: 198n

Kapiti disputed election: 250–251, 264–266
Kirk, John: 146
Kirk Labour Government: 18–19
Kirk, Norman: 21, 135, 173, 174, 194
    beliefs: 19–20
    political style: 18, 20, 191
Kunowski, Tony: 166, 193, 231

Labour party:
    1978 annual conference, features of: 139–140
    abortion policies: 138, 139
    advertising and publicity by: 145–146
    campaign, effect of: 134, 146–147
    campaign expenditures: 91
    campaign policies and strategies: 140–143
    candidate selection: 101–106, 117–118
    constituency: 45, 58, 62
    elector registration controversy: 85–87
    funding problems: 144–145
    historical background: 15, 119
    incumbents, challenging of: 110–112
    individual electorate campaigns: 143
    influence of Douglas credit on: 150–151
    internal problems: 136–137
    leadership: 20, 134–135, 194
    manifesto and other publications: 142, 145
    Maori affiliation: iv, 3
    Maori electorates, alteration of: 72–74
    membership, attitude toward: 121
    Moyle affair: 136
    opinion polls, use of: 169, 178–179
    organizational inadequacies: 135–136, 145
    precampaign regional conference issues: 138
    redistribution, effect of: 80–82, 137
    redistribution, required swing to Labour, table: 81
    slogans: 16, 17, 188, 191, 217
    tax reform proposals: 140–141
    trends in support for: 170, 173–174, 176–179
    women, support by: 206–208
    women's campaign activities: 139
    see also Candidates; Election results
Lambert, Bruce: 220
Lange, David: 139, 146, 178
La Varis, Ramon: 220
Leadership: see Party leadership; specific political parties

AEI's *At the Polls* Studies

Australia at the Polls: The National Elections of 1975, Howard R. Penniman, ed. (373 pp., $5)

The Australian National Elections of 1977, Howard R. Penniman, ed. (367 pp., $8.25)

Britain at the Polls: The Parliamentary Elections of 1974, Howard R. Penniman, ed. (256 pp., $3)

Britain Says Yes: The 1975 Referendum on the Common Market, Anthony King (153 pp., $3.75)

Canada at the Polls: The General Elections of 1974, Howard R. Penniman, ed. (310 pp., $4.50)

France at the Polls: The Presidential Elections of 1974, Howard R. Penniman, ed. (324 pp., $4.50)

The French National Assembly Elections of 1978, Howard R. Penniman, ed. (255 pages, $7.25)

Germany at the Polls: The Bundestag Election of 1976, Karl H. Cerny, ed. (251 pp., $7.25)

India at the Polls: The Parliamentary Elections of 1977, Myron Weiner (150 pp., $6.25)

Ireland at the Polls: The Dáil Elections of 1977, Howard R. Penniman, ed. (199 pp., $6.25)

Israel at the Polls: The Knesset Elections of 1977, Howard R. Penniman, ed. (333 pp., $8.25)

Italy at the Polls: The Parliamentary Elections of 1976, Howard R. Penniman, ed. (386 pp., $5.75)

Japan at the Polls: The House of Councillors Election of 1974, Michael K. Blaker, ed. (157 pp., $3)

A Season of Voting: The Japanese Elections of 1976 and 1977, Herbert Passin, ed. (199 pp., $6.25)

Scandinavia at the Polls: Recent Political Trends in Denmark, Norway, and Sweden, Karl H. Cerny, ed. (304 pp., $5.75)

Studies are forthcoming on the latest national elections in Belgium, Britain, Canada, Colombia, Denmark, Greece, India, Italy, the Netherlands, Norway, Spain, Sweden, Switzerland, and Venezuela, and on the first elections to the European Parliament. Also forthcoming is *Democracy at the Polls*, edited by David Butler, Howard R. Penniman, and Austin Ranney, a comparative examination of the electoral process in a wide range of democratic nations.